EMDR Therapy With
FIRST RESPONDERS

Marilyn Luber, PhD, is a licensed clinical psychologist in general private practice in Center City, Philadelphia, Pennsylvania. She was trained in eye movement desensitization and reprocessing (EMDR) in 1992 by Dr. Francine Shapiro, and now assists in EMDR Institute trainings as a facilitator and logistics coordinator. She has coordinated trainings in EMDR-related fields in the greater Philadelphia area since 1997. She teaches Facilitator and Supervisory trainings and other EMDR-related subjects both nationally and internationally, and was on the EMDR Task Force for Dissociative Disorders. She was on the founding board of directors of the EMDR International Association (EMDRIA) and served as the chair of the International Committee until June 1999. Currently, she is a facilitator in the EMDR Global Alliance, a group consisting of the leaders of all the EMDR associations who are working to support standards in EMDR worldwide. In 1997, Dr. Luber was given a Humanitarian Services Award by the EMDR Humanitarian Association, and later, in 2003, she was presented with the EMDR International Association's award for "outstanding contribution and service to EMDRIA." In 2005, she was awarded the Francine Shapiro Award for "outstanding contribution and service to EMDR." In 2009, she edited *Eye Movement Desensitization and Reprocessing (EMDR) Scripted Protocols: Basics and Special Situations* and *Eye Movement Desensitization and Reprocessing (EMDR) Scripted Protocols: Special Populations* published by Springer Publishing Company. Several years later, in 2012, she edited Springer's first CD-ROM books, *Eye Movement Desensitization and Reprocessing (EMDR) Scripted Protocols With Summary Sheets CD-ROM Version: Basics and Special Situations* and *Eye Movement Desensitization and Reprocessing (EMDR) Scripted Protocols With Summary Sheets CD-ROM Version: Special Populations*. In 2001, through EMDR-HAP (Humanitarian Assistance Programs), she published *Handbook for EMDR Clients* and it has been translated into eight languages. She has written the "Around the World" and "In the Spotlight" articles for the EMDRIA Newsletter four times a year since 1997. She has worked as a primary consultant for the FBI field division in Philadelphia. Dr. Luber has a general psychology practice, working with adolescents, adults, and couples, especially with complex post traumatic stress disorder (C-PTSD), trauma and related issues, and dissociative disorders. She runs consultation groups for EMDR practitioners.

EMDR Therapy With FIRST RESPONDERS

Edited by

Marilyn Luber, PhD

SPRINGER PUBLISHING COMPANY

NEW YORK

Springer Publishing Company, LLC
11 West 42nd Street
New York, NY 10036
www.springerpub.com

Acquisitions Editor: Sheri W. Sussman
Composition: S4Carlisle

ISBN: 978-0-8261-3338-0
e-book ISBN: 978–0-8261–3222-2

Content herein is excerpted from *Implementing EMDR Early Mental Health Interventions for Man-Made and Natural Disasters: Models, Scripted Protocols, and Summary Sheets*, edited by Marilyn Luber. © Springer Publishing Company, LLC. The Foreword, Preface, Acknowledgments, and section introductions have been included herein in their entirety.

Implementing EMDR early mental health interventions for man-made and natural disasters : models, scripted protocols, and summary sheets/edited by Marilyn Luber.
    p. ; cm.
   Implementing eye movement desensitization reprocessing early mental health interventions for man-made and natural disasters
   Includes bibliographical references and index.
   ISBN-13: 978–0-8261–9921-8
   ISBN-10: 0–8261-9921–6
   ISBN-13: 978–0-8261–3222-2 (e-book)
   ISBN-13: 978–0-8261–2957-4 (CD-ROM)
    I. Luber, Marilyn, editor of compilation.   II. Title: Implementing eye movement desensitization reprocessing early mental health interventions for man-made and natural disasters.
   [DNLM: 1. Stress Disorders, Traumatic—therapy.   2. Cross-Cultural Comparison.   3. Disasters.   4. Eye Movement Desensitization Reprocessing. WM 172.5]
   RC552.T7
   616.85'21—dc23   2013021409

Printed in the United States of America.

To my mother, who has been going through her own recent trauma
with the spirit and true determination
that she has always displayed throughout her life:
a role model for us all.

We are all responsible for the world we live in. Worldwide, clinicians are forging bonds that transcend countries and ideologies. Bonds that can help heal the trauma and pain that lead to ongoing violence and suffering. To make a difference that effects generations to come—don't leave it to anyone else. We all have to take a part in it.

—Francine Shapiro

Contents

PART I
EMDR Early Mental Health Interventions: First Responders

PART II
EMDR Early Intervention for Special Situations

Robbie Adler-Tapia, PhD, is a licensed psychologist who was previously a firefighter and emergency medical technician (EMT). Currently Dr. Adler-Tapia is an Employee Assistance Provider for law enforcement, firefighters, and first responders. She is a team member for the National Fallen Firefighters' Taking Care of Our Own Program. She also works with children and families with trauma, attachment, adoption, and child welfare issues. Dr. Adler-Tapia serves as an expert witness in the Juvenile and Family Courts. She is an EMDRIA Approved Consultant, an EMDR Institute Facilitator and a HAP Trainer. As a national and international speaker, she has presented for the National Fallen Firefighters' Foundation, Arizona Women in Policing, EMDRIA conferences, the ISST-D Conference, and the Rady Chadwick International Child and Family Maltreatment Conference. On a volunteer basis, Dr. Adler-Tapia runs a group for officers involved in shootings.

David Blore, PhD, BSc (Hons), DipBPsych, SRN, RMN, ENBHA, is an EMDR-Europe accredited EMDR consultant and facilitator and an accredited cognitive-behavioral therapy (CBT) therapist in York, England. He has been working with victims of psychological trauma for 25 years and using EMDR for 20 years mainly in occupational mental health. He is a consultant to the United Kingdom railway industry, police forces, the petrochemical industry, and various other organizational groupings. Dr. Blore is leader of the www.linkedin.com group on Positive Psychology and EMDR, which has over 400 members from 38 countries. He is a founder member of the Centre for Applied Positive Psychology (CAPP) and author of over 30 peer-reviewed papers and conference presentations, mainly on EMDR. He is author of *In Search of the Antonym to Trauma*, derived from his PhD studies on the lived experience of posttraumatic growth, post–road traffic accident, and post-EMDR.

Tammera M. Cooke, BA, MA, possessing a curiosity in matters of human being suffering, healing, and change, is pursuing a doctoral degree in clinical psychology (PsyD) at Antioch University Seattle. Her dissertation is a philosophical hermeneutic examination of the ideology informing the profession of psychology's professional ethics code and the major dilemma confronting contemporary psychologists: how to speak to the ills of our time without being able to draw explicitly from the moral and ethical traditions that constitute us. Her clinical practice is grounded in relational psychotherapy with a focus on rural mental health care, international psychology, and disaster relief/response.

Manda Holmshaw, PhD, is a consultant, clinical psychologist, and clinical director of Moving Minds, a national rehabilitation organization in the United Kingdom, which treats adults and children after traumatic experiences, especially road traffic accidents, assaults, and accidents at work. She is an EMDR-Europe accredited trainer and consultant. She divides her time among supervision, clinical work, research, and EMDR training, and is based in London.

Susan Rogers, PhD, has been actively involved in the treatment of war and trauma survivors since 1981. She has provided treatment and training in EMDR in the United States, as well as in Londonderry and Belfast, Northern Ireland; Cracow and Warsaw, Poland; Dhaka, Bangladesh; St. Petersburg, Russia; and Sarajevo, Bosnia-Hercegovina. She has also worked with the American National Red Cross in response to the 1995 Mississippi floods and tornadoes. She serves on the VA Emergency Response Team for Eastern Pennsylvania.

Mark C. Russell, CDR, USN (Ret.), PhD, ABPP, is dual-board certified by the American Board of Professional Psychology (ABPP) in clinical psychology and clinical child and adolescent psychology. A recently retired Navy commander and military psychologist with over 26 years of military service, he is a nationally recognized expert on war stress injuries, testifying before the congressionally mandated Department of Defense (DoD) Task Force of Mental Health regarding his efforts to prevent a military mental health crisis as chronicled by *USA Today*, including the lack of veterans' access to EMDR training, research, and treatment. A former Research Assistant to Francine Shapiro, Dr. Russell became the first EMDR Institute Trainer in the DoD, conducting seven joint DoD/VA EMDR trainings that led to the training of over 320 military mental health clinicians, including a 2011 training of the U.S. Army's 113th Combat Stress Control Unit, prior to deploying to Afghanistan. Coauthor of the book *Treating Traumatic Stress Injuries in Military Personnel* (2013), Dr. Russell has also published over 20 articles and two book chapters on treatment of war trauma. In 2006, he was awarded the Distinguished Psychologist Award by the Washington State Psychological Association. He currently chairs the PsyD program at Antioch University Seattle, and is the establishing Director of the Institute of War Stress Injuries and Social Justice, dedicated to ending cyclic failure to meet the mental health needs of war veterans.

Roger Solomon, PhD, is a psychologist and psychotherapist specializing in the areas of trauma and grief. He is on the senior faculty of the EMDR Institute and provides basic and advanced EMDR training internationally. He also provides advanced specialty trainings in the areas of grief, emergency psychology, and complex trauma. He currently consults with the U.S. Senate, NASA, and several law enforcement agencies. As a police psychologist with the South Carolina Department of Public Safety, he is Clinical Director of the Post Critical Incident Seminar (PCIS), a three-day post trauma program that draws on both psychological first aid, peer support, and EMDR therapy. Working with the South Carolina Army National Guard, he is Clinical Director of the Post Deployment Seminar, a three-day program for war veterans. Dr. Solomon has provided clinical services and training to the FBI; Secret Service; U.S. State Department; Diplomatic Security; Bureau of Alcohol, Tobacco, and Firearms; U.S. Department of Justice (U.S. Attorneys), and numerous state and local law enforcement organizations. Internationally, he consults with the Polizia di Stato in Italy and also provides a post trauma program for the police in Finland. Dr. Solomon has planned critical incident programs, provided training for peer support teams, and has provided direct services following such tragedies as Hurricane Katrina, the September 11 terrorist attacks, the loss of the shuttle Columbia, and the Oklahoma City bombing. He has authored or coauthored 34 articles and book chapters pertaining to EMDR, trauma, grief, and law enforcement stress.

Foreword

Foreword taken from *Implementing EMDR Early Mental Health Interventions for Man-Made and Natural Disasters: Models, Scripted Protocols, and Summary Sheets*, edited by Marilyn Luber. © Springer Publishing Company, LLC.

Human beings are born into the care and company of others. From our first breath, our lives are a progressive encounter and mastery of environing stresses, mediated to an overwhelming degree by the web of social relationships and cultural meanings that sustain us throughout our lives. Sometimes, our individual capacity to manage excessive stress derails us and we may need assistance to reestablish a healthy coping capability. The evolution of mental health resources in developed countries has expanded the availability and efficacy of such assistance for individuals overcome by personal traumatic stress in normal times.

But disaster is not "normal"; in fact it is a severe disruption of the normal context in which we can find our bearings and rely on familiar systems of support. Disaster brings very high levels of traumatic stress at the same time that it undermines the usual coping resources and systems of care that may mitigate trauma or support healing.

The authors collected in this volume have been creative participants in the first generation of therapists who employed EMDR as a clinical treatment for posttraumatic stress disorder and related conditions. They know firsthand what research has confirmed—that EMDR is an effective and efficacious treatment for trauma in both children and adults, across all cultures and groups where it has been employed. It was only natural that they would want to apply this therapy to the massive trauma issues arising in modern day disasters, whether these arise from natural events (earthquake, tsunami, hurricane) or man-made disasters (warfare, flight from persecution, or famine).

However, although much psychotherapy has advanced in the past century in some parts of the world, it remains substantially underdeveloped where most of the world's people live. Moreover, even in places where psychotherapy is well-established it is not widely available at all socioeconomic levels. And most important, it is not widely understood by those who coordinate disaster response nationally or internationally that psychotherapy has a valuable role in early disaster intervention.

Clinician volunteers from the EMDR Humanitarian Assistance Program (HAP) and sister organizations have not been discouraged by these circumstances. As the following chapters recount, they have rolled up their sleeves and entered into the scene of disaster determined to find out how principles of EMDR can be best utilized to reduce trauma and increase the coping capacity of disaster survivors so that the goals of recovery and adaptation can be more fully and rapidly attained.

I had the privilege of meeting and working with many of the authors collected here while I served as Executive Director of HAP. They accomplished much by their direct service to survivors and by their teaching of useful skills to local caregivers. But they also learned much about the capacity of other cultures to support the coping efforts of their members, about the need for mental health response to blend collaboratively into the overall efforts of disaster responders to also address medical, nutritional, shelter, security, economic, and other needs. They learned the importance of adapting the mental health response to the particular phase of disaster recovery, and to the need for special attention to the first responders and local human service workers confronting vicarious traumatization.

Surely one of the most universal lessons learned was that populations and public officials everywhere were rarely equipped in advance to grapple with the emergent mental health issues that arise out of a community-wide disaster. From this recognition has come a growing effort to develop in all countries a more widespread understanding of traumatic stress and its treatment. Especially because disasters tend to occur in those countries and populations that are least resilient, the efforts to build up public understanding of trauma and caregiver skills for stress reduction *before disaster strikes* seem most likely to mitigate the psychological toll of future disasters. That is why HAP has been particularly interested in developing Trauma Recovery Networks in all countries where HAP works.

In this latest insightful volume gathered and edited by Marilyn Luber, the authors have combined the lessons learned with personal accounts of how they proceeded. There is still much to be done to integrate mental health care effectively into disaster response worldwide, but this volume will help to point the way to best practices.

Robert Gelbach, PhD
Past Executive Director at EMDR Humanitarian Assistance Programs

Preface

All of us familiar with EMDR have heard about Francine Shapiro's 1987-walk in the park and how she observed her own disturbing thoughts disappear. On reflection, she realized that her eye movements seemed to be resulting in a decrease of her once distressing thoughts. She was surprised and intrigued and tried it again with other thoughts. It worked again. She decided to try it with friends and when it worked again, she tried it with clients. She took this eye movement phenomenon and crafted a protocol based on the following elements:

- Incident: "Describe the memory from which you wish relief in terms of who was involved and what had happened."
- Picture: "Isolate a single picture that represents the entire memory (preferably the most traumatic point of the incident) and indicate who and what is in the picture."
- Negative cognition (NC): "What words about yourself or the incident best go with the picture?"
- SUD scale: "Imagine the traumatic scene and the words of the belief statement ___ (state the negative cognition) and assign a SUDs (subjective units of disturbance scale) where 0 = (neutral or calm) to 10 = (the worst you can think of); how does it feel?"
- Positive cognition (PC): "How would you like to feel instead?"
- Validity of cognition (VoC) for PC: On a 1 to 7 scale where 1 feels completely false and 7 feels completely true, how true does the new statement feel to you?" (Shapiro, 1989)

She called it Eye Movement Desensitization (EMD). Over time, as she observed the processing of many traumatic incidents by many clients, she believed that the results went beyond a desensitization effect and actually reprocessed and changed clients' perceptions of their traumas; she added an "R" for "Reprocessing" and renamed EMD to EMDR (Shapiro, 1991).

In 1989, the San Francisco Bay Area earthquake not only disrupted this community, it changed the way Francine viewed trauma that had recently/just occurred. As more and more clients came to her office to process their experiences of the quake, she noticed that something was different when she used her normal protocol for EMDR: It was not generalizing. Instead of targeting the memory and having the process link to the other associations related to the traumatic memory network, she had to be more actively engaged in helping clients target the next part of their earthquake experience. It was as if the parts were not yet integrated into a whole. She realized that the memories her clients were telling her had not yet consolidated and that she needed to figure out how to help them link into the memory networks associated with the event. The premise of EMDR is the Adaptive Information Processing Model (AIP; for more in-depth descriptions, see Shapiro, 1995, 2001, 2006; Shapiro, Kaslow, & Maxfield, 2007); this means that everyone has an inborn predisposition to move toward health and the internal ability to accomplish it. When this movement is obstructed (and not related to a lack of information or organic issues), it is probable that the experiences become dysfunctionally stored and unable to connect with other adaptive information. As a result, clients may have maladaptive images, perceptual distortions, emotions, and sensations that are "stuck" in trauma time, unable to process. That is, adaptive information is unable to link into the memory networks holding the dysfunctionally stored information. The goal becomes to enable the more adaptive information held in other neural networks to link into these dysfunctionally stored memories and facilitate normal memory processing.

In response to her clients' needs, she created the Protocol for Recent Traumatic Events (Shapiro, 1995; 2001). The protocol she crafted addressed how to reprocess the elements of an unconsolidated memory with little/no linkages. She started by obtaining a "narrative history" of the event. She wisely took each of the separate aspects of the memory her clients reported and treated each one of them as a separate target with the EMDR Standard procedure up to the installation of the positive cognition (PC). She thoughtfully decided to not go beyond that because clients would then have to pay attention to body sensations that would continue to be there, she reasoned, because the whole memory had yet to be completed. If there was a most disturbing element of the memory, she started there; if not, she followed clients' chronologies of the event. After the first part of the memory was completed, she did the others in chronological order.

To check the work, she asked clients to visualize the entire sequence of the event with their eyes closed as she figured they would be better able to concentrate on their experiences and associate to it. If they did notice that there was some residual distress, she asked them to stop and then she used the EMDR Procedure including the NC and PC. She had clients continue this process and repeat it—if needed—until the whole event could be experienced with no emotional, cognitive, or somatic change. By asking clients next to open their eyes and think of the whole event from start to finish, she could observe if they could also keep one foot in the present and one in the not-so-distant past. Then, she installed the PC. After this was done, she was ready to check and see if clients had any residual distress in their bodies that needed processing; so she had them do the body scan. When all of the different elements of the event were completed and the body scan was clear, she asked for any present stimuli such as triggers that resulted in a startle response, nightmares, or other reminders of the event that were still disturbing; she processed each trigger with her clients. Although she did not write about the future template in this section of her book, she discusses the 3-Pronged Protocol throughout it and so it is assumed that she includes this as well. Out of the devastating San Francisco Bay Area earthquake of 1989 came a new treatment for recent trauma.

Over the years, recognition of EMDR as a treatment has grown. In fact the following organizations are incorporating EMDR into their treatment guidelines: Clinical Division of the American Psychological Association (Chambless et al., 1998); United Kingdom Department of Health (2001); National Council for Mental Health (Israel) (Bleich, Kotler, Kutz, & Shalev, 2002); Clinical Resource Efficiency Support Team of the Northern Ireland Department of Health, Social Services and Public Safety, Belfast (CREST, 2003); Dutch National Steering Committee Guidelines Mental Health Care (2003); Stockholm: Medical Program Committee/ Stockholm City Council, Sweden (Sjöblom et al., 2003); American Psychiatric Association (2004); Department of Veterans Affairs & Department of Defense (2004); French National Institute of Health and Medical Research (INSERM, 2004); Therapy Advisor (2004–2007); National Collaborating Center for Mental Health (2005); Australian Centre for Posttraumatic Mental Health (2007); Practice Guidelines of the International Society for Traumatic Stress Studies (Foa, 2009); California Evidence-Based Clearinghouse for Child Welfare (2010); and the Substance Abuse and Mental Health Services Administration (SAMHSA) National Registry of Evidence-Based Programs and Practices (SAMHSA, 2011) (retrieved from the EMDR Institute website [www.emdr.com] and Schubert & Lee [2009]). Only two of these guidelines include specific references to the use of EMDR with clients diagnosed with acute stress disorder (APA, 2004; Australian Centre for Posttraumatic Mental Health, 2007). The other guidelines designate EMDR as an evidence-based treatment for PTSD; however, it seems that all of the guidelines are referring to EMDR related to chronic PTSD (after 3 months).

Kutz, Resnick, and Dekel (2008) point out that information on "the biology and psychology of acute stress syndromes is relatively sparse," and they go on to suggest, based on their clinical experience with terror and accident victims, that the current idea of time-related definitions of acute, posttraumatic stress might need to be modified and gave the following example: "the border (4 weeks) between ASD and acute PTSD seems utterly arbitrary, and both ASD and acute PTSD seem to form a continuous acute stress (AS) Syndrome." In a similar vein, Mark Russell, Tammera Cooke, and Susan Rogers in their chapter, "EMDR and Effective Management of Acute Stress Injuries: Early Mental Health Intervention From a Military Perspective," ask a similar question, "What is the difference between 3 weeks and 6 days (acute stress disorder) and 4 weeks and a day (PTSD)?" They note that after 4 weeks, the ASD diagnosis automatically converts to PTSD and EMDR is one of the few "A-level" trauma-targeted psychotherapies for PTSD. Also, they cite clinical case studies reported by Russell (2006) and Wesson and Gould (2009) showing that EMDR treatment is successful when treating combat-related ASR and ASD for those on active duty in the military. They believe that this distinction is arbitrary and empirically unsupported.

Elan Shapiro (2012, p. 244), in his article looking at the field of early psychological intervention (EPI) after trauma and the place of EMDR, reports, "the state of current evidence about early response to trauma and subsequent disorders reveals a complex picture. Bryant, Creamer, O'Donnell, Silove, and McFarlane (2011), summarizing the findings of an ambitious study which investigated the extent to which ASD at 1 month predicts posttraumatic psychiatric disorders at 12 months after trauma, in a large sample from five Australian hospitals concluded that the ASD diagnosis has limited utility in identifying recent trauma-exposed individuals who are at high risk for PTSD . . . however . . . most people diagnosed with ASD will suffer some psychiatric disorder a year later. . . . In contrast the overall utility of the diagnosis as an early screening strategy . . . is very limited because the majority of people who develop a disorder will not initially display full or subsyndromal ASD" (Bryant et al., 2011, p. 5).

Shapiro (2012, p. 244) discusses practical and ethical questions concerning the importance of treatment of ASD since so many go on to develop PTSD or other psychiatric disorders (Bryant, Friedman, Spiegel, Ursano, & Strain, 2010; Roberts, Kitchiner, Kenardy, & Bisson, 2009) and the fact that PTSD is only one of several disorders that can result from trauma may mean that we could be overlooking an important group who go on to develop these disorders. Shapiro goes on to report (2012, p. 244), "The possibility of delayed-onset PTSD should also be remembered, as it was found to occur in up to 68% of cases, depending on definitions (Andrews, Brewin, Philpott, & Stewart, 2007)." Other concerns, also in Shapiro's article (2012, p. 242), are mentioned by Vanitallie (2002), such as "the dysregulation of the metabolic system, stemming from chronic stress, and attempts to accommodate it (allostatic load) contributes to the development of a variety of illnesses, as well as certain disorders of immune function" or McFarlane (2010a, 2010b) who states, "The association with cardiovascular risk factors and inflammatory markers indicates that exposure to traumatic stress leads to a general disruption of an individual's underlying homeostasis" (2010b, p. 5). The high cost to individuals and to society is evident.

Although there are a number of PTSD studies concerning the efficacy of EMDR, there are very few reports on the effect of EMDR on AS; undoubtedly, more research would be helpful in more clearly defining these diagnoses and the best interventions for them. The Cochrane review of psychological interventions looked at psychological interventions within the first 3 months after a traumatic event, and was unable to recommend any early psychological intervention for general immediate use after a critical incident (Roberts, Kitchiner, Kenardy, & Bisson, 2008, 2009). However, EMDR-based protocols are being used with increasing frequency in individual or group formats to address the traumatic symptoms subsequent to man-made and natural disasters and, from the reports and the research that is beginning to be published, survivors' traumatic symptoms are decreasing.

In this text, there are several different protocols used to address AS. Francine's original EMD Protocol was brought back into circulation in the *Military and Post-Disaster Response Manual* (Shapiro, 2004) for emergency situations such as in frontline military operations. In

EMD, the client is returned to the target frequently, the SUD level is checked, and the focus is on the target without moving down the associative tracks to other events/situations. This is a highly structured intervention meant to keep the client focused in emergency situations. Emergency room treatments have also been utilized as in Gary Quinn's Emergency Response Procedure (ERP) for stabilization and Judith Guedalia and Frances Yoeli's EMDR Emergency Room and Wards Protocol (EMDR-ER©) to help get patients who had been traumatized functioning again and able to leave the ER. Kutz, Resnick, and Dekel (2008) used a "modified, abridged, single session" EMDR protocol for AS syndromes using mainly the BLS element of the Standard EMDR Protocol without the cognitive processing elements while focusing on the most distressing sensory, bodily experience, or cognitive preoccupation related to the traumatic incident and rated with the SUDs. Sets are continued until there is a decrease in distress. Their results showed that with this intervention 50% had complete relief and 27% experienced substantial relief of their acutely stressed patients and concluded that this brief variation can be useful for victims of large scale disaster as well as trauma victims in hospitals and outpatient situations. Russell has used EMD; he targets only a single memory with the image, NC, emotions, SUDs, and location of body sensation with BLS to assist with crisis intervention and reduce the primary symptoms associated with the precipitating event without following free associations that are unrelated to the target. He uses a modified EMDR (Mod-EMDR) script that he has adapted from the EMD script; here, the target can be a single incident target memory or a representative worst memory from a group of memories related to the specific event. Russell reports using these scripts with patients after a near or immediate aftermath of exposure to a severe or potentially traumatic event or when patients present with severe acute stress responses or combat and operational stress reactions.

Elan Shapiro and Brurit Laub (2008) created a comprehensive protocol called "Recent Traumatic Episode Protocol" (R-TEP) that expands the existing protocols of EMD, ER-related protocols, and EMDR together and includes ways to contain and keep clients safe while processing. Their protocol introduces four important concepts: the Traumatic Episode, the Episode Narrative, the Google Search, and Telescopic Processing.

R-TEP was used and research done with victims of a terrorist bombing in Gungoren, Istanbul (Altan Aytun et al., 2010). The participants were children and adults who scored high on the IES and the PTSD Symptom Checklist. R-TEP (incorporating EMD and Recent Event Protocols) was used with the adult participants who were seen weekly to work only on the trauma of the bombing; participants completed an IES prior to each session. The number of sessions was restricted to the completion of EMD and R-TEP. The data analyses demonstrate that EMDR was effective with the adults and helped in the prevention of PTSD and recommended the use of EMDR as a crisis intervention tool. The positive effect was maintained at a 3-month follow up. Tofani and Wheeler (2012) applied R-TEP in three different cases, observing markers such as distance concerning the trauma, a decrease in negative affect, access to information that is more adaptive, and changes in measures such as the SUDs, the VoC scale, and the revised IES-R, indicating changes in the perception of the traumatic memory. All three clients reported therapeutic changes in behavior and functioning. The EMDR R-TEP was used with over 2,000 survivors of recent earthquakes in northern Italy with pre- and posttreatment data collected showing changes in posttraumatic stress (Shapiro & Fernandez, 2013). Also, it was used with survivors from the recent earthquake in eastern Turkey in 2012 (Shapiro, 2012, p. 244).

Ignacio Jarero and Lucina Artigas created a different modification of Shapiro's (2001) Protocol for Recent Traumatic Events that provided an individual treatment format to clients suffering from recent ongoing trauma called the "EMDR Protocol for Recent Critical Incidents" (EMDR-PRECI). It was developed in the field under extremely dangerous circumstances to treat critical incidents where related stressful events continued for an extended time (often more than 6 months) and where there was no posttrauma period of safety for memory consolidation. Two randomized controlled trials (RCT) with the EMDR-PRECI have been published with delayed treatment designs supporting the efficacy of EMDR-PRECI in reducing symptoms after a 7.2 earthquake in North Baja California, Mexico (Jarero, Artigas,

& Luber, 2011), and working with traumatized first responders responding to a human massacre situation (Jarero & Uribe, 2011, 2012).

An EMDR group protocol, the EMDR Integrative Group Treatment Protocol, was created in 1997 in Mexico after Hurricane Pauline (Artigas et al., 2000, 2009). Originally, this work was designed for children and combined the Standard EMDR Protocol with a group therapy model (Artigas et al., 2000; Jarero et al., 1999). However, it has been used with good success with disaster survivors from 7 years of age upward. There are a number of reports of its success worldwide (Aduriz, Knopfler, & Bluthgen, 2009; Errebo, Knipe, Forte, Karlin, & Altayli, 2008; Jarero et al., 2006, 2008), or with adaptations to meet the circumstances (Fernandez et al., 2004; Gelbach & Davis, 2007; Korkmazlar-Oral & Pamuk, 2002; Wilson, Tinker, Hofmann, Becker, & Marshall, 2000; Zaghrout-Hodali, Alissa, & Dodgson, 2008). Jarero and Artigas (2010) applied the EMDR-IGTP during 3 consecutive days to 20 adults in a Central American country with an ongoing geopolitical crisis. Results of this uncontrolled study showed decreases in scores on the SUDs and IES. Changes in the IES were maintained at a 14-week follow-up even with ongoing crisis. Louise Maxfield (2008, p. 75) wrote that, "EMDR-IGTP has been found effective in several field trials and has been used for thousands of disaster survivors around the world."

The Imma Protocol (2009) was adapted from the IGTP and includes the Four Elements for Stress Management and group dynamic principles. Also, the Indian response team in Gujarat created an EMDR group protocol including the Butterfly Hug that was used with approximately 16,000 children in the area with positive results and decrease in traumatic symptoms.

There have been some cases described in the literature that discuss successful treatment of adults using EMD with two women, 1 month after the Great Hanshin-Awaji earthquake. They had been diagnosed with ASD. With both women, the SUDs decreased to 0 and the changes were maintained at a 5-month follow-up (Ichii & Kumano, 1996).

Francine Shapiro's Protocol for Recent Traumatic Events was used with 9/11 survivors (Silver, Rogers, Knipe, & Colelli, 2005). They found that EMDR was a useful treatment intervention in the immediate aftermath of the event and later as well. In 2008, Colelli and Patterson found that their three cases demonstrated the usefulness of EMDR as a postdisaster treatment. It was only used in one case less than 3 months after 9/11; however, it was also found effective after 9 and 12 months. Fernandez (2002) used an average of 6.5 EMDR sessions for successful treatment with child survivors of the Molise earthquake in Italy; this was done over treatment cycles of 1 month, 3 months, and 1 year post incident. In 2008, Fernandez worked with a tsunami survivor diagnosed with acute PTSD and in a case study reported that after three EMDR sessions, the survivor was symptom-free. The different forms of the EMDR protocol are being used quite actively in the EMDR community to relieve the distress of patients post disaster as has been illustrated above. Given the amount of catastrophes that we seem to be facing in the world on a more and more regular basis, it is an appropriate time for a book such as *Implementing EMDR Early Mental Health Interventions for Man-Made and Natural Disasters: Models, Scripted Protocols, and Summary Sheets*.

The seed for *Implementing EMDR Early Mental Health Interventions for Man-Made and Natural Disasters: Models, Scripted Protocols, and Summary Sheets* grew out of this author's many exposures to recent trauma over the years: growing up under the constant threat of nuclear holocaust; living through the Vietnam era; hearing about sexual assault from my clients and about motor vehicle accidents; learning EMDR in 1992 and how to treat trauma-related issues; responding to Oklahoma City; training Israeli and Palestinian mental health practitioners to be EMDR facilitators and/or consultants and hearing their stories; meeting and working with trauma survivors of terrorist attacks in Jerusalem and Bethlehem; seeing the trauma symptoms displayed by Israeli supervisees during a supervisory course and working with their traumas after the second intifada; debriefing with the Philadelphia-based FBI group who responded to 9/11; assisting the friends and relatives of a friend after the brutal murder of his adolescent daughter; attending conferences where disaster responses were emphasized; interviewing 61 members of the EMDR community for the EMDRIA newsletter and hearing about their lives and how they have responded to many different types of disasters (e.g., hurricanes, earthquakes, terrorist attacks, war, acid attacks) in many different places (e.g., Oklahoma City, Bangladesh, New York, Serbia, Croatia, Rwanda, Mexico); and talking and connecting with many more colleagues and friends after they returned from disaster responses.

In 2009, *Eye Movement Desensitization and Reprocessing (EMDR) Scripted Protocols: Basics and Special Situations* (Luber, 2009a) was published. Although it was not a book about recent trauma per se, it did contain at least 10 out of 35 chapters that were recent-trauma related. Clearly, recent trauma was occupying this author's thoughts. This interest in recent trauma was amplified after a presentation at the EMDR European Annual Conference in Amsterdam. Konuk (2009, June) was presenting on "Mental Health Response and Training Program for Developing Countries: Turkish Model." The depth and breadth of his response to this enormous natural disaster was inspiring and seemed an important model that other EMDR disaster responders would be interested to know about. This ongoing Turkish Project began with the response to the earthquake but was continuing currently, and he discussed the elements that he thought were pertinent to a disaster response: financing, the training of mental health professionals, providing psychological services, creating a trauma therapy center, building a trauma library, preparing for other disasters by engaging consultants who had experience in this area, and research. From 1999 until the time of the presentation (2009), his group trained 550 therapists in the EMDR Basic Training. They also trained 900 students and professionals in early trauma intervention skills. In the aftermath of their 1999 disaster project, the response teams have learned so much and are so well organized that they can be on-site within 30 to 60 minutes after any disaster in many areas in Turkey. As a result, they are held in high regard nationally and have had the ability to respond to more earthquakes, floods, bombings, and an airplane crash. Emre's pithy final words were the following, *"If you intend to go into the 'disaster business' in a developing country: Find the owner; find the money; teach organizational skills; teach how to write a proposal; and teach project management!"*

However, it was after the 2011 Tohoku earthquake and tsunami in Japan occurred that the need for this type of book became pressing. This author had visited Japan less than a year before the catastrophe to do an EMDR HAP military training with Nancy Errebo at the Atsugi Naval Base several hours outside of Tokyo. In the hopes of supporting interaction between the EMDR Japan Association members and the American EMDR-trained mental health personnel on the U.S. military bases in Japan, this author made the formal introductions so that they could get to know and work with each other. When the disaster struck, we were all in touch with each other trying to find ways to support our Japanese colleagues. This author began to pull together the recent trauma-related protocols for our Japanese colleagues and helped them connect with other EMDR practitioners who were experts in the field of recent trauma—all of whom are represented in this book. It became clear that it would be far easier if all of these protocols were housed in one text and/or on a CD version; it was at that point that this author approached her editor at Springer Publishing Company, Sheri W. Sussman, with the idea. However, it was not just the protocols that were of importance; it was also how members of the EMDR community were responding to disasters globally. A proposal was written and accepted.

Implementing EMDR Early Mental Health Interventions for Man-Made and Natural Disasters: Models, Scripted Protocols, and Summary Sheets is akin to the structure in the other EMDR Scripted Protocol texts:

- *Eye Movement Desensitization and Reprocessing (EMDR) Scripted Protocols: Basics and Special Situations* (Luber, 2009a)
- *Eye Movement Desensitization and Reprocessing (EMDR) Scripted Protocols: Special Populations* (Luber, 2009b)
- *Eye Movement Desensitization and Reprocessing (EMDR) Scripted Protocols With Summary Sheets (CD-ROM Version)*: Basics and Special Situations (Luber, 2012a)
- *Eye Movement Desensitization and Reprocessing (EMDR) Scripted Protocols With Summary Sheets (CD-ROM Version): Special Populations* (Luber, 2012b)

The only exception to this structure is the inclusion of the first section on Early Mental Health Intervention Response: An International Perspective.

The following description from *Eye Movement Desensitization and Reprocessing (EMDR) Scripted Protocols: Basics and Special Situations* gives a clear understanding of the evolution and importance of this format:

> *Eye Movement Desensitization and Reprocessing (EMDR) Scripted Protocols: Basics and Special Situations* grew out of a perceived need that mental health practitioners could be served by a place to access both traditional and newly developed protocols in a way that adheres to best clinical practices incorporating the Standard EMDR Protocol that includes working on the past, present, and future issues (the 3-Pronged Protocol) related to the problem and the 11-Step Standard Procedure that includes attention to the following steps: image, negative cognition (NC), positive cognition (PC), validity of cognition (VoC), emotion, subjective units of disturbance (SUD), and location of body sensation, desensitization, installation, body scan, and closure. Often, EMDR texts embed the protocols in a great deal of explanatory material that is essential in the process of learning EMDR. However, sometimes, as a result, practitioners move away from the basic importance of maintaining the integrity of the Standard EMDR Protocol and keeping adaptive information processing in mind when conceptualizing the course of treatment for a patient. It is in this way that the efficacy of this powerful methodology is lost.
>
> "Scripting" becomes a way not only to inform and remind the EMDR practitioner of the component parts, sequence, and language used to create an effective outcome, but also to create a template for practitioners and researchers to use for reliability and/or a common denominator so that the form of working with EMDR is consistent. The concept that has motivated this work was conceived within the context of assisting EMDR clinicians in accessing the scripts of the full protocols in one place and to profit from the creativity of other EMDR clinicians who have kept the spirit of EMDR but have also taken into consideration the needs of the population with whom they work or the situations that they encounter. Reading a script is by no means a substitute for adequate training, competence, clinical acumen, and integrity; if you are not a trained EMDR therapist and/or you are not knowledgeable in the field for which you wish to use the script, these scripts are not for you.
>
> As EMDR is a fairly complicated process, and indeed, has intimidated some from integrating it into their daily approach to therapy, this book provides step-by-step scripts that will enable beginning practitioners to enhance their expertise more quickly. . . .
>
> These scripted protocols are intended for clinicians who have read Shapiro's text (2001) and received EMDR training from an EMDR-accredited trainer. An EMDR trainer is a licensed mental health practitioner who has been approved by the association active in the clinician's country of practice. (Luber, 2009a, p. xxi)

In 2012, the CD-ROM versions of the original 2009 books were published in a different format. Included in the CD-ROM were just the protocols and summary sheets (the notes were not included and are in the 2009 texts). As explained in the Preface of *Eye Movement Desensitization and Reprocessing (EMDR) Scripted Protocols With Summary Sheets (CD-ROM Version): Basics and Special Situations* (Luber, 2012a):

> The idea for *Eye Movement Desensitization and Reprocessing (EMDR) Scripted Protocols: Summary Sheets for Basics and Special Situations* grew out of the day-to-day work with the protocols that allowed for a deeper understanding of case conceptualization from an EMDR perspective. While using the scripted protocols and acquiring a greater familiarity with the use of the content, the idea of placing the information in a summarized format grew. This book of scripted protocols and summary sheets was undertaken so that clinicians could easily use the material in *Eye Movement Desensitization and Reprocessing (EMDR) Scripted Protocols: Basics and Special Situations*. While working on the summary sheets, the interest in brevity collided with the thought that clinicians could also use these summary sheets to remind themselves of the steps in the process clarified in the scripted protocols. The original goal to be a summary of the necessary data gathered from the protocol was transformed into this new creation of data summary and memory tickler for the protocol itself! Alas, the summary sheets have become a bit longer than originally anticipated. Nonetheless, they are shorter—for the most part—than the protocols themselves and do summarize the data in an easily readable format. . . .

The format for this book is also innovative. The scripts and summary sheets are available in an expandable, downloadable format for easy digital access. Because EMDR is a fairly complicated process, and often intimidating, these scripted protocols with their accompanying summary sheets can be helpful in a number of ways. To begin with, by facilitating the gathering of important data about the client from the protocol, the scripted protocol and/or summary sheet then can be inserted into the client's chart as documentation. The summary sheet can assist the clinician in formulating a concise and clear treatment plan for clients and can be used to support quick retrieval of the essential issues and experiences during the course of treatment. Practitioners can enhance their expertise more quickly by having a place that instructs and reminds them of the essential parts of EMDR practice. By having these fill-in PDF forms, clinicians can easily tailor the scripted protocols and summary sheets to the needs of their clients, their consultees/supervisees, and themselves by editing and saving the protocol scripts and summary sheets.

Consultants/Supervisors will find these scripted protocols and summary sheets useful while working with consultees/supervisees in their consultation/supervision groups. These works bring together many ways of handling current, important issues in psychotherapy and EMDR treatment. They also include a helpfu way to organize the data collected that is key to case consultation and the incorporation of EMDR into newly trained practitioners' practices. (Luber, 2012a, p. iv)

The main book is divided into eight parts with 26 chapters that include working with recent trauma models of response, resources, on-site responses, individuals, groups, special populations, special situations, and clinician self-care VII. The first part is devoted to the "Early Mental Health Intervention Response: An International Perspective." There are six chapters included in this section and all of them revolve around how disaster struck in the authors' environments and how they responded. Alan Cohen and Mooli Lahad explain the evolution of their Community Stress Prevention Center (CSPC) that was destined to become one of the earliest (1979)—if not *the* earliest—center to work with a mental health response in Israel and possibly in the world. Through the efforts of the CSPC, many people globally have learned how to respond to major disasters. Their influence is illustrated in the chapters from Turkey and Spain that follow. The second chapter is by Emre Konuk and his assistant, Zeynep Zat. As described above, Emre was part of the Turkish Psychological initiative to respond to the Marmara earthquake of 1999. They describe how, from the beginning, they incorporated a structure upon which they could improve their mental health disaster response capabilities over the years and then explain how they have gone on to accomplish it. Maria Cervera has been one of the major critical incident leaders in Spain. She describes how the Spanish psychologists—with the help of what they learned from Mooli Lahad's CSPC and the Independent Counseling and Advisory Services (ICAS)—built a national network of psychological professionals who are trained in mental health disaster response and related treatments. She explains a number of different interventions and how their ability to respond has made a difference throughout Spain. Ignacio (Nacho) Jarero and Susana Uribe take the opportunity in their chapter to describe Nacho's "The Seven Phase Model." They describe this multicomponent model for an early psychological intervention program that is carried out by the Early Psychological Intervention Team (EPIT). They discuss in detail what to do before, during, and after deployment to the disaster zone. Through their organization, Asociación Mexicana Para Ayuda Mental en Crisis (AMAMECRISIS), they have assisted and taught their method to many clinicians. The fruits of their work—the Butterfly Hug, the EMDR Integrative Group Treatment Protocol (IGTP) for Children and for Adults, and the EMDR Protocol for Recent Critical Incidents (EMDR-PRECI)—are the gifts from them that we use all around the world. Carol Martin, the Executive Director of EMDR Humanitarian Assistance Programs (EMDR HAP), and Nancy Simons, Clinical Director of EMDR HAP, have written about the lessons learned by this program over the years. They go into more depth about the Trauma Recovery Networks (TRNs) that are forming across the United States to respond to local disasters in their communities and sometimes to join other communities, if a response is needed. The last chapter in this part speaks to how a small group of volunteers from Mumbai was able to mount a huge response after the Gujarat earthquake of 2001. Sushma Mehrotra, Mrinalini Purandare, Parul Tank, and Hvovi

Bhagwagar discuss this project and what they learned about responding to a major disaster. They, too, created an EMDR group protocol to respond to the needs of the victims.

The second part is devoted to "EMDR Early Mental Health Resources." Although there were many to choose from, there are only two of the most used resources are in this section: the Butterfly Hug created by Luci Artigas and the Four Elements Exercise for Stress Management by Elan Shapiro. These two individuals have been central to the creation of a number of the chapters in this text as a result of their sensitivity, creativity, and ability to transform a difficult situation by creating something totally new and specific to their context; they truly have the gift of turning therapy into an art form. "EMDR On-Site or Hospital Response" is the third section. In these chapters, we find very resourceful ways to work with trauma victims in the immediacy of their trauma. Gary Quinn's Emergency Response Procedure (ERP) gives us an important way to stabilize patients in the emergency room or on-site. Judith Guedalia's work assisted by Frances Yoeli is called the EMDR Emergency Room and Wards Protocol (EMDR-ER©) and they walk us through a thoughtful way of helping stabilize trauma survivors and creating new narratives for their trauma patients.

The fourth part, "EMDR Early Intervention Procedures for Individuals," presents the scripted protocol for Francine Shapiro's Protocol for Recent Traumatic Events, discussed in the beginning of this Preface. It is the basis—along with the Standard EMDR Protocol—upon which we have constructed our EMDR response for recent trauma. Elan Shapiro and Brurit Laub build on this foundation with their Recent Traumatic Episode Protocol (R-TEP) and help us conceptualize Early EMDR Intervention (EEI). Nacho Jarero and Luci Artigas end this section with their EMDR Protocol for Recent Critical Incidents (EMDR-PRECI). They, too, modify the Protocol for Recent Traumatic Events to incorporate the needs of the victims with whom they work.

"EMDR Early Intervention for Groups" is the subject of the fifth part. The first chapter is the ubiquitous EMDR Integrative Group Treatment Protocol (IGTP) for Children and the second chapter is a newer version of the IGTP modified for adults. The IGTP has been the basis for group treatment since its inception in the late '90s and has been used around the world. The Imma EMDR Group Protocol by Brurit Laub and Esti Bar-Sade is a modification of the IGTP and offers some interesting and dynamic changes for working with children. Aiton Birnbaum is another creative individual who brought his talents to introducing a workbook format for EMDR. This new approach can be used with individuals or groups and can be helpful especially for those clients who are more visual. It also offers an option for a more private way of working with traumatic material. In this chapter, you will find an actual workbook that you can copy or print out for each client.

First responders are our society's designated protectors. Whether they are firefighters, emergency medical service professionals, the police, or the military, they are trained to respond when many of us would run in the other direction. In the first chapter of Part VI of this book, "EMDR Early Mental Health Interventions: First Responders," Robbie Adler-Tapia delves into the world of first responders/protective service workers including firefighters and emergency medical services (EMS) professionals and helps us understand what we need to know to work with this population. Roger Solomon has been working with the police and law enforcement in many different capacities throughout the course of his career. He blends his knowledge of EMDR with his experience of the police to help us understand what we need to know to work with these officers of the law. Mark Russell is retired from the military with 26 years of service. He has translated his experience, with the help of his assistant, Tammera Cooke, and his colleague, Susan Rogers, a long-time provider of treatment to war and trauma survivors, to introduce us to the world of the military. All of these chapters introduce modifications when working with EMDR to accommodate the needs of first responders.

Part VII concerns "EMDR Early Intervention for Special Situations." The first chapter by David Blore is a protocol that addresses the particular issues regarding underground trauma. With his experience working with miners, David helps us enter into their domain so that we have a better appreciation for what the underground world is like and how to approach it when trauma strikes. The next chapter, which David wrote with Manda Holmshaw, grew out of his experience with clients who were uncomfortable revealing the content of their traumas and concerns. Through the EMDR "Blind to Therapist Protocol," they help clients reprocess their material with privacy and dignity.

The last section in the book, Part VIII, "EMDR and Clinician Self-Care: Recent Trauma Response," is at the heart of any well-designed disaster response. It is often the case that we take better care of our clients than ourselves. When it comes to disaster response, this attitude can be another type of disaster in the making. Neal Daniels's chapter discusses how we can inoculate ourselves against burnout and secondary PTSD by taking care to process residual material from our work on a regular basis. In Karen Alter-Reid's chapter about her own FR-TRN response to the Newtown shooting tragedy, self-care is a primary ingredient in the organization of their work. There are a number of checks and support systems that create a holding environment for the team so that no one slips through the cracks to face the aftermath of disaster response alone. Derek Farrell responded to the call for facilitators and volunteers to assist in Turkey after the earthquake. His chapter teaches us how even the most perceptive of clinicians can miss something in the face of such overwhelming destruction. Derek teaches us the signs and symptoms of vicarious trauma and then uses this knowledge to create better caretaking for himself and his clients. The last chapter in this section and the book is about the worst case scenarios in recent trauma response. Nacho and Susana again use the format that they did in Chapter 4 of pre-, during, and postdeployment to create checklists to assure that one has thought of all the variables when responding to disaster.

Appendix A includes the scripts for the 3-Pronged Protocol that includes past memories, current triggers, and future templates. These scripts are there to assist practitioners so that they can place them in clients' charts to use with a particular issue or as a reminder of all of the elements needed for the work to be complete.

Appendix B is an updated list of all of the EMDR associations and regional associations globally. In this way, it is possible to know where practitioners of EMDR are to be found in any part of the world. This list also includes the EMDR Humanitarian Assistance Programs that exist to help victims of man-made and natural disasters. There are also resources that catalogue information such as the Francine Shapiro Library, an invaluable source of knowledge for any EMDR practitioner. There are also links to the *EMDR Journal* and other e-journals where trauma-related information can be found.

This book is meant to go with you to disasters. Here, you will find a great deal of information that will support you in responding to the challenges that you might face when designing a disaster response or responding to a disaster. Each one of these protocols has been tried in the field. Although there is no definitive research about them, it has begun to trickle in, and you can be the next author of research in this area. Try these suggestions and protocols in your own community and join your Humanitarian Assistance Program groups and/or TRNs to create an EMDR disaster response that is felt around the world.

REFERENCES

Aduriz, M. E., Knopfler, C., & Bluthgen, C. (2009). Helping child flood victims using group EMDR intervention in Argentina: Treatment outcome and gender differences. *International Journal of Stress Management, 16,* 138–153.

Altan Aytun, O., Ozcan, G., Ciftci, A,. Konuk, E. Yuksek, H., Karakus, D., . . . Vatan Ozcelik, D. (2010, June). The effects of early EMDR interventions (EMD and R-TEP) on the victims of a terrorist bombing in Istanbul. In *Treatment of children/acute stress.* Symposium conducted at the annual meeting of the EMDR Europe Association, Hamburg, Germany.

American Psychiatric Association (APA). (2004). *Practice guideline for the treatment of patients with acute stress disorder and posttraumatic stress disorder.* Arlington, VA: American Psychiatric Association Practice Guidelines.

Andrews, B., Brewin, C. R., Philpott, R., & Stewart, L. (2007). Delayed-onset posttraumatic stress disorder: A systematic review of the evidence. *American Journal of Psychiatry, 164*(9), 1319–1326.

Artigas, L., Jarero, I., Mauer, M., López Cano, T., & Alcalá, N. (2000, September). *EMDR and traumatic stress after natural disasters: Integrative treatment protocol and the Butterfly Hug.* Poster presented at the EMDRIA Conference, Toronto, Ontario, Canada.

Artigas, L., Jarero, I., Alcalá, N., & Lopez-Cano, T. (2009). The EMDR Integrative Group Treatment Protocol (IGTP). In M. Luber (Ed.) *Eye movement desensitization and reprocessing (EMDR) scripted protocols: Basic and special situations* (pp. 279–288). New York, NY: Springer.

Australian Centre for Posttraumatic Mental Health. (2007). *Australian Guidelines for the Treatment of Adults with Acute Stress Disorder and Posttraumatic Stress Disorder.* Melbourne, Victoria: Author.

Bleich, A., Kotler, M., Kutz, I., & Shalev, A. (2002). *Guidelines for the assessment and professional intervention with terror victims in the hospital and in the community.* A position paper of the (Israeli) National Council for Mental Health, Jerusalem, Israel.

Bryant, R. A., Friedman, M. J., Spiegel, D., Ursano, R., & Strain. J. (2010). A review of acute stress disorder in *DSM-5. Depression and Anxiety, 28*(9), 802–817.

Bryant, R. A., Creamer, M., O'Donnell, M., Silove, D., & McFarlane, A. C. (2011). The capacity of acute stress disorder to predict posttraumatic psychiatric disorders. *Journal of Psychiatric Research, 46*(2), 168–173.

California Evidence-Based Clearinghouse for Child Welfare. (2010). *Trauma treatment for children.* Retrieved from www.cebc4cw.org

Chambless, D. L., Baker, M. J., Baucom, D. H., Beutler, L. E., Calhoun, K. S., Cris-Christoph, P., . . . Woody, S. R. (1998). Update on empirically validated therapies, II. *The Clinical Psychologist, 51*, 3–16.

Chemtob, C. M., Tolin, D. F., van der Kolk, B. A., & Pitman, R. K. (2000). Eye movement desensitization and reprocessing. In E. A. Foa, T. M. Keane, & M. J. Friedman (Eds.). *Effective treatments for PTSD: Practice guidelines from the International Society for Traumatic Stress Studies.* New York, NY: Guilford.

Clinical Resource Efficiency Support Team. (2003). *The management of posttraumatic stress disorder in adults.* A publication of the Clinical Resource Efficiency Support Team of the Northern Ireland Department of Health, Social Services and Public Safety, Belfast.

Colelli, G., & Patterson, B. (2008). Three case reports illustrating the use of the protocol for recent traumatic events following the World Trade Center terrorist attack. *Journal of EMDR Practice and Research, 2*(2), 114–123.

Department of Veterans Affairs and Department of Defense. (2004). *VA/DoD clinical practice guideline for the management of post-traumatic stress.* Washington, DC: Veterans Health Administration, Department of Veterans Affairs and Health Affairs, Department of Defense. Office of Quality and Performance publication 10Q-CPG/PTSD-04.

Dutch National Steering Committee Guidelines Mental Health Care. (2003). Multidisciplinary Guideline Anxiety Disorders. Utrecht, Netherlands: Quality Institute Health Care CBO/Trimbos Institute.

Errebo, N., Knipe, J., Forte, K., Karlin, V., & Altayli, B. (2008). EMDR-HAP training in Sri Lanka following 2004 tsunami. *Journal of EMDR Practice & Research, Fernandez (2002) 2*(2), 124–139.

Fernandez, I. (2002, Dicembre). I disturbi post-traumatici da stress Fattori di rischio, aspetti diagnostici e trattamento con l'EMDR (The post-traumatic stress disorder factors of risk, diagnostic aspects and treatment with the EMDR). Rivista Scientifica di Psicologia, Sommario 01, 15–124.

Fernandez, I. (2007). EMDR as treatment of post-traumatic reactions: A field study on children victims of an earthquake. *Educational and Child Psychology, 24*(1), 65–72.

Fernandez, I. (2008). EMDR after a critical incident: treatment of a tsunami survivor with acute posttraumatic disorder. *Journal of EMDR Practice and Research, 2*(2), 156–159.

Fernandez, I., Gallinari, E., & Lorenzetti, A. (2004). A school-based intervention for children who witnessed the Pirelli building airplane crash in Milan, Italy. *Journal of Brief Therapy, 2*, 129–136.

Foa, E. B. (2009). *Effective treatments for PTSD: Practice guidelines from the International Society for Traumatic Stress Studies*, 2nd ed. New York, NY: Guilford.

Gelbach, R., & Davis, K. (2007). Disaster response: EMDR and family systems therapy under community-wide stress. In F. Shapiro, F. W. Kaslow, & L. Maxfield (Eds.), *Handbook of EMDR and family therapy processes* (pp. 387–406). New York, NY: John Wiley.

Grainger, R. D., Levin, C., Allen-Byrd, L., Doctor, R. M., & Lee, H. (1997). An empirical evaluation of eye movement desensitization and reprocessing (EMDR) with survivors of a natural disaster. *Journal of Traumatic Stress, 10*, 665–671.

Ichii, M., & Kumano, H. (1996). Application of eye movement desensitization (EMD) to the acute stress disorder victims suffered from the Great Hanshin-Awaji Earthquake. *Japanese Journal of Brief Psychotherapy, 5*, 53–68.

Ichii, M., & Kumano, H. (1996). Eye movement desensitization by Kobe earthquake victims with acute stress disorder (EMD) application. *Japanese Association of Brief Psychotherapy, Research Brief, 5*, 53–70.

INSERM. (2004). *Psychotherapy: An evaluation of three approaches.* Paris, France: French National Institute of Health and Medical Research.

Jarero, I., & Artigas, L. (2010). The EMDR Integrative Group Treatment Protocol: Application with adults during ongoing geopolitical crisis. *Journal of EMDR Practice and Research, 4*(4), 148–155

Jarero, I., Artigas, L., & Hartung, J. (2006). EMDR Integrative Group Treatment Protocol: A post-disaster trauma intervention for children and adults. *Traumatology, 12*, 121–129.

Jarero, I., Artigas, L., & Luber, M. (2011). The EMDR Protocol for Recent Critical Incidents: Application in a disaster mental health continuum of care context. *Journal of EMDR Practice and Research, 5*(3), 82–94.

Jarero, I., Artigas, L., Mauer, M., López Cano, T., & Alcalá, N. (1999, November). *Children's post traumatic stress after natural disasters: Integrative treatment protocol.* Poster presented at the annual meeting of the International Society for Traumatic Stress Studies, Miami, Florida.

Jarero, I., Artigas, L, & Montero, M. (2008). The EMDR Integrative Group Treatment Protocol: Application with child victims of mass disaster. *Journal of EMDR Practice & Research, 2*(2), 97–105.

Jarero, I., & Uribe, S. (2011). The EMDR Protocol for Recent Critical Incidents: Brief report of an application in a human massacre situation. *Journal of EMDR Practice and Research, 5*(4), 156–165.

Jarero, I., & Uribe, S. (2012). The EMDR Protocol for Recent Critical Incidents: Follow-up report of an application in a human massacre situation. *Journal of EMDR Practice and Research, 6*(2), 50–61

Korkmazlar-Oral, U., & Pamuk, S. (2002). Group EMDR with child survivors of the earthquake in Turkey. *Journal of the American Academy of Child and Adolescent Psychiatry, 37*, 47–50.

Konuk, E. (June, 2009). *Mental Health Response and Training Program for Developing Countries: Turkish Model.* Paper presented at the EMDR Europe Association Conference, Amsterdam.

Kutz, I., Resnick, V., & Dekel R. (2008). The effect of single-session modified EMDR on acute stress syndromes. *Journal of EMDR Practice and Research, 2*(3), 190–200

Laub, B., & Bar-Sade, E. (2009a). In M. Luber (Ed.), *Eye movement desensitization and reprocessing (EMDR) scripted protocols: Basics and special situations.* New York, NY: Springer.

Luber, M. (2009b) (Ed.). *Eye movement desensitization and reprocessing (EMDR) scripted protocols: Special populations.* New York, NY: Springer.

Luber, M. (2012a) (Ed.). *Eye movement desensitization and reprocessing (EMDR) scripted protocols with summary sheets (CD-Rom version): Basics and special situations.* New York, NY: Springer.

Luber, M. (2012b) (Ed.). *Eye movement desensitization and reprocessing (EMDR) scripted protocols with summary sheets (CD-Rom version): Special populations.* New York, NY: Springer.

McFarlane, A. C. (2010a). *Abstract to plenary presentation.* Paper presented at EMDR Europe Annual Conference, Hamburg, Germany.

McFarlane, A. C. (2010b). The long-term costs of traumatic stress: intertwined physical and psychological consequences. *World Psychiatry, 9*, 3–10.

Maxfield, L. (2008). EMDR treatment of recent events and community disasters. *Journal of EMDR Practice & Research, 2*(2), 74–78.

National Collaborating Centre for Mental Health. (2005). *Post traumatic stress disorder (PTSD): The management of adults and children in primary and secondary care.* London, England: National Institute for Clinical Excellence.

National Institute for Clinical Excellence (2005, March). *Post-traumatic stress (PTSD): The management of PTSD in adults and children and secondary care.* London, England: National Collaborating Centre for Mental Health.

Roberts, N. P., Kitchiner, N. J., Kenardy, J., & Bisson, J. I. (2009). Multiple session early psychological interventions for the prevention of post-traumatic stress disorder. The Cochrane Library (Issue 3). [DOI: 10.1002/14651858.CD006869.pub2].

Roberts, N. P., Kitchiner, N. J., Kenardy, J., & Bisson, J. I. (2009). Systematic review and meta-analysis of multiple-session early interventions following traumatic events. *American Psychiatric Association, AJP in Advance.* Retrieved fromajp.psychiatryonline.org

Russell, M. C. (2006). Treating combat-related stress disorders: Multiple case study utilizing eye movement desensitization and reprocessing (EMDR) with battlefield casualties from the Iraqi war. *Military Psychology, 18*, 1–18.

SAMHSA's National Registry of Evidence-based Programs and Practices. (2011). Retrieved from http://nrepp.samhsa.gov/ViewIntervention.aspx?id = 199

Schubert, S., & Lee, C. W. (2009). Adult PTSD and its treatment with EMDR: A review of controversies, evidence, and theoretical knowledge. *Journal of EMDR Practice and Research, 3*(3), 117–132.

Shapiro, E. (2009). EMDR treatment of recent trauma. *Journal of EMDR Practice and Research, 3*(3), 141–151.

Shapiro, E. (2012, October). EMDR and early psychological intervention following trauma. *European Review of Applied Psychology, 62*(4), 241–251.

Shapiro, E., & Fernandez, I. (2013, June). *Early EMDR intervention (EEI): Theory, practice and research application in a mass disaster.* Presentation at the annual meeting of the EMDR Europe Association, Geneva, Switzerland.

Shapiro, E., & Laub, B. (2008). Early EMDR intervention (EEI): A summary, a theoretical model, and the recent traumatic episode protocol (R-TEP). *Journal of EMDR Practice and Research, 2*(2), 79–96

Shapiro, F. (1989). Eye movement desensitization: A new treatment model for post-traumatic stress disorder. *Journal of Behavior Therapy and Experimental Psychiatry, 20*, 211–217.

Shapiro, F. (1991). Eye movement desensitization and reprocessing procedure: From EMD to EMDR-a new treatment model for anxiety and related traumata. *Behavior Therapist, 14*, 122–125.

Shapiro, F. (1995) *Eye movement desensitization and reprocessing: Basic principles, protocols and procedures.* New York, NY: Guilford Press.

Shapiro, F. (2001). *Eye movement desensitization and reprocessing: Basic principles, protocols and procedures.* 2nd ed. New York, NY: Guilford Press.

Shapiro, F. (2004). *Military and post-disaster response manual*. Hamden, CT: EMDR Humanitarian Assistance Program.

Shapiro, F. (2006). *EMDR: New notes on adaptive information processing with case formulation principles, forms, scripts and worksheets*. Watsonville, CA: EMDR Institute.

Shapiro, F., Kaslow, F. W., & Maxfield, L. (2007). *Handbook of EMDR and family therapy processes*. Hoboken, NJ: Wiley.

Silver, S. M., Rogers, S., Knipe, J., & Colelli, G. (2005, February). EMDR therapy following the 9/11 terrorist attacks: A community-based intervention project in New York City. *International Journal of Stress Management, 12*(1), 29–42.

Sjöblom, P. O., Andréewitch, S., Bejerot, S., Mörtberg, E., Brinck, U., Ruck, C., & Körlin, D. (2003). *Regional treatment recommendation for anxiety disorders*. Stockholm, Sweden: Medical Program Committee/ Stockholm

Therapy Advisor (2004–2007), Retrieved from www.therapyadvisor.com

Tofani, L. R., & Wheeler, K. (2012). Le protocole de l'épisode traumatique récent: Evaluation et analyse des résultats de trois études de cas [The protocol for recent traumatic episode: Evaluation and analysis of the results of three case studies]. *Journal of EMDR Practice and Research, 6*(4), 46E–63E.

United Kingdom Department of Health. (2001). *Treatment choice in psychological therapies and counselling evidence based clinical practice guideline*. London, England: Author.

U.S. Department of Veterans Affairs, Veterans Health Administration & Department of Defense. (2004, January). VA/DoD clinical practice guideline for the management of post-traumatic stress. Version 1.0. Washington, DC: Veterans Health Administration, and Department of Defense.

Vanitallie, T. B. (2002). Stress: A risk factor for serious illness. *Metabolism, 51*(6 Suppl. 1), 40–45.

Wesson, M., & Gould, M. (2009). Intervening early with EMDR on military operations. *Journal of EMDR Practice and Research, 3*(2), 91–97.

Wilson, S., Tinker, R., Hofmann, A., Becker, L., & Marshall, S. (2000). *A field study of EMDR with Kosovar-Albanian refugee children using a group treatment protocol*. Paper presented at the annual meeting of the International Society for the Study of Traumatic Stress, San Antonio, TX.

Zaghrout-Hodali, M., Alissa, F., & Dodgson, P. (2008). Building resilience and dismantling fear: EMDR group protocol with children in an area of ongoing trauma. *Journal of EMDR Practice & Research, 2*(2), 106–113.

Acknowledgments

As a young girl and on into my adolescence, I had the good fortune to grow up in an international community. In this oasis of the International School of Geneva (Ecolint) and under the greater global community fostered by the many international organizations that were headquartered there, I lived in a place where we all coexisted in a type of harmony that—it turns out—is rare. Our school community had its wrinkles but the bullying and the rage that one hears about so frequently now was not apparent, at least to me. We learned to think and reason and negotiate. Through our Students' United Nations, we fought the battles of our world through words and compromise. Simply put, we all got along with each other and if we had a problem, we worked it out. My first year of college shattered that pristine experience of cooperation and tolerance; it was 1968 and the end of my first year when the streets of Paris erupted and chaos ensued as "La revolution de mai" held the whole city hostage. Returning to the States in the middle of the Vietnam War opened my eyes to the fact that the lessons I learned in Geneva were certainly not happening where I now found myself, and I discovered later that my friends from Ecolint felt that same way. Since then, I have learned a great deal about trauma and, sadly, it is everywhere.

I would like to acknowledge the need for us—as an EMDR international community—to be part of an initiative to turn this state of affairs around. This book, *Implementing EMDR Early Mental Health Interventions for Man-Made and Natural Disasters: Models, Scripted Protocols, and Summary Sheets*, is an attempt to help my colleagues in the EMDR community learn more about what is needed to respond in the face of disaster and help victims heal and reclaim their lives.

I had two major experiences that pushed me toward the formulation of this book: hearing Emre Konuk present and the 2011 Tōhoku earthquake and tsunami in Japan. First, I would like to acknowledge my friend and colleague, Emre Konuk. It was Emre's presentation at the 2009 EMDR Europe Conference on the Turkish Model for a mental health response that inspired me to learn more about disaster response. As I got to know Emre better through attending conferences and a trip to Turkey, I heard more and more about the breadth and depth of his projects and felt that his gifts of organization and of creating projects for the greater good was information that we all needed to access.

The 2011 disaster in Japan was of a more personal nature for me. I first traveled to Japan in 1976 with my parents, who had a small business selling Japanese prints. I opened a Japanese art gallery that same year with my father and for a short time I ran the gallery before I decided to go back to teaching and then become a clinical psychologist. The gallery continued and the walls of my world have literally been filled with the aesthetic of Japan since then. I have been back several more times since my first trip for personal, art, and EMDR-related work.

I would like to acknowledge the work of Masaya Ichii who—in fact—was one of the first to use EMD with earthquake survivors after the 1995 Kobe earthquake. Masaya has gone on to become a trainer and create J-HAP, and has been an important force in helping EMDR develop in Japan. I would also like to acknowledge Shigeyuki Ota who did much to support the Japanese response in Tōhoku, as well as Elan Shapiro, Brurit Laub, Nacho Jarero, Masamichi Honda, Kiwamu Tanaka, Masako Kitamura, Robert Gelbach, Derek Farrell, Sushma Mehrotra, Richard Smith, Emre Konuk, Miyako Shirakawa, Akiko Kikuchi,

Keisuki Niki, Pam Brown, Rashid Qayyum, and many other EMDR colleagues from all over the world who helped sustain the EMDR response in Japan.

From the early days of EMDR, Roger Solomon's name was synonymous with working in the area of recent trauma. With his knowledge and experience with the police and other law enforcement agencies, Roger was the person to whom we all went when we had questions concerning early EMDR intervention, critical incident response, and traumatic grief. I would like to acknowledge Roger for all of the work that he has done in this area for all of us in the EMDR community. And let me say to you, Roger, "Thank you for your support over the years and the grace with which you answered all the questions that I had or assisted me with your insights concerning areas of recent trauma, no matter where you were or what you were doing. Also, for reconnecting me with my old friend, Jim McIntosh, who as an FBI agent helped me understand more clearly the impact of recent trauma and the horrors of 9/11."

I would like us all to remember and celebrate Jim who passed away after his own long battle with illness for his service to his family, friends, and country.

I would like to recognize my friend, Robert Wittman, fellow traveler, FBI agent, and Japanese aficionado who always knows how to climb over any mountain to get to the other side.

There are a number of other people whom I would like to acknowledge concerning this book as it would not have happened without the learning that I gained from our discussions; the hashing out and back and forth of our conversations helped me have a greater appreciation for the nuances of these ideas. To my friends, Elan Shapiro and Brurit Laub, words cannot express how much our discussions have meant to me in the understanding of early EMDR intervention and my respect for their continuing creativity and kindness of spirit. To the three gentleman who underwrote my "trauma fact-finding trip" to Kiryat Schmona (Alan Cohen), Jerusalem (Gary Quinn), and Tel Aviv (Udi Oren) to help me understand the impact of recent trauma and find ways to raise money for more EMDR trainings in the Middle East. To all of the consultants who attended the many consultancy trainings that we (often with Elan) created together in Israel—their willingness to share the innermost parts of themselves during our work together created a profound learning experience that touched me deeply.

I would like to acknowledge Nacho Jarero, Lucy Artigas, and Susana Uribe, a braver group of people I cannot imagine. Let me say: "Thank you for your friendship and the joy that you take in the most simple of pleasures, even as you go into 'battle' or put on your hazmat suits. I have learned more about the spirit that one needs to face the evils of the world and come out on the other side well and—always—with the 'Ministry of Presence.'"

I would like to acknowledge the strength and heart of my female friends and colleagues: Lucy Artigas, Sushma Mehrotra, Mona Zaghrout, Maria Cervera, Robbie Dunton, Rosalie Thomas, Peggy Moore, Susanna Uribe, Kerstin Bergh Johannesson, Phyllis Klaus, Zara Yellin, Zona Scheiner, Barbara Hensley, Catherine Fine, Irene Geissl, Elaine Alvarez, Barbara Grinnell, Robbie Adler-Tapia, Carolyn Settle, Kate Wheeler, Sandra Wilson, Victoria Britt, Sheila Bender, Marsha Heiman, Delphine Pecoul, Maria Elena Aduriz, Ligia Barascout de Piedra Santa, Louise Maxfield, Joany Spierings, Reyhana Ravat, Jennifer Lendl, Deany Laliotis, Francisca Garcia Guerra, Esly Carvalho, Eva Muenker-Kramer, Nancy Errebo, Luise Reddemann, Phyllis Goltra, Priscilla Marquis, Barbara Parrett, Carlijn de Roos, Linda Cohn, Jocelyne Shiromoto, Christine Rost, Martine Tiedt-Schutte, Elfrun Magloire, Eva Zimmerman, Esther Ebner, France Haour, Hanne Hummel, Shelley Weber, Hope Riley, Brenda Byrne, Veronika Engl, Isabel Fernancez, Sandy Shapiro, Ruth Heber, Ellen Latenstein, Karen Alter Reid, Sue Evans, Susan Schaefer, Lulu Medina, Debby Korn, Brurit Laub, Sandra Wilson, Elizabeth Snyker, Hellen Hornsveld, Renee Beer, Christie Sprowls, Barbara Korzun, Patti Levin, Jocelyn Barrett, Reg Morrow, Carol Crow, Carol Forgash, Esti Bar Sade, Isabelle Meignant, Tessa Prattos, Jenny Ann Rydberg, Fran Yoeli, Katy Murray, Sandra Paulsen, Donna D'Aloia, Katy O'Shea, Sandra Kaplan, Nancy Smith, Dorothy Ashman, Wendy Freitag, Pam Brown, Laurie Tetrault, Ana Gomez, Kay Werk, Debra Wesselmann, Maria Masciandaro, Betsy Prince, Jill Strunk, Denise Gelinas, Sandi Richman, Shelley Uram, Frankie Klaff, Edith Taber, Celia Grand, Cynthia Kong, Blanche Freund, Francine Shapiro, and all of the extraordinary women I have met on this journey.

To Derek Farrell who has become a friend—not just a colleague—over the past several years: "Thank you for your ability to keep grounded despite the difficulties around you and for the gift of your experience that you have given to all of us."

To Richard Mitchell, my old friend and fellow voyager on our trip to Bethlehem that opened our eyes and souls; to Jim Knipe who has been a great support; to Bob Gelbach, Howard Wainer, Donald Nathanson, and Stuart Wolfe who have been strong supporters of my writing; and to AJ Popky who introduced me to EMDR.

To Steve Silver: "Thank you for all that I have learned from you while doing EMDR supervision groups together, for your willingness to answer questions, and for always looking for the 'light in the heart of darkness.'" I would like to acknowledge Susan Rogers and Elaine Alvarez for stepping in at a time when I needed assistance and making everything clear. Thank you also to Elan Shapiro, Brurit Laub, Nacho Jarero, and Roger Solomon for helping when another set of eyes or four was needed.

I would also like to remember Kathy Davis who left us with the legacy of her wisdom, her knowledge, and her kindness.

I would like to thank the Springer staff, especially my editor, Sheri W. Sussman, for her encouragement and support in the face of many demands on my time during this period of writing.

Always, I want to thank and acknowledge Francine. "Your discovery, your creativity, your persistence, and your ability to open a new door that is EMDR has been one of the greatest gifts in my life and in the lives of uncountable others."

I am dedicating this book to my mother who has been going through her own recent trauma with the spirit and true determination that she has always displayed throughout her life; a role model for us all.

EMDR Early Mental Health Interventions: First Responders

I

One of the most striking elements that unites the chapters in this section on first re-sponders is that each member group that is represented has its particular culture replete with its own language, abbreviations, uniform, attitude, stoicism, ability to compartmentalize, code of ethics, outlook, comradeship, and focus on the mission. It is from their culture that its members draw the strength and unadulterated courage to go into the most gruesome of situations.

Critical incidents and first responders go hand and hand. When everyone else moves away from the struggles, the strikers, the gun-wielding perpetrators, the motor vehicle crash victims, the stranded occupants of homes that are burning, the battles, the hand-to-hand combat, or the cats in impossible places to reach, the first responders are the ones who move forward; they step up and override the basic fear mechanism that warns them of danger and go in the opposite direction of what their gut is signaling them. They are simply extraordinary in their intention to go in and fight the battles, recover the wounded, calm the masses, save the dying, and take care of their own. These first responders are close cousins to us as mental health practitioners sharing the same need or intention of taking care of and/or protecting others; however, they are on the front lines of these actions.

Robbie Adler-Tapia is a talented psychologist who has experience in child welfare, forensics, and working with law enforcement, firefighters, and first responders. Her clear, incisive thinking and ability to problem solve supported her choice as a mental health consultant with the National Fallen Firefighters' Foundation. Her chapter, "Early Mental Health Intervention for First Responders/Protective Service Workers Including Firefighters and Emergency Medical Services Professionals," is a testimony to the importance of understanding the first responders with whom you work. These men and women are in the front lines of every kind of catastrophe and—as she points out—this makes them at risk for direct and vicarious traumatization. As no first responder's job is the same, it is important *not* to generalize about what they do and make sure that you are informed about the nature of their experience. Again, her emphasis is on how important it is to really know the culture. She underscores, often, that "earning individual and group trust is the biggest hurdle to efficacy in responding to critical incidents with first responders." Also, when mental health practitioners are working with first responders, they are usually coordinating with the Department and Command Staff about their clients and have to know how to handle the types of demands and rules that are pertinent in functioning under this umbrella. Understanding in the beginning what is expected is crucial to the work that we do and our relationship with our clients. In this chapter, we hear again about how important it is for first respond-ers to learn how to participate in emotional self-care and there is a discussion about ways to actualize this. Robbie also emphasizes the importance of teaching her clients how to contain the psychological and physiological experiences they are having—but not to keep them closed off forever—by instructing them on how to use "containers" for this purpose.

Knowing the nature of the types of targets to which this population are exposed, Robbie has produced a helpful form, the "Parade of Faces," to support remembering the targets and help her responders organize them to use in EMDR processing. She activates both the negative and positive cognitions within the format of her "Parade of Faces," a task that is clear and helpful in eliciting these self-statements. Robbie cautions therapists to understand that this population has learned to disregard their physiological responses while on duty; therefore, coming to the Body Scan may be difficult and need our support and psychotherapeutic tools for dealing with disturbing experiences. In this chapter, Robbie enables us to understand more clearly the world of the first responders of which she has such thorough knowledge.

From the mid-seventies, Roger Solomon has spent most of his career working nationally and internationally as a psychologist and consultant with the police and other branches of law enforcement and the military. He was the EMDR trainer in the early days of EMDR, along with Kay Werk; both were known for their commitment to working with recent trauma and critical incidents. As a result of his connections with law enforcement and his association with Jeffrey Mitchell, founder of the International Critical Incident Stress Foundation (ICISF), Roger's EMDR Institute's Basic Trainings were filled with the stories of the many police, federal agents, NASA workers, and grieving spouses with whom he worked and for whom he was always designing new and innovative programs to address their circumstances even more effectively. Through Roger, we enter the world of the law enforcement officer and learn to lead with our more left-brain, cognitive selves. In his chapter, "Early Mental Health EMDR Intervention for the Police," he gives suggestions about how to provide coping strategies as well as how to work with the EMDR Protocol for Recent Traumatic Events. He warns that therapists working in this area need to be aware of their own responses to the terrible stories they hear so that they do not affect the officers' ability to tell their narratives. As in working with any client, it is also helpful to mark the positive moments where the officer demonstrated competence. He discusses the types of positive and negative cognitions and cognitive interweaves most used with this population with helpful examples to round out our understanding.

Mark Russell knows the military. Born into a military family and on a Marine base, he has formally served 26 years in the military and retired as a Navy commander and military psychologist. He is an outspoken advocate of military personnel, both while he was in the military and in his current position outside the service. As a recognized military expert on war stress injuries, he responded to a request to testify before a congressionally mandated Department of Defense (DoD) Task Force on Mental Health regarding his efforts to prevent a military mental health crisis. Mark is passionate about helping the men and women in the United States military get the assistance that they need when they are traumatized as a result of anything that occurs while serving their country from war-related stress injuries, to vicarious traumatization, to sexual assaults. He has been an advocate in stressing the importance of EMDR for service men and women and has called for the DoD and Veterans Administration (VA) to allow more of their mental health practitioners access to EMDR training to treat their patients, and for researchers of PTSD to fund research on EMDR and treatment in the military. Currently, he is the chair for the PsyD Program at Antioch University in Seattle and is the founding Director of the Institute of War Stress Injuries and Social Justice, dedicated to stopping the cycle of ignoring the mental health needs of war veterans.

In Chapter 3, Mark, Tammera Cooke (his assistant), and Susan Rogers (a psychologist who has been actively involved in the treatment of war and trauma survivors since 1981) help us understand the military perspective on Acute Stress-Related Disorders and Syndromes by guiding us through the alphabet of military definitions so that we can understand and begin to learn this code. The fact is that the goal of frontline psychiatry is always to keep the individual battle-ready. The United States military discourages pathologizing universal stress reactions as symptoms and after a brief respite to restore the soldiers' psychological and physiological well-being, they support returning them to their units. Psychotherapy is considered inappropriate for Acute Stress Response or Combat Stress Reactions until evacuated away from the front lines. They discuss Mark's model for an Acute Stress Injury Spectrum from mild through severe and how to screen for Acute Stress Injuries.

The use of EMDR for early intervention in the military is the heart of this chapter. There is a great deal of literature and governmental sanction for EMDR as a treatment for PTSD. Mark, Tammera, and Susan question making the distinction between a client with trauma-related symptoms 3 weeks and 6 days (ASD) and 4 weeks and 1 day (PTSD). As EMDR is an evidence-based, "A-level" trauma-focused intervention for PTSD, they propose that this is an arbitrary and empirically unsupported distinction. They also point out that there are several peer-reviewed publications with case studies on how EMDR can be used for combat-related ASR and ASD while working with soldiers on active duty with excellent results.

To adapt EMDR to a military setting, they propose and explore seven considerations: referral question; strength of the therapeutic alliance; client treatment goals; timing and environmental constraints; clinical judgment regarding client safety; suitability for standard trauma-focused EMDR reprocessing protocol; and utilization of any adjunctive intervention and referral need. In this process, they review protocols that are used as EMDR early intervention protocols and scripted protocols by Mark such as his version of Eye Movement Desensitization (EMD) and the Modified-EMDR (Mod-EMDR) script. They also discuss resources and a script for Combat/Tactical Breathing. It is clear that Mark has given a great deal of thought to how to work with the people in the service to whom he has dedicated his life's work.

The chapters in this section give us as clinicians a way to understand the different worlds of first responders/protective service workers, the police, and members of the military. Summary sheets accompany each chapter to remind us of the important points in the chapter and a place to incorporate the data of our clients. The next step is to turn to the next page and enter these worlds.

Early Mental Health Intervention for First Responders/Protective Service Workers Including Firefighters and Emergency Medical Services Professionals

Robbie Adler-Tapia

"We wait, we hope, we pray, until you come home again."

—Oprah Winfrey

Introduction

First responders or protective service workers who respond to man-made and natural disasters experience daily career exposure to acute stress and trauma. By working in professional positions in law enforcement, fire sciences, emergency medical services and search and rescue and as 911 operators and dispatchers, emergency room staff (including doctors and nurses), child welfare workers, and even psychotherapists, these individuals experience direct or secondary trauma from the work environment. The work of caring for the emotional and physical needs of others takes its toll on those in the trenches. In these inimitable circumstances, the exposure can lead to direct traumas and/or vicarious trauma for the professional in a first responder role.

This chapter will focus on clinical skills for providing emergency mental health services to first responders while adhering to the eye movement desensitization and reprocessing (EMDR) protocol in the treatment of those professionals who are exposed to trauma in the line of duty. Case conceptualization is considered through the lens of the Adaptive Information Processing Model (AIP). The reader will learn how to develop a comprehensive treatment plan with methods for advanced resourcing skills and treating professional traumas specific to first responders. Psychotherapy requires a dance between ongoing encounters with trauma in the line of duty while considering complicated forensic issues. Personal and professional trauma arises out of the mission of first responders whose role it is to protect and serve the public.

The Mission of First Responders

This chapter will focus on all other "first responders" also referred to as "protective service workers." First responder is a broad term that attempts to capture those who serve in many roles caring for the health and safety of the community in emergency and crisis situations. There are structural, wildland, and aerial firefighters; emergency medical services (EMS) that include paramedics, emergency medical technicians (EMT), search and rescue professionals, as well as emergency personnel in hospitals and other medical facilities including doctors, nurses, physician's assistants, and ancillary staff. First responders have also included mental health professionals who work in crisis treatment roles, child welfare workers who care for abused and neglected children, and emergency dispatchers/911 operators who take the calls and dispatch first responders. Structural firefighters commonly work in more urban areas responding to fires and safety issues in structures, to transportation accidents such as those that occur with automobiles and trains, and to injured persons. Wildland firefighters often fight fires in the open spaces in forests and deserts. Aerial firefighters are those who fight fires from the air by dropping water and/or fire retardant. No matter what the title or assignment, the mission of these professionals is to respond to natural and man-made disasters, and crisis situations that threaten the safety and welfare of others. First responders go to the scene, exposing themselves to personal and psychological traumas in order to care for the health and safety of others.

There are no international statistics published on the numbers of first responders in the world; however, the Centers for Disease Control and Prevention (CDC) reported in 2006 that

> Approximately 800,000 firefighters in the United States are volunteer firefighters and 300,000 are career firefighters. Volunteer firefighters primarily serve communities with fewer than 25,000 inhabitants, whereas most career firefighters serve communities of more than 25,000 persons. (CDC, 2006)

In addition, "a 2003 survey of State EMS directors found 669,278 licensed providers in 48 States and 4 territories" (www.ems.gov/pdf/EMSWorkforceReport_June2008.pdf).

Internationally, the numbers of first responders predictably includes millions of individuals who are exposed to trauma in the line of duty. These professions expose individuals to a higher rate of personal threat both physically and psychologically while also witnessing the horrific traumas to others.

The Cost of the Career

The daily wear and tear of the job takes a toll on the individual, departments, and families. Compared with the general population, with an estimated 6.8% lifetime prevalence rate of posttraumatic stress disorder (PTSD) for American adults (as reported by the 2005 National Comorbidity Survey Report), firefighters are at increased risk for developing PTSD. The International Association of Fire Chiefs' Foundation (1991) stated that

> Stress is one of the most serious occupational hazards in the fire service, affecting health, job performance, career decision-making, morale, and family life. Emotional problems, as well as problems with alcohol and drugs, are becoming increasingly evident. High rates of attrition, divorce, occupational disease, and injury continue . . . [and] suicide is a real and tragic alternative for some. (www.IAFCF.org)

First Responders with high PTSD scores are also at a three times greater risk for developing metabolic syndromes, such as dyslipidemia, high blood pressure, and glucose intolerance (First Responders Foundation; www.1strf.org). Therefore, in addition to mental health issues, first responders are at higher risk for chronic health issues and injuries including hypertension, cardiac crisis, obesity, and diabetes from shift work. For first responders, the cost of the career is evident in many areas as the role includes chronic exposure to traumatic events. Some of the events are unique to the line of duty.

First Responder Trauma

Professional trauma is responding to and witnessing an actual or **perceived** threat to the safety/integrity of self or others that may result in intense fear or helplessness in response to an event. Research suggests "powerless in the face of an event" often is what causes the client to experience the event as traumatic. For first responders, responding to and witnessing a critical event or a series of distressing life events over time can lead to medical and/ or physical symptoms and long-term consequences. The perception of any event varies depending on the individual, but any event with sufficient impact to produce significant emotional reactions in the present or future may need to be reprocessed. Critical incidents are commonly considered to be extremely unusual in the range of ordinary human experiences, but are daily occurrences for first responders. Such critical incidents may include: crew member's death in line of duty, the death or serious injury of a child, multiple fatalities or seriously injured survivors, attempted or successful suicides, natural disasters, personal mishaps involving death or permanent injury and otherwise high emotional impact, deadly force incidents, grotesque injuries, acts of terrorism, or acts of violence resulting in injury or death. Ultimately, professional trauma is anything that negatively impacts the psyche and changes the course of healthy development.

Targets of Professional Exposure

In addition to witnessing and experiencing horrific natural and man-made events as part of the career, targets of professional exposure include death notifications, personal exposure, when professional colleagues are hurt or killed in the line of duty, unique sensory flashbacks, and the residual impact of habitual stoicism, depersonalization, and derealization. Targets for reprocessing for first responders can be organized with the "Parade of Faces." See the form for "Parade of Faces" in Phase 1 of this chapter.

Professional Trauma

Professional trauma is responding to and witnessing an actual or **perceived** threat to the safety/integrity of self or others that may result in intense fear or helplessness in response to an event. Research suggests powerless in the face of an event often is what causes the client to experience the event as traumatic. For first responders, responding to and witnessing a critical event or a series of distressing life events over time can lead to medical and/or physical symptoms and long-term consequences. The perception of any event varies depending on the individual, but is any event with sufficient impact to produce significant emotional reactions in the present or future may need to be reprocessed. Critical incidents are commonly considered to be extremely unusual in the range of ordinary human experiences, but are daily occurrences for first responders. Such critical incidents may include: crew members death in line of duty, the death or serious injury of a child, multiple fatalities or seriously injured survivors, attempted or successful suicides, natural disasters, personal mishaps involving death or permanent injury and otherwise high emotional impact, deadly force incidents, grotesque injuries, acts of terrorism, acts of violence resulting in injury or death. Ultimately, trauma is anything that negative impacts the psyche and changes the course of healthy development.

In addition to the horrific experiences first responders are exposed to responding to natural and man-made disasters, there are traumas unique to the field. First responders experience "line-of-duty traumas," "line-of-duty deaths" (LODD), and Postshooting Trauma in Law Enforcement (PSTLE) (Adler-Tapia, 2012).

- *Line-of-Duty Traumas* are those experienced during work that include witnessing death or near death experiences of individuals in the community, other professionals, or risk to self.
- *Line-of-Duty Death (LODD)* are deaths that occur when professionals die in the line of duty. When a LODD occurs, all the other professionals responding to the call are now in an even more stressful position of trying to rescue and treat a comrade.

Finally, there are traumas that occur after the professional event including:

- *Postshooting Trauma in Law Enforcement (PSTLE)* (Adler-Tapia, 2012) are traumas that occur after the professional event. PSTLE is an acronym to explain the process that professionals must endure following a shooting. Law enforcement and first responders alike may be witnesses to a criminal investigation. The ongoing stress further complicates the treatment process. There are firefighters who are also law enforcement such as those who serve in arson investigation roles and scene management/security; therefore, the line between law enforcement and other first responders is not always clear.

- *Betrayal Trauma—the* experience that some professionals face when not feeling supported by department and/or command, media, public, and family.

Similarities and Differences With First Responders

Learning the common terms and how the individual professional conceptualizes his or her duty is a crucial part of psychotherapy as each individual is unique. However, with the global term of first responders, it is important for mental health professionals to recognize that there are similarities and differences in the roles that have to do with the duty assignment. The similarities are in the mission as defined above. The differences may be in the assignment and enactment of the job.

Emergency Services Dispatchers or 911 Operators in the United States dispatch other professionals to the scene of a disaster when help is needed, but rarely go to the scene. While waiting for other professionals to arrive, these "first, first responders" may need to console a child, give emergency medical directions, and organize the response of the other professionals all from auditory input. These individuals may later struggle with the visual creations that occurred when he/she was verbally dispatching assistance. These first responders often work in a call center or facility away from the incident.

Law Enforcement Professionals are more likely to work alone, while other first responders work in teams. Law enforcement professionals may respond to provide assistance to other professionals from the same squad, department, or area, but are often alone in the field responding to calls. Law enforcement professionals may also be in the field observing and trying to prevent crimes from occurring. Communities tend to have a negative perspective of law enforcement because these professionals are tasked with upholding laws.

Other First Responders are rarely alone. A fire crew often includes at least two professionals who depend on each other and tend to live and work together. Professional fire professionals often sleep at the fire department in order to respond faster to calls. Wildland fire professionals may spend weeks together camping in forests and less populated areas as they attempt to prevent and/or control fires that cover large areas. Whatever the assignment, these individuals can spend more time together than they do with their own families; therefore, the role of caring for "brothers and sisters" on the squads or teams of professionals becomes even more stressful and traumatic if someone is injured or killed in the line of duty. Losing "one of our own" impacts everyone more than in most professional work environments. These professionals not only put their own safety and lives on the line for the public, but also for each other. "I've got your six" is a term often used to describe that one professional is watching out for the back of another professional.

Ultimately it is important for therapists to ask the individual or the squad, "Tell me about your role and your assignment." Never assume that just because a client is a first responder, that you have any idea what he or she does; however, therapists need to understand that there are some commonalities in the culture of first responders. The similarities with first responders include psychological defense mechanisms and commitment to "family."

Culture of Stoicism, Depersonalization, and Derealization

Stoicism, depersonalization, and derealization are three common psychological defense mechanisms used by first responders to deal with the wear and tear of the career.

- *Stoicism* is a cultural expectation in that first responders are expected to *not* be impacted by the events to which they respond. This expectation manifests in a unique sense of humor, which can be interpreted as cold and/or disrespectful by others. The uniform and mask of first responders is used to cope with the career and is expected by the culture.

- *Depersonalization* is experiencing an event, but feeling like it is happening to someone else.
- *Derealization* is experiencing an event, but feeling like it isn't real.

Many first responders habitually use these defense mechanisms as the impact of chronic trauma exposure accumulates and becomes destructive both physically and psychologically. At times, the habitual use of depersonalization and derealization can result in delayed onset of PTSD. It is important for therapists to understand that these are ways in which first responders learn to cope when inundated with traumatic events and are part of the professional culture.

With some first responders, there are childhood and/or family traumas that accumulate over time and impact the health of the professional. Recognizing the family impact is significant when providing psychotherapy to first responders.

The Families of First Responders

First responders have two families including the traditional family and the professional family. Both families are part of the individual's life and impact his/her response to his/her career.

The Traditional Family

This family includes spouses and significant others, parents, siblings, children, and extended family and friends. One study found empirical support for the presence of secondary trauma among the wives and significant others of firefighters. Research has documented the need for the identification and treatment of firefighters with PTSD and their secondarily affected significant others (Gawrych, 2010). Additional stressors for first responders are the health and safety of family members. Stress at work and at home often collide to cause a high rate of symptoms in first responders. Research also suggests that the health and support of the professional department and command have a significant influence on how well first responders cope with the daily trauma exposure.

The Professional Family

"My goal is to get home safe to my family and my brothers get home safe to their families, too." With first responders, the professional family includes the squad and the department. Many first responders and especially firefighters, EMS, and search and rescue live together as part of the job for at least some time during the week. There are several types of firefighters including structural, wildland, and aerial. Most spend some time living together— structural at the station and wildland usually spend the summers together camping in areas to protect the environment and fight fires. EMS professionals usually travel in pairs or as part of a larger team of first responders. Corrections officers are locked in together in one of the most dangerous positions that exist. Because of the coexistence required of the job, these professional families not only protect the community, but each other; therefore, when there are LODDs or injuries, the entire family is impacted.

Treating Trauma Exposure for First Responders

Because of the ongoing exposure, departments may need a variety of mental health services before, during, and after a critical incident. Ideally, training will begin during the training academy and continue throughout the professional's career. Service needs for the department may include:

- Pre-incident training
- Critical incident stress management
- On-scene support services

- Anniversary meetings
- Command consultation
- Family crisis intervention
- Follow-up services
- Postincident services
- Individual treatment for duty
- Workman compensation services

Any of these services may be part of what is requested for first responders.

How Do Mental Health Professionals Prepare for and Organize a Disaster Response?

Mental health professionals may be involved with preparing for and responding to traumatic incidents and disaster situations. These may include incidents limited to the department and/or larger community situations. In order to respond most effectively, it is important to assess the following needs:

To What Type of Disaster Are You Responding?

- Are you responding to a *natural disaster* (wildland and/or forest fires, earthquakes, a tsunami, hurricane, flood, epidemic, structural collapse)?
- Or, a *man-made event* (torture, acts of terrorism, war, drug cartel wars, school shootings, gang warfare, robbery, arson, bombs, etc.)?

First responders train for many types of disasters, but the larger the event with the greater amount of individuals displaced and injured, the greater the exposure that can create response and management issues.

Logistics of a Mental Health Disaster Response

When mental health professionals are invited to provide services by the department and/or by the command staff, there are important logistical issues to consider.

- *Location*—Where will you implement the response?
- *Demobilization*—Will the first responders have time off after the critical incident before returning to work? Or, will the first responders be expected to respond to calls during the intervention? Providing mental health services for professionals who remain on duty may be quite difficult, but for some volunteer and smaller departments, there is no back up so that the first responders can be off-duty.
- *Participation*—Who needs your help and who will be part of the team of responders? What are the needs of the group to be helped?
- *Professional Response*—How many professionals are needed? Do you have enough professionals or, if not, how do you organize your disaster responders?
- *Logistics*—How long is the intervention? Who will organize food and drinks for the group? Feeding first responders is an important part of building relationships and gaining trust. Logistics may also include mental health interventions to augment department practices. Departments may contact mental health professionals following an "After Action Review" (AAR), when concerns arise about the impact of the event on the first responders.
- *Confidentiality*—Will confidentiality and privacy be honored? How will they be maintained? Will records be maintained for services? Are there differences between professional and civilian interventions? If so, what are they?
- *Costs/Payment*—What are the costs/budget? Is this a voluntary or paid position? How will billing and payment be handled?

Postincident Services

Working With the Department and Command to Provide Postincident Services

Working with the Department and Command staff of first responders varies for each situation and department. The Department is the employer of the first responder that interacts with other employees, other departments, and local, state, and national government entities. At times, Department and Command may seek preincident services such as pre-employment assessments, training, and education. Postincident services may include consultation from mental health professionals and/or assistance with interventions for first responders and/or communities involved in the incident. Postincident services are more likely to be provided in the field such as at the scene or at the department, rather than at the therapist's office.

Who Invited the Involvement of the Mental Health Professional?

When therapists work with first responders, one of the most important considerations is who invited the involvement: self-referral or a department referral. The dynamics about the original referral or request impact how the therapist should proceed since first responders are not always comfortable with mental health professionals and may be suspicious of the services.

Note: Earning individual and group trust is the biggest hurdle to efficacy in responding to critical incidents with first responders.

Considering the referral and the following questions are important in making clinical decisions when working with first responders.

Referrals for Mental Health Services

Along with providing information about PFA and resources included at the end of this chapter, one of the most important interventions for first responders following a natural or manmade disaster is to provide information on how to find a mental health specialist. Most first responders who realize the need for treatment are not sure how to access services; therefore, it is helpful to explain the different types of mental health professionals, and how to access services.

When responding to the needs of first responders following a natural or manmade disaster, it is helpful for the therapist to assess what services if any are available to the individual.

- Is there an Employee Assistance Program (EAP)?
- Is the EAP internal to the department or an external EAP where the individual is referred to providers in the community?
- What concerns arise from an EAP referral?
- Is there trust with the EAP providers and are the providers knowledgeable about this population and the culture of first responders?
- Is it possible for the first responder to be referred to a private practitioner? For some first responders, the concern exists that seeking mental health treatment may impact professional careers or any legal processes in which the individual is involved.
- If a first responder is a witness, will the therapist's records be protected from the legal proceedings?

Helping first responders understand what services are available and responding to any concerns about seeking treatment is an important intervention. Once this information is available, the therapist many need to provide some education about the type of treatments that are available to first responders (see the Treatment section below)

Self-Referral

If the individual first responder sought out therapy at the mental health professional's office, what are the expectations? This process is similar to a private referral that most therapists encounter, but unique in that there are complicated legal and professional issues involved as previously discussed.

Department Referral

If the Department contacted the mental health professional, there are many more issues to consider.

- What and how will confidentiality be managed?
- What do the individual and/or department expect?
- What is the purpose of the intervention requested?
- What and how will confidentiality be managed?
- Are on-scene services requested? If so, is there a risk to the mental health service provider?
- Does Command/Leadership expect updates about the services?
- If so, how will the therapist correspond with the Department?
- Are there privacy issues that need to be resolved?
- Will there be an Industrial Commission/Workman's Compensation Case?
- Are there criminal issues that impact this mental health process? For example, was the critical incident arson started by someone else?
  - ☐ Will this first responder have to testify about the call or any other call? First responders may not be as likely as law enforcement to be involved in criminal proceedings; however, it is imperative that mental health providers consider this possibility from the point of the initial referral and then determine what/if any impact this will have on treatment.

After Action Review (AAR)

An "After Action Review" is a common term used in military, law enforcement, and first responders. An AAR is a meeting of the professionals who responded to an event and later conduct debriefing of the response in order to improve services and safety for professionals. An AAR often includes the following questions posed to the professionals who responded to the event. Information on the AAR can be found at the following link: www.queri.research .va.gov/ciprs/projects/after_action_review.pdf

- What was expected to happen? What was our mission?
- What actually occurred?
- What went well and why?
- What can be improved and how?
- What could have gone better?
- What might we have done differently?
- Who needs to know?

Psychological Component of the AAR

Capitalizing on a known process for first responders, therapists may consider adding a psychological component to the AAR, using a critical incident stress debriefing (CISD)/critical incident stress management (CISM) model of response, or a combination of the two. The following questions can expand the AAR to address the psychological impact of the event.

- How did it impact me?
- What do I need to do to care for myself?
- How do I get closure?
- Who else is struggling?

- What if anything do I need/want to do for my brothers and sisters who also experienced this exposure?
- How does this impact our next call? Our next shift?

By teaching first responders to consider these questions, an awareness of the impact of the exposure begins to grow. With this acknowledgement, first responders then need tools to deal with the ongoing and cumulative effect of trauma exposure. One common initial service that is a tradition for first responders is CISM services.

Mental Health Services for First Responders

Critical Incident Stress Debriefing (CISD) and Critical Incident Stress Management (CISM)

CISM services are an integrated, comprehensive, and multidimensional crisis intervention system that includes CISD services. These services are intended to help individuals exposed to critical incidents. CISM services can be offered to individuals, but with first responders are most often provided to the group of professionals who responded to the incident. The focus is to provide "psychological first aid" (PFA) as an immediate debriefing in order to minimize the harmful effects of job stress, specifically in crisis or emergency situations. CISD/CISM is most helpful when the department has prepared with preincident training.

CISM services include seven steps (adapted from Everly & Mitchell, 1997):

1. *Precrisis Preparation:* this includes preincident stress management training, education, and skill building.
2. *Disaster or Large-Scale*, as well as, school and community support programs that include demobilizations, informational briefings, "town meetings," and staff advisement.
3. *Defusing* is a three-phased, structured group activity that is after or soon after the event for assessment, triaging, and acute symptom mitigation.
4. *CISD* refers to the "Mitchell Model" (Mitchell & Everly, 1996). This is a seven-phase, structured group discussion, usually provided 1 to 10 days post crisis, and designed to mitigate acute symptoms, assess the need for follow up, and if possible provide a sense of postcrisis psychological closure.
5. *One-on-One Crisis Intervention/Counseling or Psychological Support* throughout the full range of the crisis spectrum.
6. *Crisis Intervention and Organizational Consultation.*
7. *Follow Up and Referrals for Assessment and Treatment*, if necessary.

Note: In addition, mental health professionals may provide assessment of individuals and case management for individuals with ongoing needs.

With this overview of CISM, the remainder of this chapter addresses postincident services including referrals, assessment and case management, and treatment.

Psychological First Aid

The PFA Field Operations Manual was written to help professionals dealing with man-made and natural disasters. This comprehensive manual provides valuable information for professionals along with training and handouts for survivors of all ages. The manual is available online at the following web site: www.ptsd.va.gov/professional/manuals/manual-pdf/pfa/PFA_2ndEditionwithappendices.pdf (retrieved January 15, 2013).

In addition, there are downloadable applications that all first responders can carry on computers and smart phones to provide immediate assistance in dealing with individuals of all ages from infancy to adult. This tool is helpful to therapists and should be made available to all first responders for self-care and to assist in the line of duty. PFA also provides a way to educate first responders about the impact of exposure to man-made and natural disasters while allowing the possibility that he/she too could be impacted. (www.mentalhealthfirstaid.org)

With information and education, therapists who work with first responders need to consider how to intervene and what services are necessary when first responders seek out the expertise of a therapist.

Assessment and Case Management

Assessment and case management following a critical incident may require the management of personal health. This may include safety planning, assessment for danger to self (DTS), and/or danger to others (DTO), assessment of individual first responders, referrals for medication assessment and management, assisting individuals in locating appropriate mental health services, and treatment.

Mental health professionals need to consider the legal and ethical complications of multiple roles in training and education, assessment, and treatment. Training and consultation roles may be necessary in order for the mental health professional to act in accordance with professional standards of care. Mental health professionals can respond to the department and/or to the individual; however, it is important to be aware of boundaries, confidentiality, and dual relationships. When in doubt, the mental health professional should seek consultation with his/her professional organization and or other colleagues.

Safety Planning

Mental health professionals may be contacted to assess the safety of the first responders. As part of the process, therapists many need to address the following questions.

- How does the therapist intervene if the first responder is still on the job?
- What documentation, if any, will the department request?
- Is there a risk to the public, the individual, and/or other first responders? This risk needs to be assessed in light of the possibility that the first responder is an armed professional.
- Are mental health services a requirement for return to duty?
- What assessment will the mental health provider be asked to provide to the department, if any? In some cases, the mental health services are part of a "Fitness for Duty" process where the department command is trying to determine if the first responder is capable of carrying out his or her duties as a professional.

If the mental health professionals are not part of the Fitness for Duty team, they need to ask about the fitness for duty process in order to make case management and clinical decisions when working with first responders.

- Is a safety plan necessary?
- If so, who needs to know?
- How do you protect a career?
- Is a DTO assessment necessary?
- Is a DTS assessment necessary? How will this occur?

Assessment of DTS can include the Modified SAD PERSONAS Scale, which helps assess suicide risk *(Campbell)* (www.medicine.missouri.edu/psychiatry/uploads/Psychiatric -Interview.pdf Retrieved March 2, 2013).

SAD PERSONAS Scale

• Sex
• Age
• Depression
• Previous attempt
• Ethanol abuse

• Rational thinking loss
• Social supports lacking
• Organized plan
• No spouse
• Availability of lethal means
• Sickness

After assessing the risk of DTS or others, the therapist must make an appraisal of how to manage the risk. This may include immediate intervention, contact with department and staff, referral to a higher level of care, and medication management.

Assessment of Individual First Responders

Assessment is a multifaceted process including a clinical interview and standardized measures. The assessment should consider both exposure to traumatic events and life stressors along with the evaluation of subsequent symptoms. Resources for locating assessment tools are included at this end of this chapter.

Referrals for Medication Assessment and Management

In addition to emergency psychological services and ongoing mental health treatment, some first responders may need to be referred for medication management and or addictions treatment. Determining the process for this to occur and how the individual first responder's care will be monitored needs to be determined at the onset. Some first responders need assistance in identifying and accessing care. There are different treatment modalities for which first responders can be referred for individual psychotherapy.

Treatment

Treatment Modalities may include debriefings for groups such as CISD/CISM, and/or individual psychotherapy, including cognitive-behavioral therapy (CBT), cognitive processing therapy (CPT), prolonged exposure (PE) therapy, and EMDR. For the purposes of the remainder of this chapter, the treatment of first responders will be conceptualized through the phases of the EMDR Protocol (Shapiro, 2001).

This chapter does not replace training in the Standard EMDR Protocol (Shapiro, 2001) and the EMDR Basic Training. The remainder of this chapter will provide a review of the EMDR phases, and scripted protocols with suggestions for modifications when working with first responders.

Early Mental Health Intervention for First Responders/Protective Service Workers, Including Firefighters andEmergency Medical Services (EMS) Professionals Script Notes

Note: The purpose of the Script Notes is to help the clinician have a greater understanding of how to use the script that follows after this section.

Case Conceptualization With EMDR: Treatment Planning and Intervention

There are certain issues to consider that affect EMDR case conceptualization and treatment planning when working with first responders and may alter the "flow" or how to proceed with psychotherapy. One of the most significant factors is the overlay of legal issues. Legal/forensic issues may include criminal and/or civil litigation.

Criminal investigations may occur when first responders are responding to an event that is a crime such as arson, homicide, or other criminal events. When proceeding with

EMDR, the therapist needs to discuss these issues with the client and determine if there are any issues that may impact the flow of treatment. Furthermore, will the therapist's notes be subpoenaed or will the therapist need to testify? It is prudent to proceed with every client as if there may be forensic involvement.

Civil court issues may occur if there will be a civil lawsuit filed against the department and/or against the parties in a case. This could occur in a car accident in which one vehicle driver sues another driver. The first responder may be a witness in a civil case; therefore, the client's records may be requested in the case. The first responder also might have a workman's compensation case against the department if physical and/or psychological injuries are suffered on duty. In this case, the therapist again needs to consider how the treatment process may be forensically complicated.

With any type of litigation, it is important for the therapist to have complete and comprehensive records in compliance with ethical and legal standards. It is helpful to seek consultation from professional organizations and legal professionals in accordance with the mental health professionals' license and training.

If a first responder is referred by his/her department, the therapist must consider that there could be employment issues that also need to be clarified before proceeding with treatment. For example, did the first responder's command staff refer him/her for treatment? If so, what will be expected from the therapist? Will the treatment be comprehensive or focused specifically on work-related issues? Is treatment a condition of fitness for duty and/or return to duty?

Comprehensive Versus Work-Focused Treatment

The therapist must determine if this is comprehensive treatment or event-focused treatment. Event-focused treatment occurs when trauma reprocessing is restricted to the specific event or critical incident that brought the first responder into care. When this occurs, the therapist may need to use EMD rather than EMDR. With event-focused reprocessing phases of EMDR, there are specific steps included in the treatment.

Treatment With EMDR

In Phase 1 (History-taking, Case Conceptualization and Treatment Planning), the treatment involves gathering a biopsychosocial intake that includes the history of the client's symptoms, developing rapport, conceptualizing the client's needs, and creating a treatment plan. Also, it is important to assess for trauma and dissociation. Use standardized assessments, if possible, for future assessment and documentation. With first responders, a recent incident may have precipitated the treatment referral.

Targets of Opportunity

What brought the individual into the office? The target of opportunity may be the one that is most easily accessed and presented by the client as the precipitating factor for the treatment visit. Those targets may be from a recent professional event, a personal event, or a combination. It is important that mental health professionals honor the information that the client presents as the precipitating event while also educating the client about the possible associated events. This clinical decision will not only impact the treatment process, but also the therapist–client relationship and the client's willingness to participate in treatment. At times, the precipitating event may be the result of professional exposure.

Targets of Professional Exposure

Targets of professional exposure include death notifications, personal exposure, when professional colleagues are hurt or killed in the line of duty, unique sensory flashbacks, and the residual impact of habitual stoicism, depersonalization, and derealization. Organizing targets for reprocessing for first responders can be organized with the "Parade of Faces." See the form for "Parade of Faces," in the Preparation Phase of this chapter.

Diagnostic Challenges

Therapists working with first responders need to consider the diagnostic issues with which the first responder presents for treatment. Some are obvious and some are more subdued.

- How does the diagnostic process impact the individual's job and career?
- With the specific diagnosis, is the first responder willing and/or able to return to the line of duty?
- If there is a concern regarding the first responder's well-being, what safety planning is necessary?

In the Preparation Phase (Phase 2), there are many resources/tools for first responders to manage the line of duty exposure. There are many resources available to first responders both from the department and from the community. Internet resources are listed below. First responders need to be taught and encouraged to participate in emotional self-care. Emotional Self-Care for first responders includes having the right EQUIPMENT (see script).

Containers

Training as a first responder is essential but not complete without learning how to contain the intense psychological and physiological experiences from the line of duty. Rather than stoicism, dissociation, depersonalization, and derealization, first responders can be taught various types of containers to cope with the work-related exposure. It is important to remind the first responder that a container is not intended to be closed indefinitely, but, instead, to hold the individual's response that would interfere with the work in the present, until the job is done. Sometimes professionals may respond to sequential events and need many containers during a shift. It can be a healthy process to contain traumatic events until a more appropriate time and then address the trauma; however, many first responders never get around to emptying the container. This is the point where first responders need to learn unique skills for being able to respond to calls day after day—year after year.

Early Mental Health Intervention for First Responders/ Protective Service Workers Including Firefighters and Emergency Medical Services (EMS) Professionals Script

Phase 1: History Taking

Target Identification of Parade of Faces for First Responders: Parade of Faces Script

Use the Parade of Faces as the metaphor for creating a targeting sequence plan. A Parade of Faces is a metaphor for all the calls that linger and haunt first responders, contributing to the onset of physical and mental health issues. The calls that linger often include the following.

- First and worst calls
- Child-related calls and fatalities
- Suicides
- Calls where the professional felt personally threatened or was injured
- Calls with intense odors and/or human remains
- Associations with professional's personal life

The Haunted: Parade of Faces form below can be used to organize targets and resources for EMDR with first responders.

Haunted: Parade of Faces— The Calls That Haunt	NAME: _____ DATE: _____		
DISTURBING EVENTS "Tell me about the calls that haunt you even now."	**Timeline Weeks/ Months**	**SIGNIF. REL.**	**POSITIVE EVENTS/RESOURCES** **The calls that reinforce why I do the job. "Tell me about the calls where you felt successful."**
	Before the academy		
	Academy		
	Rookie		
	1		
	2		
	3		
	4		
	5		
	6		
	7		
	8		

Using the Parade of Faces form, the therapist can begin collecting targets for trauma reprocessing with EMDR. This first call can actually have occurred long before the client became a first responder. Often the individual witnessed something in childhood. For example, police officers might have witnessed someone being beaten such as domestic violence or a bully. EMS personal have reported witnessing horrific injuries when they felt helpless.

Say, *"When you think about the calls that haunt you, what calls are the most difficult?"*

_____

_____

Say, *"What is the first call that haunts you?"*

_____

_____

Say, *"Image the calls like a parade that you watch from the first to the most recent call. Those may include calls about suicides, children, severe bodily injuries, and/or body odors such as blood, brain matter, decomposition, burning flesh. When you think about that parade of faces of the calls that haunt you, what's your negative belief about yourself now? Those might be things like, 'I should have done something?' ' I'm powerless?' 'I can't forget or get over it.'"*

_____

_____

After documenting the negative cognition, say the following:

"Now tell me about the first call that made you proud about becoming a first responder."

_____

_____

Say, *"Now I want you to think about your positive belief about yourself when you think of your career. What would that be?"*

_____

_____

Say, *"I want you to imagine the parade of the calls that haunt you on a television channel and you have the remote. On what channel would you put all of the calls that haunt you?"*

_____

_____

The therapist now documents the channel for the critical events, and then identifies a channel for the positive events.

Note: The therapist needs to use the terms the first responder identifies about being successful in the field.

Say, *"What channel would you use for all the calls where you felt successful and helpful?"*

_____

_____

Say, *"How did it impact you?"*

_____

_____

Say, *"What do you need to do to care for yourself?"*

_____

_____

Say, *"How do you get closure?"*

_____

_____

Say, *"Who else is struggling?"*

_____

_____

Say, *"What if anything do you need/want to do for your brothers and sisters who also experienced this exposure?"*

_____

_____

Say, *"How does this impact your next call? Your next shift?"*

_____

_____

- Intake _____
- Assessment _____
- Documentation _____
- Flow of EMDR _____
- Treatment planning while on duty _____
- Treatment planning while on light duty _____
- Decisions to return to work as targets for EMDR _____

Phase 2: Preparation Phase

The goals of the Preparation Phase of EMDR include identifying the resources the client has and teaching additional resourcing skills. The second goal of this phase is teaching the mechanics of EMDR.

Resources

Find out what resources the client has.

Say, *"What are the types of resources that you count on?"*

_____

_____

After the client responds, then ask about the needed resources.

Say, *"What resources do you need? Ask yourself the following questions:"*

_____

_____

Say, *"Do you need to assess your diet and improve your eating?"*

_____

_____

Say, *"Do you need to improve sleep hygiene?"*

_____

_____

Say, *"Do you need to care for your physical health?"*

_____

_____

Say, *"Do you need to learn stress management skills?"*

_____

_____

Say, *"Do you need to explore your spiritual needs?"*

_____

_____

Say, *"Do you need to use the skills you already have?"*

_____

_____

Say, *"Do you need to learn interpersonal skills in order to have healthier personal and professional relationships?"*

_____

_____

Say, *"What residual effects do you carry from your childhood that interfere with your current life?"*

_____

_____

Say, *"What residual effects do you carry around from your personal life that you need to deal with?"*

_____

_____

Say, *"What residual effects do you carry around from your professional life that you need to process?"*

_____

_____

RESILIENCE AND HARDINESS

Note: Training in resilience and hardiness improves the first responder's ability to cope with the career and the "wear and tear" of doing the job.

Say, *"How are you assessing the current impact of these issues in your life?"*

_____

_____

If the first responder assesses that there is an impact on his life, find out how he processes current stressors and traumas.

Say, *"What skills and/or tools do you use?"*

_____

_____

Say, *"What skills and/or tools do you need?"*

_____

_____

PROFESSIONAL GRIEF AND LOSS RESOURCES

Because first responders enter in the middle of the story, they often don't see the beginning or end.

Say, *"How do you get closure?"*

_____

_____

Say, *"What are your religious and spiritual needs?"*

_____

_____

Say, *"Is it appropriate/helpful for you to attend funeral services or practice closure other types of closure?"*

_____

_____

Using Resources for Management of a Career as a First Responder

Say, *"One of the ways that you can remember how to take care of yourself emotionally and maintain your health while in the line of duty is to have the right EQUIPMENT. EQUIPMENT stands for:*

- Engage your resources and acquire new ones.
- Quality of Life is important each day!
- Utilize medical and mental health services
- Improve your longevity by participating in daily self-care—diet, exercise, and hearth health
- Prepare for survival by practicing and learning new skills
- Mentor others by modeling healthy professional behavior both on duty and off.
- Educate yourself about the long-term impact of trauma exposure and keep acquiring new resources for coping
- Never forget that you are as important as those you protect, serve, and rescue!
- Take care of each other—at work and at home.*"

Resources/Tools for First Responders to Manage the Line of Duty Exposure

Containers

Teaching first responders how to use various types of containers will help them cope with work related exposure.

Note: Containers are not intended to be closed indefinitely, but, instead, to hold the individual's response that would interfere with the work in the present, until the job is done.

CONTAINERS SCRIPT

Say, *"Sometimes we have thoughts, or feelings, or body sensation that get in the way at work or at home. Do you ever have thoughts or feeling like that? I want you to know that if we need to we can put those thoughts or feelings in a container like a box or something really strong that they can't get out. What do you think you would need to hold those thoughts or feelings?"*

_____

_____

Next say, *"I want you to be able to put all of those thoughts or feelings, or what we worked on today in that container. Sometimes we need different containers for different thoughts or feelings. Sometimes, it helps to draw pictures of the_____(container) and make sure it's strong enough to hold everything that you need it to hold.*
Let's imagine that everything you worked on today is put in the container and we lock it away/seal it away until we meet next time when we can take it out to work on it again. When we get together we will work to empty your container so there's always room for new stuff if you need it. If you start thinking about things that bother you that are too hard to handle or it seems to come out before our next session, you can just imagine putting it into the container and sealing it in there until we meet again."

"Finishing the Call"—Getting Closure

First responders need skills to get closure on calls. This may include spiritual and/or religious rituals. First responders many need/want to attend funerals, or participate in some type of grief response. Some first responders benefit from knowing more about the patient/victim. One first responder continued to have a picture of the bloody face of the child he rescued. He was later able to see a school picture of the child so he could get closure on the flashbacks of her face and gain some closure on this call that haunted him.

Say, *"It is important for you to get closure on calls. This may include spiritual and/or religious rituals, attending a funeral, grieving, learning more about what happened to the victim/patient."*

_____

_____

MAKE A PLAN

Say, *"How will the department handle this issue?"*

_____

_____

Say, *"What would be a plan to help you?"*

_____

_____

Assess current resources—what resources are available and what does the individual/group need to manage this event? The mental health professional needs to help the first responder assess what resources currently exist.

Say, *"What resources are available to you?"*

_____

_____

Say, *"What does the individual/group need to manage this event?"*

_____

_____

Learn new skills—what new skills may the individual/group/department need to cope with the current situation?

Say, *"What new skills may you, the group and/or department need to cope with the current situation."*

_____

_____

Accurately assess on-going stress and trauma—first responders need to be taught and encouraged to regularly assess the impact of the career. Resources included at the end of this chapter are helpful to provide to the individual and department during and after the mental health intervention.

Empty containers on a daily basis—Having daily rituals to empty the containers the first responder has used to contain the thoughts, emotions, and body sensations from the critical incident needs to be routinely emptied.

Say, *"What can you do on a daily basis to clear the calls you have responded to that shift?"*

_____

_____

Health is an ongoing holistic process.
After Action Psychological Review can be used as in Phase 1 above.

Phase 3: Assessment Phase

In the assessment phase (Phase 3), the goal is to access and activate the memory network for trauma reprocessing. One clinical decision point when using this protocol is whether to do EMD (Shapiro, 1989) or EMDR (Shapiro, 2001). EMD is dedicated to "restricted reprocessing" (Outcalt, 2012, personal communication) focused on reprocessing one target at a time rather than using the full EMDR (Shapiro, 2001) protocol in which all potential associative links are addressed. After a critical incident with first responders, the therapist may decide to proceed with EMD. EMD then restricts the reprocessing to the incident while containing other associative links. This phase is focused on the specific event, while containing all other associations. The Assessment Phase can be remembered using the acronym TICES: target, image, cognition, emotion, and sensation.

- *T*–The *target* is the critical incident. This can be selected from the "Parade of Faces." When responding to a recent critical incident with first responders, the target is the event.

  Say, *"We discussed the parade of faces that haunt you. For today we agreed that we are going to focus on this critical event_____(Therapist repeats the target)."*

- *I*–The *image* is the worst part of that specific critical incident. If the critical incident is more recent, there may be multiple images that arise. Of the images, the therapist can make a chronological list of the images and start with the first one specific to that critical incident.

Say, *"When you bring up that event we agreed to work on today, what image comes up for you as the worst part of the event?"*

_____

_____

If the critical incident is recent, the therapist can say, "When you bring up that event, what image is the first image that comes up for you as the worst part of the event?"

_____

_____

- C–The *cognitions* are those associated with the critical incident. The negative and positive cognitions need to be consistent and then the therapist needs to assess the validity of cognition (VoC).

NEGATIVE COGNITION

The therapist may use the negative cognition (NC) previously elicited while completing the "Parade of Faces" protocol.

Say, *"When you think about that event, what is the negative belief you have about yourself now?"*

_____

_____

POSITIVE COGNITION (PC)

Say, *"When you think about that event, what would you rather believe instead?"* Or you can say, *"What's the good thought that you want to tell yourself instead?"*

_____

_____

ELICITING THE VOC

Say, *"When you think about those words,_____(PC), how true do those words feel to you now on a scale of 1 completely false to a 7 meaning completely true?"*

_____

_____

- E–Eliciting emotions:

Say, *"When you bring up that critical incident, what emotions come up for you now?"* Once the emotion(s) are identified, the therapist needs to assess the Subjective Units of Disturbance (SUDs) on a 10 point scale with 0 no disturbance and 10 the most disturbance the first responder is experiencing in relation to the critical incident.

_____

_____

To elicit the SUDs:

Say, *"When you think about that incident and those emotions, how disturbing does it feel to you now on a scale of zero meaning no disturbance and 10 the worst you have ever experienced?"*

_____

_____

- *S*–The *sensations* are the physical sensations the client is experiencing in relation to the critical incident and the corresponding emotions. In order to elicit the body sensations associated with the target, the therapist

Says, *"When you bring up that incident and those emotions, where do you feel that in your body now?"*

_____

_____

After eliciting the procedural steps of the Assessment Phase, the therapist continues with the Desensitization Phase of EMDR.

Phase 4: Desensitization Phase

During the Desensitization Phase, the therapist is regularly helping the client to contain other associations and focus on the specific critical incident that is the focus of this episode of care. Other associated incidents do need to be documented for possible future care.

To begin desensitization:

Say *"I'd like you to bring up that event_____ (label and describe using client's words), and the words_____ (repeat the NC in client's words), the_____feeling, and notice where you are feeling it in your body and _____"* (therapist uses whatever bilateral stimulation [BLS] previously identified.)

Begin the BLS. (You established the BLS method and speed during the introduction to EMDR). The type of BLS may need to be changed often in order to assist the individual in sustaining attention.

If the client appears to be too upset to continue reprocessing, it is helpful to reassure the client by saying the following:

Say, *"It's normal for you to feel more as we start to work on this. Remember we said it's like_____(metaphor) so just notice it. It's old stuff."* (This is not always necessary.)

After a set of BLS, instruct the individual by saying the following:

Say, *"Take a deep breath."* (It is often helpful if the therapist takes an exaggerated breath to model for the client, as the therapist asks the client for brief feedback on the process.)

And then say, *"What did you get now?"* Or *"Tell me what you got?"*

_____

_____

Or if the client needs coaching, say, the following: "What are *you thinking, feeling, how does your body feel, or what pictures are you seeing in your head?"*

_____

_____

After the client recounts his/her experience, the therapist says the following:

Say, *"Continuing with that incident we're working on, just notice what comes up, and go with that,"*

Do another set of BLS. (Do not repeat the client's words/statements.)

As an optional phrasing you can say, *"Just notice that."*

The therapist does not need to understand what is happening; only the client does because what matters is how the individual has maladaptively stored the information.

Again ask the following: say, *"What do you get now?"*

_____

_____

If new negative material presents itself, continue down that channel with further sets of BLS.

Continue with sets of BLS until the client's responses indicate that he/she is at the end of a memory channel. At that point, the client may appear significantly calmer with no new disturbing material is emerging. Then, return to the target by having the client evaluate the progress.

Say, *"When you think about that incident we first talked about today, what happens now?"*

_____

_____

Note: Remember, first responders may not show affect because of the culture of stoicism.

There may be no more disturbing material for them to access or describe about the target memory. After the client recounts his/her experience, add a set of BLS.

Say, *"Go with that."*

_____

_____

If positive material is reported, add one or two sets of BLS to increase the strength of the positive associations before returning to target.

Say, *"Go with that."*

If the therapist assesses that the client has reprocessed the critical incident because the material reported is neutral or positive then say the following:

Say, *"When you go back to that incident we talked about today, what do you get now?"*

_____

_____

No matter how the client responds, add a set of BLS.

Say, *"Go with that."*

If no change occurs, then check the SUD.

Say, *"On a scale of 0 to 10, where 0 is no disturbance or neutral and 10 is the highest disturbance you can imagine, how disturbing does it feel now?"*

0	1	2	3	4	5	6	7	8	9	10
(no disturbance)										(highest disturbance)

If the SUD is greater than 0, continue with further sets of BLS, time permitting.

Say, *"Go with that."*

If the SUD is 0, do another set of BLS to verify that no new material emerges and then proceed to the installation of the PC.

Say, *"Go with that"*

Note: Only proceed to Installation Phase after you have returned to target, added a set of BLS, no new material has emerged, and the SUD is 0.

Phase 5: Installation Phase

During the Installation Phase, the therapist has the first responder hold together the incident and assess the efficacy of the PC, exploring for more expanded PCs. The first responder may find that his/her perceptions of the career may have changed and begin to impact professional performance. This change may need to be discussed with the individual.

Say, *"When you bring up that incident and the words_____(PC), does that one still fit or does something else fit better now?"*

_____

Say, *"Go with that."*

The individual may have a new PC that is now installed with BLS.

Say, *"When you think of the incident* (or picture), *how true do those words _____(clinician repeats the PC) feel to you now on a scale of 1 to 7, where 1 feels completely false and 7 feels completely true?"*

1	2	3	4	5	6	7
(completely false)			(completely true)			

Use a set of BLS and then repeat this statement until the PC is at a 7.

Say, *"Go with that."*

Say, *"What do you get now when you think of the incident* (or picture), *how true do those words_____(clinician repeats the PC) feel to you now on a scale of 1 to 7, where 1 feels completely false and 7 feels completely true?"*

Once the PC is installed, the final phase of trauma reprocessing is the body scan.

Phase 6: Body Scan Phase

This phase focuses on the first responder's physiological response to the critical incident. Many first responders learn early in their career to disregard personal body sensations while in the line of duty. The Body Scan Phase may be surprising and even disturbing to first responders who have never experienced or dealt with even personal exposure from the career. Since many first responders use dissociation and have to learn to ignore physical sensations, paying attention to those for the first time may be difficult and even alarming. The therapist needs to teach the client mindfulness while also helping him/her to understand what is happening.

> Say, *"Close your eyes and keep in mind the original memory and the positive cognition. Then bring your attention to the different parts of your body, starting with your head and working downward. Any place you find any tension, tightness, or unusual sensation, tell me."*

Then use another set of BLS.

Say, *"Go with that."*

Continue until the client reports a clear body scan. Once the critical incident has cleared, the therapist may need to determine if the first responder wants to continue with additional trauma work or if EMD for this one event is sufficient.

Phase 7: Closure

Complete as much work as time and circumstances allow, leaving adequate time for closure and debriefing. With first responders, the therapist needs to ensure that activated material is sufficiently contained especially if the individual will be continuing to be in the field during EMDR.

> Say, *"It is important that you continue to practice the resources we previously identified between sessions in order to cope with the wear and tear of your career."*

Incomplete Session

If the session is incomplete, remind the client of the Container Exercise and other relaxation techniques to prepare for ending the session. Skills for first responders were discussed earlier in this chapter. Remind the individual to practice relaxation skills and containers in order to continue being successful in the line of duty.

> Say, *"You've addressed a great deal of intense issues today and reprocessing could continue over the next few days. Remember to use your container that we talked about earlier and the relaxation techniques we've practiced in your sessions. Feel free to contact me if you need additional support."*

If you have completed the session, say the following:

> Say, *"Things may come up or they may not. If they do, great. Write it down and it can be a target for next time. You can use a log to write down what triggers images, thoughts or cognitions, emotions, and sensations; you can rate them on our 0-to-10 scale where 0 is no disturbance or neutral and 10 is the worst disturbance. Please write down the positive experiences, too."*

> *"If you get any new memories, dreams, or situations that disturb you, just take a good snapshot. It isn't necessary to give a lot of detail. Just put down enough to remind you so we can target it next time. The same thing goes for any positive dreams or situations. If negative feelings do come up, try not to make them significant. Remember, it's still just the old stuff. Just write it down for next time. Then use the tape or the Safe Place exercise to let as much of the disturbance go as possible. Even if nothing comes up, make sure to use the tape every day and give me a call if you need to."*

Phase 8: Reevaluation

With each new session, the therapist obtains feedback on experiences/observations since last session. The client continues to check the Parade of Faces for new traumatic or positive events. The therapist needs to check the SUD and VoC on the previous incident, and for any unprocessed material from previous sessions and probe for any new material that might have emerged.

> Say, *"When you think about the incident we worked on last week, what do you get now?"*

_____

_____

After the client responds the following:

> Say, *"On a scale of 0 to 10, where 0 is no disturbance or neutral and 10 is the highest disturbance you can imagine, how disturbing does it feel now?"*

0	1	2	3	4	5	6	7	8	9	10

(no disturbance)   (highest disturbance)

If SUD rating on previous week's incident is greater than 0, continue reprocessing.

> Say, *"Bring up that incident, those words_____(repeat the NC), and notice where you feel it in your body."*

Begin BLS.

If the SUDs is zero, but the VoC rating for the previous week's incident is less than 7 continue to reprocess this target.

If the previous week's target appears to be resolved (SUDs = 0, VoC = 7), then complete the body scan and move on to the next target on the treatment plan target list OR move on to target current triggers associated with the critical incidents.

This provides a scripted protocol for proceeding through the eight phases of the EMDR Protocol specifically focused on working with first responders and protective service personnel.

Summary

This chapter provided an overview of how to organize mental health services for first responders who experience daily exposure to critical incidents and traumatic events. Services may be offered for training as preincident services. Other services may be requested during a critical incident or postincident. The first responder is a perpetual witness to the suffering of others while at other times the first responder may also become a victim when responding to a critical incident. Significant research documents the physical and psychological consequences of a career as a first responder. With this foundation, first responders need ongoing self-care and efficacious mental health services in order to weather the storm of the career. Responding to the needs of first responders requires familiarity with the culture, earning the respect and trust of the community, awareness of the complicated forensic issues, and adjustments to mental health services such as have been offered with EMDR. Mental health professionals can provide invaluable services to protect the first responder and his/her family.

Resources for First Responders

- A Manager's Guide: Traumatic Incidents at the Workplace, United States Office of Personnel Management, OWR Publication 20 | February, 2003. http://archive.opm .gov/employment_and_benefits/worklife/officialdocuments/handbooksguides/ trauma/index.asp
- American Red Cross—www.redcross.org
- Centers for Disease Control and Prevention (CDC)—www.bt.cdc.gov/disasters
- Center for the Study of Traumatic Stress—www.cstsonline.org
- Critical Incident Stress Management (CISM), Office of Work-Life Programs, U.S. Department of Homeland Security, United States Coast Guard www.uscg.mil/directives/ ci/1000–1999/CI_1754_3A.pdf www.uscg.mil/worklife/critical_incident_stress.asp
- Defense Centers of Excellence (DCoE) for Psychological Health and Brain Injury— www.dcoe.health.mil/default.aspx
- Federal Emergency Management Agency (FEMA)—www.fema.gov
- Insure You Can Save a Life!—www.lifeinsure.com/education-center/life-insurance -tips/insure-you-can-save-a-life
- International Association of Firefighters (IAFF)—www.iaff.org
- International Critical Incident Stress Foundation—www.icisf.org
- National Fallen Firefighters Foundation—www.firehero.org
- National Institute for Occupational Safety and Health (NIOSH)—www.cdc.gov/NIOSH
- National Integration Center (NIC) Incident Management Systems Integration Division (FEMA) www.fema.gov/national-incident-management-system
- Navy and Marine Corps Public Health Center Portal—www.med.navy.mil/sites/ nmcphc/Pages/Home.aspx
- Navy Operational Stress Control (OSC) Official Blog Site—www.navynavstress.com
- Psychological First Aid: Field Operations Guide www.ptsd.va.gov/professional/ manuals/manual-pdf/pfa/PFA_2nd Editionwithappendices.pdf
- Substance Abuse and Mental Health Services Administration (SAMSHA) www .samhsa.gov/index.aspx
- The Stress Continuum www.uscg.mil/worklife/docs/pdf/stress_continuum.pdf
- U.S. National Response Team (NRT) www.nrc.uscg.mil/nrsinfo.html
- U.S. Office of Personnel Management (OPM)—*A Manager's Handbook: Handling Traumatic Events*, February 2003—www.opm.gov/policy-data-oversight/worklife/ reference-materials/traumaticevents.pdf

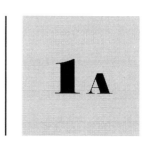

SUMMARY SHEET:
Early Mental Health Intervention for First Responders/ Protective Service Workers Including Firefighters and Emergency Medical Services Professionals

Robbie Adler-Tapia
SUMMARY SHEET BY MARILYN LUBER

☑ Check when task is completed, response has changed, or to indicate symptoms.

Note: This material is meant as a checklist for your response. Please keep in mind that it is only a reminder of different tasks that may or may not apply to your incident.

Basic Information for the Mental Health Practitioner—The Mission of First Responders

First Responder Trauma

Trauma = anything that negatively impacts the psyche and changes the course of healthy development.

Targets of Professional Exposure = witnessing horrific events plus include death notifications, personal exposure, when professional colleagues are hurt or killed in the line of duty, unique sensory flashbacks, and the residual impact of habitual stoicism, depersonalization, and derealization.

Professional Trauma = anything that negatively impacts the psyche and changes the course of healthy development.

- ☐ *Line of Duty Traumas* = those experienced during work that include witnessing death or near-death experiences of individuals in the community, other professionals, or risk to self.
- ☐ *Line of Duty Death (LODD)* = deaths that occur when professionals die in the line of duty. Can be more stressful for other professionals in trying to rescue and treat a comrade.
- ☐ *Postshooting Trauma in Law Enforcement (PSTLE)* = traumas after professional event. The *official* process that professionals must endure following a shooting. The ongoing stress further complicates the treatment process.
- ☐ *Betrayal Trauma* = the experience that some professionals face when not feeling supported by department and/or command, media, public, and family.

Similarities and Differences With First Responders

☐ *Emergency Services Dispatchers or 911 operators* in the U.S. dispatch other profession-als to the scene of a disaster when help is needed, but rarely go to the scene. May later struggle with visual creations that occurred when verbally dispatching assistance.
☐ *Law Enforcement Professionals* are more likely to work alone.
☐ *Other First Responders* are rarely alone.

Culture of Stoicism, Depersonalization, and Derealization

☐ *Stoicism* is a cultural expectation in that first responders are expected to not be impacted by the events to which they respond.
☐ *Depersonalization* is experiencing an event, but feeling like it is happening to some-one else.
☐ *Derealization* is experiencing an event, but feeling like it isn't real.

The Families of First Responders

The Traditional Family = concerned about the health and safety of family members
The Professional Family = squad and department

Treating Trauma Exposure for First Responders

Service needs for the department may include:

☐ Pre-incident training
☐ CISM (Critical Incident Stress Management)
☐ On-Scene Support Services
   ☐ Anniversary meetings
   ☐ Command consultation
   ☐ Family crisis intervention
   ☐ Follow-up services
   ☐ On-scene support services
   ☐ Post-incident services
   ☐ Individual treatment for duty
   ☐ Workmen's Compensation Services

Note: Earning individual and group trust is the biggest hurdle to efficacy in responding to critical incidents with first responders.

How Do Mental Health Professionals Prepare for and Organize a Disaster Response/Elements of a Mental Health Disaster Response?

Who Contacted the Mental Health Professional? _____

Who Will Be the Department Contact? _____

To What Type of Disaster Are You Responding?

☐ *Natural disaster* (wildland and/or forest fires, earthquakes, a tsunami, hurricane, flood, epidemic, structural collapse, etc.)?
☐ *Man-made event* (torture, acts of terrorism, war, drug cartel wars, school shootings, gang warfare, robbery, arson, bombs, etc.)?

Where Did the Incident Occur? _____

What Is the Size of the Incident?

How many professionals are estimated to have been impacted? _____

How many civilians are estimated to have been impacted? _____

Logistics of a Mental Health Disaster Response

Location—Where will you implement the response? _____

Demobilization

☐ *Time off postincident before back to work*

☐ *No time off—first responders expected to respond to call*

Participation

Who needs help? _____

Who are the team of responders? _____

What are the needs of the group to be helped? _____

Professional Response

How many professionals needed? _____

Are there enough?   ☐ Yes ☐ No

If not, effect on organization: _____

Logistics

Duration of intervention? _____

Who organizes food and drink for group? _____

How much time will be available for the response?   _____Hours? _____Days?

Confidentiality

Will confidentiality and privacy be honored?   ☐ Yes ☐ No

How will confidentiality and privacy be maintained?

Will records be maintained for services?   ☐ Yes ☐ No

Are there differences between professional and civilian interventions?   ☐ Yes ☐ No

If so, what are they? _____

How will referrals be addressed? _____

Costs/Payment

What are the costs/budget?

Is this a voluntary or paid position? Telephone number: _____ Voluntary? _____ Paid?

How will billing and payment be handled? _____

Postincident Services

Working With Department and Command to Provide Postincident Services

Who Invited the Involvement of the Mental Health Professional?

☐ Self-referral/Individual referral (Circle)

Who?_____ Telephone number: _____

☐ Department referral

Who?_____ Telephone number: _____

What Type of Service Is Requested? _____ ☐ *Individual?* ☐ *Group?*

When Was the Contact Made? _____

Referrals for Mental Health Services

EAP available	☐ Yes	☐ No
EAP internal/external to department	☐ Internal	☐ External

Concerns about RAP referral _____

_____

EAP providers knowledgeable about first responders	☐ Yes	☐ No
Option to go to private practitioner	☐ Yes	☐ No
Will there be any ongoing civil or criminal investigations/litigation?	☐ Yes	☐ No
If a witness, will therapist's records be protected from legal proceedings?	☐ Yes	☐ No

Self-Referral

Self-referral—what are the expectations? _____

_____

Department Referral

- What and how will confidentiality be managed? _____

  _____

- What do the individual and/or department expect? _____

  _____

- What is the purpose of the intervention requested? _____

  _____

- What and how will confidentiality be managed? _____

  _____

• Are on-scene services requested?	☐ Yes	☐ No
If so, is there a risk to the mental health service provider?	☐ Yes	☐ No
• Does command/leadership expect updates about the services?	☐ Yes	☐ No
If so, how will the therapist correspond with the Department?		
• Are there privacy issues that need to be resolved?	☐ Yes	☐ No
• Will there be an Industrial Commission/Workman's Compensation Case?	☐ Yes	☐ No
• Are there criminal issues that impact this mental health process?	☐ Yes	☐ No
• Will this first responder have to testify about the call or any other call?	☐ Yes	☐ No

After Action Review (AAR) = a meeting of the professionals who responded to an event and conduct a debriefing of the response in order to improve services and safety for professionals.

Psychological Component of the AAR—**Therapists may add a psychological component to the AAR, using a CISD/CISM model of response:**

- How did it impact me? _____

- What do I need to do to care for myself? _____

- How do I get closure? _____

- Who else is struggling? _____

- What if anything do I need/want to do for my brothers and sisters who also experienced this exposure? _____

- How does this impact our next call? Our next shift? _____

Mental Health Services for First Responders

Critical Incident Stress Debriefing (CISD) or Critical
Incident Stress Management (CISM)   ☐ Yes   ☐ No

Focus is to provide "Psychological First Aid" as an immediate debriefing in order to minimize the harmful effects of job stress, specifically in crisis or emergency situations. CISM services include seven steps (adapted from Everly & Mitchell, 1997):

1. *Precrisis Preparation, which includes* preincident stress management training, education, and skill building.
2. *Disaster or Large-Scale,* as well as school and community support programs that include demobilizations, informational briefings, "town meetings," and staff advisement.
3. *Defusing is* a 3-phase, structured group activity that is after or soon after the event for assessment, triaging, and acute symptom mitigation.
4. *Critical Incident Stress Debriefing (CISD)* refers to the "Mitchell Model" (Mitchell and Everly, 1996) This is a 7-phase, structured group discussion, usually provided 1 to 10 days postcrisis, and designed to mitigate acute symptoms, assess the need for follow up, and if possible provide a sense of postcrisis psychological closure.
5. *One-On-One Crisis Intervention/Counseling or Psychological Support* throughout the full range of the crisis spectrum
6. *Crisis Intervention and Organizational Consultation*
7. *Follow Up and Referrals for Assessment and Treatment,* if necessary

Note: In addition, mental health professionals may provide assessment of individuals and case management for individuals with on-going needs.

Psychological First Aid (PFA)   ☐ Yes   ☐ No
   (www.ptsd.va.gov/professional/manuals/psych-firstaid.asp)
   ☐ PFA Field Operations Manual available online
   ☐ PFA apps for smart phones available
   ☐ Mental Health First Aid (www.mentalhealthfirstaid.org)   ☐ Yes   ☐ No
   ☐ Referrals for Medication Assessment and Management may be Needed   ☐ Yes   ☐ No

Assessment and Case Management   ☐ Yes   ☐ No

Safety Planning—Questions to Assess Safety

- How to intervene if first responder is still on the job? _____ _____

  _____

- What documentation, if any, will the department request? _____

  _____

- Risk to the public, the individual, and/or other first responders, i.e., first responder is armed   ☐ At-Risk   ☐ Not A Risk

- Are mental health services a requirement for return to duty?   ☐ Yes   ☐ No

- What assessment will the mental health provider be asked to provide to the department, if any? _____

Fitness for Duty Process = to make case management and clinical decisions with first responders. (Only if the mental health professional is qualified to conduct fitness for duty assessment).

- Is a safety plan necessary?   ☐ Yes ☐ No

  If so, who needs to know? _____

- How do you protect a career? _____

- Is a DTO assessment necessary?   ☐ Yes ☐ No

- Is a DTS assessment necessary?   ☐ Yes ☐ No

  How will this occur?_____

Assessment of Individual First Responders   ☐ Yes ☐ No

Modified SAD PERSONAS Scale helps assess suicide risk
- ☐ Sex
- ☐ Age
- ☐ Depression
- ☐ Previous attempt
- ☐ Ethanol abuse
- ☐ Rational thinking loss
- ☐ Social supports lacking
- ☐ Organized plan
- ☐ No spouse
- ☐ Availability of lethal means
- ☐ Sickness

☐ After assessing the risk of danger to self or others, the therapist must make an appraisal of how to manage the risk.
- ☐ Immediate intervention
- ☐ Contact with department and staff
- ☐ Referral to a higher level of care
- ☐ Medication management

Treatment—Is treatment necessary?   ☐ Yes ☐ No
Format:

- ☐ Group
  - ☐ CISD/CISM
  - ☐ EMDR Group Protocol

- ☐ Individual Psychotherapy
  - ☐ CBP
  - ☐ CPT
  - ☐ PE
  - ☐ EMDR

Early Mental Health Intervention for First Responders/Protective Service Workers Including Firefighters and Interventions: Emergency Medical Services (EMS) Professionals, Notes, Case Conceptualization and Script

Case conceptualization With EMDR: Treatment Planning and Interventions

Important to consider if there are legal issues

- Any issues impacting flow of treatment?   ☐ Yes ☐ No

- Will notes be subpoenaed?   ☐ Yes ☐ No

- Is it prudent to proceed if forensic involvement?   ☐ Yes ☐ No

☐ Are your records complete and in compliance with ethical
and legal standards?   ☐ Yes ☐ No

☐ If departmental referral, what are the expectations? _____

_____

☐ Is it appropriate to continue with treatment?   ☐ Yes ☐ No

Comprehensive versus work-focused
    ☐ Comprehensive
    ☐ Work-focused

Individual Treatment With EMDR

Phase 1: Client History and Treatment Planning

    ☐ Biopsychosocial Intake
    ☐ Assess for trauma and dissociation
    ☐ Target Selection

        ☐ TARGETS OF OPPORTUNITY = most easily accessed and precipitating factors in treatment visit such as targets from recent professional event, personal event, or both.

        _____

        ☐ TARGET OF PROFESSIONAL EXPOSURE = death notifications, personal exposure, when professional colleagues are hurt or killed in the line of duty, unique sensory flashbacks, and the residual impact of habitual stoicism, depersonalization, and derealization.

        _____

        ☐ TARGET IDENTIFICATION OF PARADE OF FACES FOR FIRST RESPONDERS: PARADE OF FACES SCRIPT

The calls that linger often include:
    ☐ First and worst calls
    ☐ Child-related calls and fatalities
    ☐ Suicides
    ☐ Calls where the professional felt personally threatened or was injured
    ☐ Calls with intense odors and or human remains
    ☐ Associations with professional's personal life

Questions:

Most difficult call that haunts you: _____

_____

First call that haunts you: _____

_____

Image the calls like a parade that you watch from the first to the most recent call. Those may include calls about suicides, children, severe bodily injuries, and/or body odors such as blood, brain matter, decomposition, burning flesh. When you think about that parade of faces of the calls that haunt you, what's your negative belief about yourself now? Those might be things like, "I should have done something?" "I'm powerless?" "I can't forget or get over it."

    NC: _____

    First call that made you proud about becoming a first responder: _____

    _____

Positive belief about yourself when you think of your career: _____

_____

Image the parade of the calls that haunt you on a television channel and you have the remote. What channel would you put all of the calls that haunt you?

Channel for Haunting Calls:_____

Channel for Positive Events: _____

Channel for Calls Where Feel Successful and Helpful: _____

_____

Other Questions Concerning Critical Event

How did it impact you? _____

_____

What do you need to do to care for yourself? _____

_____

How do you get closure? _____

_____

Who else is struggling? _____

_____

What if anything do you need/or want to do for your brothers and sisters who also experienced this exposure? _____

_____

How does this impact our next call? Your next shift? _____

_____

Diagnostic Challenges

☐ How does diagnosis impact job and career? _____

_____

☐ With specific diagnosis able to/willing to return to line of duty?   ☐ Yes ☐ No

☐ Safety plan necessary?   ☐ Yes ☐ No

If yes, what steps will be taken?_____

Note: It is important for mental health professionals to assess response to the department and/or command. This could impact the first responder's career and future in the profession

Phase completed   ☐ Yes ☐ No

Phase 2: Preparation

☐ *Teach Mechanics of EMDR*   ☐ Completed

☐ *Resources*

Resources you count on: _____

_____

☐ Resource review concerning client needs in following areas:

Diet and eating: _____

Sleep hygiene: _____

Physical health: _____

Stress management skills: _____

Spiritual needs: _____

Skills already has: _____

Interpersonal skills for healthier personal and professional relationships: _____

_____

Residual effects from childhood interfering in current life: _____

_____

Residual effects from personal life: _____

_____

Residual effects from professional life: _____

_____

☐ RESILIENCE AND HARDINESS

Assessment of current impact of coping with career and "wear and tear" of career on life:

_____

Skills and/or tools I use: _____

Skills and/or tools I need: _____

☐ PROFESSIONAL GRIEF AND LOSS RESOURCES

How can get closure since only seeing middle of critical incident: _____

_____

Spiritual and religious needs: _____

_____

Appropriate/helpful to attend funeral services/practice closure/other types of closure:

_____

_____

Using Resources for Management of a Career as First Responder

EQUIPMENT *is an acronym for first responders to remind them to maintain their health while in the line of duty.*

☐ Engage your resources and acquire new ones.
☐ Quality of Life is important each day!
☐ Utilize medical and mental health services
☐ Improve your longevity by participating in daily self-care—diet, exercise, and hearth health
☐ Prepare for survival by practicing and learning new skills
☐ Mentor others by modeling healthy professional behavior both on duty and off.
☐ Educate yourself about the long-term impact of trauma exposure and keep acquiring new resources for coping
☐ Never forget that you are as important as those you protect, serve, and rescue!
☐ Take care of each other- at work and at home.

Resources/Tools for First Responders to Mange the Line of Duty Exposure

☐ Containers = way to contain intense psychological and physiological experiences from line of duty vs using stoicism, dissociation, depersonalization and/or derealiza-tion. Important to remind them that it is not to be closed indefinitely but just to hold the material that would interfere with the work in the present until the job is done

CONTAINERS SCRIPT

> Say, *"Sometimes we have thoughts, or feelings, or body sensations that get in the way at work or at home. Do you ever have thoughts or feeling like that? I want you to know that if we need to we can put those thoughts or feelings in a container like a box or something really strong that they can't get out of. What do you think you would need to hold those thoughts or feelings?"*

> _____

> Next say, *"I want you to be able to put all of those thoughts or feelings, or what we worked on today in that container. Sometimes we need different contain-ers for different thoughts or feelings. Sometimes, it helps to draw pictures of the_____(container) and make sure it's strong enough to hold every-thing that you need it to hold.*
> *Let's imagine that everything you worked on today is put in the container and we lock it away/seal it away until we meet next time when we can take it out to work on it again. When we get together we will work to empty your container so there's always room for new stuff if you need it. If you start thinking about things that bother you that are too hard to handle or it seems to come out before our next session, you can just imagine putting it into the container and sealing it in there until we meet again."*

Container *Script Taught*   ☐ Yes ☐ No
Phase Completed   ☐ Yes ☐ No

"Finishing the Call"—Getting Closure

☐ PLAN FOR GETING CLOSURE:

_____

_____

How will the department handle this issue? _____

☐ ASSESS RESOURCE (see above)

☐ NEW SKILLS NEEDED TO COPE (see above)

☐ ASSESS ON-GOING STRESS AND TRAUMA (see resources at end of chapter)

☐ EMPTY CONTAINER ON DAILY BASIS

Phase 3: Assessment

During assessment, major decision point for case conceptualization is which protocol to use:

> ☐ EMD
> ☐ EMDR

PAST   ☐ Completed
Complete TICES (acronym for target, image, cognition, emotion,
and sensation)   ☐ Completed

Target=Critical Incident (see Parade of Faces): _____

_____

Image=worst part of specific critical incident. If multiple images, make chronological list and start with first one specific to critical incident: _____

_____

Cognitions:

NC (elicited during Parade of Faces): _____

PC (elicited during Parade of Faces): _____

VoC: ___/7

Emotions in relation to critical incident: _____

SUD: ___/10

Sensation in relation to critical incident: _____

_____

Phase completed   ☐ Yes ☐ No

Phase 4: Desensitization (According to Standard EMDR Protocol/EMD Protocol)

With EMD, the therapist is active in helping client contain other associations and focus on specific critical incident. Document associated incidents for possible use later.

Note: Remember, first responders may not show affect because of the culture of stoicism.

Phase completed   ☐ Yes ☐ No

Phase 5: Installation (According to Standard EMDR Protocol/EMD Protocol)

PC: ☐ Completed

New PC (if new one is better): _____

VoC: _____/7

Incident + PC + BLS

Phase completed   ☐ Yes ☐ No

Phase 6: Body Scan   ☐ Completed

Note: First responders learn to disregard personal body sensations while in line of duty so Body Scan may be surprising/disturbing. Help them to be mindful while helping them understand what is happening.

Unresolved tension/tightness/unusual sensation: _____

_____

Unresolved tension/tightness/unusual sensation + BLS

Decision point:

☐ Continue with additional trauma work

☐ EMD for one event sufficient

Phase completed   ☐ Yes ☐ No

Phase 7: Closure (According to Standard EMDR Protocol/EMD Potocol)   ☐ Completed

Incomplete Session

☐ Use Container Exercise and/or other relaxation techniques to prepare for end of session.

☐ Remind first responder to practice relaxation skills and containers to continue being successful in line of duty.

☐ Remind to practice resources previously identified to cope with wear and tear of career.

Phase completed   ☐ Yes   ☐ No

Phase 8: Reevaluation

☐ *EMD: Re-evaluate Incident:*

   ☐ SUDS of Incident: _____/10

   ☐ VoC of Incident: _____/7

   ☐ Body Sensations: Clear? _____   ☐ Yes   ☐ No

☐ *EMDR: Check Parade of Faces for new traumatic or positive events:*

Check Parade of Faces for new traumatic or positive events:

TRAUMATIC MATERIAL: _____

_____

_____

POSITIVE EVENTS: _____

_____

SUDS OF INCIDENT:_____/10

   ☐ If > than 0, continue processing.
   ☐ If SUD = 0 but VoC <7, continue to reprocess.
   ☐ If SUD = 0 and VoC = 7, complete body scan and move to next target/move to current triggers.

☐ *Reprocessed Necessary Targets:*   ☐ Completed

☐ *Check for Current Triggers:* _____

_____

_____

☐ *Check for Future Template:* _____

_____

_____

EMDR helpful in daily life: ☐ Yes   ☐ No

Phase Completed   ☐ Yes   ☐ No

   Notes: _____

_____

_____

_____

Early Mental Health EMDR Intervention for the Police

Roger Solomon

Introduction

In the aftermath of a critical incident, most law enforcement agencies and other emergency service personnel have access to psychosocial programs (e.g., critical incident stress management [CISM] interventions; Mitchell & Everly, 2003). CISM involves a number of different interventions, including structured group interventions that facilitate sharing of experiences, normalization of reactions, and psychosocial education on trauma and coping, as well as individual support. Only personnel who have had special training should do these kinds of interventions. However, further therapeutic support may be needed, and EMDR is an effective intervention for police officers (Lamphear, 2010; McNally & Solomon, 1999).

Law enforcement officers are resilient individuals who have gone through background checks, pre-employment psychological screening, rigorous training, and usually a year of probation where their performance is evaluated. However, the therapist should have some knowledge of the police occupation and culture to optimize credibility and effectiveness.

For the EMDR therapist who is providing therapeutic support in the aftermath of a disaster or critical incident, it is hoped the following information will facilitate understanding of the law enforcement profession and culture.

The LEO and Critical Incidents

Law enforcement can be very stressful. The law enforcement officer's (LEO) role is multifaceted and multidimensional in enforcing the law, protecting the public, and responding to emergencies and crises of all types. LEOs are often the first to respond to traumatic events and crisis situations to keep the peace and comfort the victims and consequently are involved in many critical incidents. A *critical incident* is a term used to describe a potentially traumatizing event that occurs in the performance of one's duty, and that potentially overwhelms the LEO's sense of vulnerability and control. Examples of critical incidents include:

- Line of duty death
- Suicide of an emergency worker
- Multi-casualty incident/disaster
- Significant event involving children
- Knowing the victim of the event
- Serious line of duty injury

- Line of duty shooting
- Excessive media interest
- Prolonged incident with loss

Involvement in such incidents may (or may not) result in PTSD. It must be understood that what is traumatizing for one LEO may not be traumatizing for another. Officers involved in the same situation can experience different levels of response.

LEOs may be traumatized not only by direct threat, but also vicariously when dealing with other people's tragedies. Witnessing death, seeing the worst society has to offer, working with victims (especially children), and the like can lead to vicarious traumatization (Solomon, 1988).

It can be helpful to think of emotional recovery and coping in terms of phases. However, it must be understood that not everybody exposed to stressful conditions or critical incidents will have a traumatic reaction. Critical incidents are certainly tragedies, but not necessarily traumatizing. In addition, people deal with the emotional impact in their own way and their own timetable. The following structure serves as a framework with which to understand the possible emotional aftermath experienced by LEOs.

The LEOs' Physiological and Mental Mobilization Responses

During a critical incident, an LEO experiences many physiological and mental mobilization reactions in the service of survival. Some of these responses can be confusing, such as time distortion (e.g., slow motion), auditory distortions (e.g., auditory exclusion), and visual distortions (e.g., tunnel vision), but are quite normal (Solomon & Horn, 1986). The LEO is usually in "operational" or "survival" mode, and therefore is task oriented and focused on fulfilling his/her mission. Because the LEO typically is focused on the job at hand (e.g., securing a crime scene), the emotional impact often hits later. Some officers, however, do experience significant stress and emotional reactions on scene, often successfully dealt with and remedied by psychological first aid and brief rest.

The LEOs' Emotional Responses

After the incident is over, the transition from operational/survival mode to experiencing the emotional impact may take a few days, but can be several weeks or longer. It is common for some officers to experience initial stress reactions, such as difficulty sleeping, difficulty concentrating, anxiety reactions, depressive reactions, intrusive and/or racing thoughts related to the incident, avoidance symptoms, and physiological arousal symptoms (Artwahl, 2002; Honig & Roland, 1998; Mitchell & Everly, 2003; Solomon & Horn, 1986).

The emotional impact—that is, the realization of one's vulnerability or lack of control (helplessness/powerlessness)—may be accompanied with intrusive, avoidance, and arousal symptoms. With time, most LEOs are able to reflect, realize, and start absorbing what happened. Integration of the incident is typified by an acceptance that one is vulnerable but not helpless. Even though one may not be able to control the events that will be encountered, one is in control of one's response to it. Further, with time, most LEOs can come out stronger, experiencing post-traumatic growth (Tedeschi & Calhoun, 2004).

The Law Enforcement Culture

Important factors to understand about Law Enforcement Officers are the following:

Resiliency: LEOs tend to be hardy, resilient individuals on the healthier end of the mental health continuum. Police officers undergo a background investigation, psychological screening, supervised field training, and a probation period. Police officers tend to be action oriented and have a practical orientation, which are helpful characteristics for law enforcement.

Conflicting Roles and Demands: LEOs have to deal with the worst society has to offer: crime, death, "man's inhumanity to man," and every type of emergency. There are many conflicting roles and demands required of our LEOs today. One minute the police officer is fighting a mugger, and the next he is comforting a child after a tragedy. The officer must be forceful with the criminal element and compassionate with victims. In so doing, the police officer strives to maintain an image of control. Police officers are not allowed to be angry, scared, or sad and are expected to take control of chaotic situations and exercise good judgment in the midst of rapidly changing stressful circumstances. As a result, police officers learn how to suppress and compartmentalize emotions, file away their fear, enabling them to go into places that everyday people run away from. Because getting in touch with emotions is not as easy as putting on or taking off a uniform, many officers become accustomed to compartmentalization and avoiding emotion.

Always Ready for Danger: Law enforcement officers are required to always be on alert for danger. A typical shift may be filled with many mundane and routine matters, but danger is ever present. Often, LEOs describe their job as "hours of boredom and seconds of terror." Though other jobs (e.g., construction) have more injuries, when a police officer gets hurt, it is often because someone intentionally wanted to harm him/her. Hence, a police officer must be constantly vigilant and always be prepared to go from "0 to 100" in the flash of a second. This *occupational suspiciousness* can also become part of everyday living, with officers suspicious of any "outsider," especially "shrinks" who try to get in their head. This occupational suspiciousness is normal and an occupational necessity given that police deal with people who are dangerous and often lie or try to "con" them.

Clannish Nature: Police officers tend to be *clannish* for a variety of reasons. First of all, they depend on one another in times of danger. If there is a fight, chances are it will be a fellow officer, not a citizen, who will jump in to help. Also, police officers are reluctant to open up to outsiders, because they feel misunderstood and are often subjected to criticism by the general public. Law enforcement officers are often more comfortable talking with fellow officers who share and understand their perspective.

Administrative Stress: A major stressor in law enforcement, as well as other professions, is the administrative stress. LEOs are expected to operate autonomously, exercise discretion and good judgment, and many find it stressful coping with a bureaucracy that has strict policy and guidelines. A misunderstanding and often critical public adds to the stress. Officers often feel in a double bind, having to make split-second decisions that later will be second-guessed by the administration, courts, the press, and the general public. Work environment issues, such as lack of organizational support, may also contribute to stress symptoms (Maguen et al., 2009; Solomon, 1988).

Early Mental Health EMDR Intervention for the Police Notes

Initial Treatment Sessions

LEOs and Emotions

An LEO is action-oriented and practical and may be initially reluctant to talk about emotions (especially feelings of vulnerability). Hence, rather than the clinician exploring feelings right away, it may be more helpful to start treatment with getting the general idea of what happened in the form of a narrative of the event(s) and any current symptoms. Then, approach emotional reactions when the officer feels ready to express them by saying, *"Tell me what happened."* or *"How is this experience impacting you (e.g. What kinds of reactions are you having? Difficulty sleeping, takes racing or intrusive thoughts, etc.)?"*

Normal Reactions to Intense Situations

The therapist should be familiar with trauma reactions and emphasize how their reactions are normal reactions to intense situations when appropriate. Many police officers, with their emphasis on keeping the image of control, may wonder if they are going "nuts" for having nightmares, flashbacks, startle responses, difficulty sleeping, and other typical post-trauma reactions. Normalizing and validating these reactions when they occur enables the officer to realize it is okay to have feelings of vulnerability and powerlessness and to express them.

Supporting the Officer

The therapist should be familiar with and supportive of the role of law enforcement. For example, police officers are authorized to use lethal force when their life or someone else's life is in jeopardy. Some therapists naively ask, *"Why didn't you wound the bad guy?"* The reality is police officers shoot to stop or eliminate the threat, which involves aiming at center mass (e.g., chest). In most instances an officer will keep firing until there is no longer a threat. Further, a wounded suspect can still use lethal force against a citizen or a police officer. Police officers deal with heartbreaking situations and have to take a tough stand in upholding the law. An understanding therapist can see the double bind situations that LEOs are exposed to and be supportive.

Provide Coping Strategies

Along with providing EMDR interventions, it can be helpful for the clinician to provide concrete strategies for coping with stress, as well as the usual safe place and resources. Examples include:

- Talk it out (with people you are comfortable with).
- Work it out (exercise for stress reduction).
- Write it out (writing down one's thoughts and feelings has been proven to be helpful in reducing stress and helping one to come to grips with what happened).
- Think it out (the internet is a good source for useful information for the LEO coping with a critical incident).
- Be careful about reading news reports, editorials, blogs, and the like (not uncommonly, critical opinions are expressed in the media, and can be upsetting to read).
- Eat healthy meals.
- Avoid drinking alcohol to excess (alcohol is a depressant that can make things worse).
- Get the rest you need.
- Keep up your routine (one's life routines provide structure and a sense of control).
- Engage in hobbies and recreation that help you get away from the job.
- Reach out to others (talking to peers who have been involved in a similar incident can be helpful. However, it is also helpful to talk to people outside of law enforcement, to get a broader perspective on life).

Not for the Squeamish Therapist

Police officers are involved in events that can involve awful images and horrible circumstances. Listening to these stories can have a significant impact on the therapist. LEOs, being trained observers, may be able to detect when their story is too upsetting for the therapist. This can result in the officer shutting down and/or the therapist losing credibility. It is normal for the therapist to have emotional reactions to upsetting material, but it is important to remain attentive, empathic, and be therapeutically present with the officer.

Utilization of EMDR

EMDR can be an efficient and effective approach for LEOs (Lamphear, 2010). The author has found that even with LEOs who are skeptical, if they are willing to participate in the process, EMDR is effective.

Pacing of EMDR

The first session can be devoted to getting to know the officer, getting an overview of the incident, how it is impacting him/her, a description of previous incidents, providing information on coping, explaining EMDR, and answering questions. The clinician can pace when to go over the incident in more detail, and provide EMDR, depending on the needs and readiness of the officer.

Typically, EMDR can be provided when shock and numbing is giving way to emotional impact, and the officer can talk about what happened and stay present with the affect. This is usually within a few days to a couple of weeks. The author has provided EMDR as soon as 18 hours following the event and up to several months later. EMDR can often effectively be applied shortly after a Critical Incident Stress Debriefing (which is usually provided within three days to a month or more; Solomon, 2008). However, an officer may need more time to fully understand his/her feelings about the event, reduce stress and arousal, have further psychosocial education on stress, trauma, and coping, and, if appropriate, explore family of origin issues or previous traumas that may have been triggered.

Previous Critical Incidents

In the initial session(s), along with getting an overview of the critical incident that brought the LEO in, it can be useful to get a brief history of previous critical incidents. It is common for an officer to have experienced many critical incidents and these may have a cumulative effect. It is not uncommon for a current traumatic incident to trigger past traumatic situations. If there are significant past critical incidents being triggered, you can discuss whether to target the most recent, or the worst one.

For example, an officer was more upset by a past auto accident that involved personal contact with people who later died, than the more recent incident involving fatalities. In this case, the earlier event was processed first. In another example, the officer was suffering from an incident involving the death of a fellow officer who was killed in circumstances similar to his father's death. The death of the fellow officer was more intrusive and so was processed first, and then the earlier event regarding his father was treated.

Often, dealing with family of origin issues is not necessary when treating an occupational trauma. However, it is not uncommon for a critical incident to trigger such issues that also have to be dealt with. For example, an officer experienced a moment of "freezing" during a critical incident that was linked to childhood experiences of his mother's yelling. After initial processing of the more recent event (which was experienced acutely), childhood traumatic memories were processed. The processing of these childhood memories enabled further resolution of the more recent trauma.

Positive Moments of Effective Action, Courage, and/or Ability to React Competently

Getting the frame-by-frame narrative, though not always necessary for effective EMDR processing, is helpful preparation for later processing. It is useful to identify positive moments (e.g., moments of effective action, courage, ability to react competently). This not only enhances awareness of self-efficacy but also can be used for cognitive interweaves if needed during memory processing.

For example, an officer was stabbed and was able to subdue the suspect. Later, when he saw the extent of his injuries, and realized how seriously he was injured, he experienced trauma symptoms related to his awareness of vulnerability. During processing, when he was stuck on the moment of being stabbed, being reminded of his actions afterward to subdue the suspect and gain control of the situation enabled successful processing.

Regarding Negative and Positive Cognitions:

- *Responsibility Plateau:* Police officers, as is typical of all first responders, are "responsibility absorbers," and not uncommonly blame themselves for events outside of their control, e.g., *"I should have been able to do more."* Consequently negative cognitions of *"It's my fault"* are common. The positive cognition, *"I did the best I could,"* is often an appropriate response to this negative cognition.

- *Safety Plateau:* Police officers may experience moments of extreme vulnerability. Negative cognitions of *"I'm in danger"* or *"I am going to die"* are common, with the positive cognitions being *"I am safe now"* or *"I survived."*

  Note: Many clinicians get confused over the negative cognition, *"I am going to die,"* because it is regarded as a true statement. It is a true statement in regard to the future, but irrational in regard to the past, since the officer survived and is sitting in your office.

- *Control Plateau:* Negative cognitions may be *"I'm powerless"* or *"I'm helpless,"* because there was nothing the officer could do to prevent, control, or change the situations. Positive cognitions usually revolve around *"I have some control"* or *"I have choices."* Positive cognitions may also involve the realization that what could be done was done, hence, *"I did the best I could"* or *"I did what I could do."* During EMDR an officer may realize, *"It was beyond my control"* (e.g. *"There was nothing I, or anybody else, could have done"),* resolving issues of self-blame that often accompanies feelings of powerlessness. Consequently, it is not uncommon for an officer to choose, *"It was beyond my control"* or *"There was nothing more I could do"* or *"It was not my fault,"* as a positive cognition at the beginning of the Installation Phase.

  Note: If there was a mistake/miscalculation/misperception made, EMDR seems to lead the person to taking responsibility for what happened, realizing what factors may have influenced the decisions and actions resulting in the mistake/miscalculation/misperception, and learning from it.

SUDs

SUDs may not always go to zero, especially if the event was recent. It is normal and ecological for tragic sights and sounds to resonate emotionally. For example, after working a gruesome incident or an incident involving a life-threatening event, the SUDs may ecologically not go below 1 or 2, or, when processing a situation where a close friend was killed two months after the event, the SUDs would not go below a 2, because there was sadness and some distress at his death and the circumstances. However, it is important to make sure to check by doing another set of BLS.

Useful Cognitive Interweaves

There are certain types of cognitive interweaves that this author has found helpful in working with LEOs.

Responsibility: If an officer is looping on issues of responsibility, such as *"It's my fault,"* (taking responsibility or blaming onself for things beyond one's control) helpful interweaves may be, *"Who was in control?"* or *"What other options were there, realistically?"* If an officer is blaming himself/herself for a reasonable decision or action that did not lead to the intended outcome, ask, *"There was a reason you did what you did (or made the decision you did), what was going on in your mind* at the time?" This latter interweave helps the LEO get in touch with, understand, and give credibility to his/her perception at the time that guided decisions and actions.

Safety: If an officer is stuck on moments of vulnerability, it may be helpful to ask, *"What happened next?"* or, *"When did you realize the event was over . . . that you survived?"*

Choice/Control: Similarly, if an officer is looping on a moment(s) of helplessness/ powerlessness, asking, *"What happened next?"* may help the officer realize forthcoming actions and decisions where control was exercised. Asking, *"Given the circumstances* (or your perception of circumstances at the time), *could anybody have done more?"* can help the officer realize that, *"There is a boundary where being a human stops and God begins,"* which is a useful interweave in itself.

If an officer is "stuck" during the processing and it is not resolving through changing bilateral stimulation (BLS), going back to target, or interweaves, a float back or affect scan may reveal other past traumatic moments that were triggered by the event. For example, an officer was stuck on the image of the eyes of a murdered child. A float back revealed that years before he had worked another case involving a drowned child, and the blank stare of the eyes looked the same.

Frame-by-Frame

Common practice is to get a "frame-by-frame" narrative of the traumatic situation(s) in which the officer was involved. In the context of EMDR therapy, in utilizing the Recent Traumatic Events Protocol, this can be done in the Assessment Phase. It identifies difficult moments that can be targeted, facilitates integration, provides an assessment of the officers' functional capacity, and—with an understanding and empathic therapist—helps build a trusting relationship.

A "frame-by-frame" is asking the officer to describe what happened frame by frame, leading up to the significant moments, with accompanying perceptions, thoughts, and feelings. What happened after the critical incident ended is also important. LEOs often remember, with great clarity, what was said to him/her after the incident. A negative statement (e.g., "What have you done?" or "Oh boy, are you in trouble now") cuts deep, while positive statements (e.g., "We are here for you" or "What can we do to help?") go a long way toward reducing stress. The hours after a critical incident, the investigative process, what happened at home, and reactions by family and friends are also important to discuss.

Early Mental Health EMDR Intervention for the Police Including the Recent Traumatic Events Protocol Script

The following are guidelines to keep in mind when working within the eight Phases of the EMDR protocol.

Phase 1: Client History Taking

Initially, get a brief overview of the recent critical incident and how it is impacting the officer. Later, as part of the Recent Traumatic Events Protocol, a more thorough narrative (frame-by-frame) will be obtained. Further, ask about what reactions and symptoms an officer may be experiencing.

Say, *"Please tell me what happened."*

_____

_____

Say, *"How is this experience impacting you (e.g.,* what kinds of reactions are you having—difficulty sleeping, racing or intrusive thoughts, etc.)?

_____

_____

Ask for a brief history of previous critical incidents.

Say, *"Could you give me a brief history of previous critical incidents that you have experienced?"*

_____

_____

_____

_____

Phase 2: Preparation

Explanation of EMDR

As with all EMDR LEOs, it is helpful to explain trauma as experiences that get "stuck" in the brain, "living in trauma time," and that EMDR therapy is a therapeutic methodology for processing.

> Say, *"When a trauma occurs it seems to be locked in the nervous system with the original picture, sounds, thoughts, and feelings. The eye movements we use in EMDR seem to unlock the nervous system and allow the brain to process the experience. That may be what is happening in REM or dream sleep—the eye movements may help to process the unconscious material. It is important to remember that it is your own brain that will be doing the healing and you are the one in control."*

Resources

Relaxation skills (e.g., including but not limited to safe place exercise) and strategies for lowering physiological arousal can be helpful.

Identify positive moments of effective action, courage, and/or ability to react competently to be used as resources and as cognitive interweaves.

> Say, *"In regard to the incident, what were the moments of strength, moments you feel good about, or positive aspects?"*

_____

_____

_____

> *Other Relaxation Strategies:* Deep breathing exercises, mindfulness, visualization, and

other coping strategies may be helpful and provided as needed.

Past Memories

Phase 3: Assessment

Go through the incident frame-by-frame and identify prominent moments and aspects. Treat each separate aspect or moment as a separate target with the full Standard EMDR Procedure and Protocol. Process the material through the installation of the PC. Do not do a Body Scan until all targets are processed.

1. Narrative History

Go through the incident frame-by-frame and identify the prominent moments and aspects. Recounting the incident can be helpful by priming the client for processing. Further, the focused concentration on the incident prevents other memories or emotional material from opening up. Treat each separate aspect or moment as a separate target with the full Standard EMDR Procedure and Protocol. Process the material through the installation of the PC. Do not do a Body Scan until all targets are processed.

> Say, *"Let's go through the incident moment by moment, frame-by-frame, from your point of view. This will enable us to identify each significant moment that we will later treat with EMDR."*

_____

_____

_____

_____

_____

_____

_____

_____

_____

_____

2. Target Most Disturbing Aspect or Moment of the Memory

Target the most disturbing aspect or moment of the memory (if necessary), otherwise target events in chronological order.

> Say, _"What was the most disturbing aspect or moment of the memory of the event?"_

_____

_____

Picture

> Say, _"What picture represents the disturbing aspect or moment of the event?"_

_____

_____

If there are many choices or if the officer becomes confused, the clinician assists by asking the following:

> Say, _"What picture represents the most traumatic moment of the event?"_

_____

_____

When a picture is unavailable, the clinician merely invites the officer to do the following:

> Say, _"Think of the disturbing aspect or moment of the event."_

_____

_____

Negative Cognition (NC)

> Say, _"What words best go with the picture that express your negative belief about yourself now?"_

_____

_____

Positive Cognition (PC)

> Say, _"When you bring up that disturbing aspect or moment of the event, what would you like to believe about yourself now?"_

_____

_____

Validity of Cognition (VoC)

Say, *"When you think of the disturbing aspect or moment of the event* (or picture) *how true do those words_____* (clinician repeats the positive cognition) *feel to you now on a scale of 1 to 7, where 1 feels completely false and 7 feels completely true?"*

1   2   3   4   5   6   7
(completely false)   (completely true)

Sometimes it is necessary to explain further.

Say, *"Remember, sometimes we know something with our head, but it feels different in our gut. In this case, what is the gut-level feeling of the truth of_____* (clinician state the positive cognition), *from 1 (completely false) to 7 (completely true)?"*

1   2   3   4   5   6   7
(completely false)   (completely true)

Emotions

Say, *"When you bring up the picture or the disturbing aspect or memory of the event and those words_____*(clinician states the negative cognition), *what emotion do you feel now?"*

_____

_____

Subjective Units of Disturbance (SUD)

Say, *"On a scale of 0 to 10, where 0 is no disturbance or neutral and 10 is the highest disturbance you can imagine, how disturbing does it feel now?"*

0   1   2   3   4   5   6   7   8   9   10
(no disturbance)   (highest disturbance)

Location of Body Sensation

Say, *"Where do you feel it* (the disturbance) *in your body?"*

_____

_____

3. Target Remainder of the Narrative in Chronological Order

Picture

Say, *"Now let's target the first stand-out moment of the event and go from there."*

_____

_____

When a picture is unavailable, the clinician merely invites the officer to do the following:

Say, *"Think of the stand-out moment."*

_____

_____

Negative Cognition (NC)

Say, *"What words best go with the picture of this stand-out moment that express your negative belief about yourself now?"*

_____

_____

Positive Cognition (PC)

Say, *"When you bring up that picture or stand-out moment, what would you like to believe about yourself now?"*

_____

_____

Validity of Cognition (VoC)

Say, *"When you think of the stand-out moment* (or picture), *how true do those words_____*(clinician repeats the positive cognition) *feel to you now on a scale of 1 to 7, where 1 feels completely false and 7 feels completely true?"*

1   2   3   4   5   6   7
(completely false)   (completely true)

Sometimes it is necessary to explain further.

Say, *"Remember, sometimes we know something with our head, but it feels different in our gut. In this case, what is the gut-level feeling of the truth of_____* (clinician states the positive cognition), *from 1* (completely false) *to 7* (completely true)?"

1   2   3   4   5   6   7
(completely false)   (completely true)

Emotions

Say, *"When you bring up the picture* (or stand-out moment) *and those words_____*(clinician states the negative cognition), *what emotion do you feel now?"*

_____

_____

Subjective Units of Disturbance (SUD)

Say, *"On a scale of 0 to 10, where 0 is no disturbance or neutral and 10 is the highest disturbance you can imagine, how disturbing does it feel now?"*

0   1   2   3   4   5   6   7   8   9   10
(no disturbance)   (highest disturbance)

Location of Body Sensation

Say, *"Where do you feel it* (the disturbance) *in your body?"*

_____

_____

Continue with Phases 4 through 5. Phases 6 through 7 are completed after the final segment of the memory has been reprocessed and all of the targets have been treated. It is at that point that the body tension can dissipate.

Note: Repeat the sequence above for each moment that stands out in chronological order.

4. Visualize Entire Sequence of Event With Eyes Closed

Have the officer visualize the entire sequence with eyes closed and reprocess it as any disturbance arises. The officer should have a full association with the material as it is being reprocessed. If there is disturbance, the officer should stop and inform the clinician. Repeat until the entire event can be visualized from start to finish without emotional, cognitive, or somatic distress.

Say, *"Please visualize the entire sequence of the event with eyes closed. If there is any disturbance, please open your eyes and we will reprocess the material together. Let me know when your disturbance decreases."*

_____

_____

Repeat this until the officer can visualize the entire event from start to finish without distress.

If or when there is no disturbance, visualize the entire sequence of the event with eyes open. See the following section.

5. Visualize Entire Sequence of Event With Eyes Open and Install Positive Cognition (PC)

Have the officer visualize the event from start to finish with *eyes open*, and install the PC.

Say, *"Please visualize the entire sequence of the event with your eyes open and think of_____(state the positive cognition). Scan the videotape mentally— even though the images will not be clear—and give the stop signal when you are finished. Go with that (or any other bilateral stimulation [BLS] you are using)."*

Use a long set of BLS.

Phase 6: Body Scan

6. Do Body Scan

Conclude with Body Scan. Only do Body Scan at the end of the processing of *all* of the targets or moments of the event.

Say, *"Close your eyes and keep in mind the original memory and the_____ (repeat the selected positive cognition). Then bring your attention to the different parts of your body, starting with your head and working downward. Any place you find any tension, tightness, or unusual sensation, tell me."*

_____

_____

If any sensation is reported, do BLS.

Say, *"Go with that."*

If a positive or comfortable sensation, do bilateral stimulation to strengthen the positive feeling.

Say, *"Go with that."*

If a sensation of discomfort is reported, reprocess until discomfort subsides.

Say, *"Go with that."*

Phase 7: Closure

Say, *"Things may come up or they may not. If they do, great. This is normal. I am not saying things are going to come up or supposed to come up, only that if they do, it is normal. Write it down, and it can be a target for next time. If you get any new memories, dreams, or situations that disturb you, just take a good snapshot. It isn't necessary to give a lot of detail. Just put down enough to remind you so we can target it next time. The same thing goes for any positive dreams or situations. If negative feelings do come up, try not to make them significant. Remember, it's still just the old stuff. Just write it down for next time. Then use any of the relaxation resources that we have worked with to let as much of the disturbance go as possible. Even if nothing comes up, make sure to practice the relaxation exercises every day and give me a call if you need to.*

Phase 8: Reevaluation

There should always be follow up to evaluate the effects of the EMDR processing. Often, over time, the meaning of the incident to the officer changes and continues to unfold, and further processing may be needed.

For example, one officer involved in a shooting situation initially *felt guilty* that he could not do more to prevent the shooting. An EMDR session resulted in a low level of SUDs and a positive cognition that he did his job and there was nothing more he could do. Two weeks later, he was experiencing significant *feelings of vulnerability* ("I could have been killed"). Another EMDR session resulted in a low level of SUDs and a positive cognition of "I survived and am safe now." Two weeks later at a follow up session, he was experiencing distress regarding the *lack of control* in these situations. The event was again targeted to deal with feelings of powerlessness resulting in a low level of SUDs and the cognition, "I can respond competently." In other words, with time, the event took different meanings. Present triggers and future templates were also completed with this officer.

Present Triggers

7. Present Stimuli or Triggers

After a critical incident is over, the officer may return to normal duty. Because everyday work involves the possibility of danger, dealing with similar situations where there is the potential for danger can trigger the previous trauma. After processing the event (with the Recent Traumatic Event Protocol), these present triggers need to be identified and processed. Further, the clinician, in subsequent sessions (e.g., Phase 8, Reevaluation), can identify what reminders or situations occurred during the week that triggered the incident or brought up feelings of vulnerability/lack of control.

List the situations that elicit the symptom(s). Examples of situations, events, or stimuli that trigger LEOs could be the following: another trauma, the sound of a car backfiring, or being touched in a certain way.

Say, *"What are the situations, events, or stimuli that trigger your trauma _____ (state the trauma)? Let's process these situations, events, or stimuli triggers one-by-one."*

Situations, Events, or Stimuli Trigger List

_____

_____

_____

_____

_____

Identify events where officer is triggered.

Picture

Say, *"What picture represents the situation or event?"*

_____

_____

Negative Cognition (NC)

Say, *"What words best go with the picture that express your negative belief about yourself now?"*

_____

_____

Positive Cognition (PC)

Say, *"When you bring up that picture, situation, or event where the startle response occurs, what would you like to believe about yourself now?"*

_____

_____

Validity of Cognition (VoC)

Say, *"When you think of the startle response* (or picture) *how true do those words_____(clinician repeats the positive cognition) feel to you now on a scale of 1 to 7, where 1 feels completely false and 7 feels completely true?"*

1	2	3	4	5	6	7
(completely false)				(completely true)		

Sometimes, it is necessary to explain further.

Say, *"Remember, sometimes we know something with our head, but it feels different in our gut. In this case, what is the gut-level feeling of the truth of_____ (clinician states the positive cognition), from 1 (completely false) to 7 (completely true)?"*

1	2	3	4	5	6	7
(completely false)				(completely true)		

Emotions

Say, *"When you bring up the picture* (the situation or event where the startle response occurs) *and those words_____*(clinician states the negative cognition), *what emotion do you feel now?"*

_____

_____

Subjective Units of Disturbance (SUD)

Say, *"On a scale of 0 to 10, where 0 is no disturbance or neutral and 10 is the highest disturbance you can imagine, how disturbing does it feel now?"*

0   1   2   3   4   5   6   7   8   9   10
(no disturbance)   (highest disturbance)

Location of Body Sensation

Say, *"Where do you feel it* (the disturbance) *in your body?"*

_____

_____

Continue with Phases 4 through 7 for the situation, event, or stimulus that triggers you from above and any others. After processing the first situation that results in a startle response, check to see if any of the others mentioned are still active; if not, proceed to the next question. If there are more startle responses that need to be processed, go ahead and reprocess that experience.

Future Templates

8. Create a Future Template

Future templates are very important for the law enforcement officer. The officer has to face the possibility that the critical incident he/she has just been involved in can occur again. Officers commonly use mental rehearsal methods to prepare for future encounters. The Future Template, which has mental rehearsal elements, can be very helpful. It is important to prepare for challenges and for the possibility of things going wrong.

For example, an officer involved in a shooting may process past and present triggers, and then do a Future Template focusing on another shooting situation. The officer also has to prepare for what will be done if he or she fires and misses, or is wounded. Many officers, after a critical incident, realize more training is needed. As one officer put it, *"You have to ask yourself if this same incident occurs again, will it be easier to deal with or more difficult? This motivated me to enhance my skills."*

IMAGE AS FUTURE TEMPLATE: IMAGINING POSITIVE OUTCOMES

Imagining positive outcomes—assisted with BLS—seems to assist the learning process, build confidence, and enhance optimal, adaptive future behavior. Connecting imagined adaptive behaviors with a positive cognition may increase generalization and self-efficacy. It is especially important when working with LEOs to build in dealing with potential challenges.

For example, an officer may imagine a future situation where he/she has to use fatal force. A potential challenge would be what would be done if the officer missed or was wounded.

Say, *"I would like you to imagine yourself coping/performing effectively with or in_____(state the situation that is being mentally rehearsed) in the future. With the positive belief_____ (state the positive belief) and your new sense of_____(state the quality: i.e., strength, clarity, confidence, calm), imagine stepping into this scene." "Notice what you see and how you are handling the situation." "Notice what you are thinking, feeling, and experiencing in your body."*

_____

_____

_____

Again, here is the opportunity to catch any disturbance that may have been missed.

Say, *"Are there any blocks, anxieties, or fears that arise as you think about this future scene?"*

_____

_____

_____

If yes, say the following:

Say, *"Then focus on these blocks and follow my fingers (or any other BLS)."*

Say, *"What do you get now?"*

_____

_____

_____

If the blocks do not resolve quickly, evaluate if the LEO needs any new information, resources, or skills to be able to comfortably visualize the future coping scene. Introduce needed information or skills.

Say, *"What would you need to feel confident in handling the situation?"*

Or say, *"What is missing from your handling of this situation?"*

_____

_____

If the block still does not resolve and the LEO is unable to visualize the future scene with confidence and clarity, use direct questions, the Affect Scan, or the Float-Back Technique to identify old targets related to blocks, anxieties, or fears. Remember, the point of the Three-Prong Protocol is not only to reinforce positive feelings and behavior in the future, but again, to catch any unresolved material that may be getting in the way of an adaptive resolution of the issue(s). Use the Standard EMDR Protocol to address these targets before proceeding with the template (see Worksheets in Appendix A).

If there are no apparent blocks and the LEO is able to visualize the future scene with confidence and clarity, say the following:

Say, *"Please focus on the image, the positive belief, and the sensations associated with this future scene and follow my fingers (or any other BLS)."*

_____

_____

Process and reinforce the positive associations with BLS. Do several sets until the future template is sufficiently strengthened.

Say, *"Go with that."*

Then say, *"Close your eyes and keep in mind the image of the future and the positive cognition. Then bring your attention to the different parts of your body, starting with your head and working downward. Any place you find any tension, tightness, or unusual sensation, tell me."*

If any sensation is reported, do BLS.

Say, *"Go with that."*

If it is a positive or comfortable sensation, do BLS to strengthen the positive feelings.

Say, *"Go with that."*

If a sensation of discomfort is reported, reprocess until the discomfort subsides.

Say, *"Go with that."*

When the discomfort subsides, check the VoC.

Say, *"When you think of the incident* (or picture), *how true do those words _____(clinician repeats the positive cognition) feel to you now on a scale of 1 to 7, where 1 feels completely false and 7 feels completely true?"*

1   2   3   4   5   6   7
(completely false)   (completely true)

Continue to use BLS until reaching the VoC = 7 or there is an ecological resolution. When the image as future template is clear and the PC true, move on to the movie as future template.

MOVIE AS FUTURE TEMPLATE OR IMAGINAL REHEARSING

During this next level of future template, LEOs are asked to move from imagining this one scene or snapshot to imagining a movie about coping in the future, with a beginning, middle, and end. Encourage LEOs to imagine themselves coping effectively in the face of specific challenges, triggers, or snafus. Therapists can make some suggestions in order to help inoculate them with future problems. It is helpful to use this type of future template after LEOs have received needed education concerning social skills and customs, assertiveness, and any other newly learned skills.

Say, *"This time, I'd like you to close your eyes and play a movie, imagining yourself coping effectively with or in_____(state where LEO will be) in the future. With the new positive belief_____(state positive belief) and your new sense of_____(strength, clarity, confidence, calm), imagine stepping into the future. Imagine yourself coping with ANY challenges that come your way. Make sure that this movie has a beginning, middle, and end. Notice what you are seeing, thinking, feeling, and experiencing in your body. Let me know if you hit any blocks. If you do, just open your eyes and let me know. If you don't hit any blocks, let me know when you have viewed the whole movie."*

If the LEO hits blocks, address as above with BLS until the disturbance dissipates.

Say, *"Go with that."*

If the material does not shift, use interweaves, new skills, information, resources, direct questions, and any other ways to help LEOs access information that will allow them to move on. If these options are not successful, usually it means that there is earlier material still unprocessed; the Float-Back and Affect Scan are helpful in these cases to access the material that keeps the LEO stuck.

If LEOs are able to play the movie from start to finish with a sense of confidence and satisfaction, ask them to play the movie one more time from beginning to end and introduce BLS.

Say, *"Okay, play the movie one more time from beginning to end. Go with that."*

Use BLS.

In a sense, you are installing this movie as a future template.

After LEOs have fully processed their issue(s), they might want to work on other positive templates for the future in other areas of their lives using the above future templates.

Conclusion

Law enforcement officers are a resilient, hardy group of people who have a stressful job and are exposed to potential traumatizing events on a daily basis. EMDR is an effective therapeutic methodology for processing traumatic events. The clinician who understands police work and the law enforcement culture can more effectively align with the officer and implement EMDR.

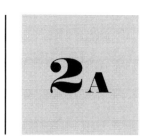
Roger Solomon
SUMMARY SHEET BY MARILYN LUBER

Name: _____ Diagnosis: _____

Medications: _____

Test Results: _____

☑ Check when task is completed, response has changed, or to indicate symptoms.

Note: This material is meant as a checklist for your response. Please keep in mind that it is only a reminder of different tasks that may or may not apply to your incident.

Early Mental Health EMDR Intervention for the Police Notes

Initial Treatment Sessions

☐ Helpful for therapist to reinforce and/or remember the following:
☐ Trauma reactions are normal reactions to intense situations
☐ LEOS are often involved in difficult situations. It is important for the clinician to be attentive, empathic, and therapeutically present even in the face of awful images and horrible circumstances

Provide Coping Strategies   ☐ Completed

    ☐ Talk it out
    ☐ Work it out
    ☐ Write it out
    ☐ Think it out
    ☐ Careful about the media
    ☐ Eat healthy meals
    ☐ Avoid excess drinking
    ☐ Rest
    ☐ Keep up routine
    ☐ Hobbies/recreation away from job
    ☐ Reach out to others

Utilization of EMDR

Common Negative and Positive Cognitions for LEOs

☐ Responsibility—*NC: "It is my fault"; PC: "I did the best I could."*
☐ Safety—NC: *"I am in danger"* or *"I am going to die"; PC: "I am safe now"* or *"I survived."*
☐ Control—NC: *"I am powerless"* or *"I am helpless"; PC: "I did the best I could"* or *"I did what I could do."* or *"I have some control,"* or *"I have some choices."*

Useful Cognitive Interweaves When LEO Is Looping

- Responsibility: *"Who was in control?"* or *"What other options were there, realistically?"* or, *"There was a reason you did what you did at that moment. What was going on in your mind?"*
- Safety: *What happened next?"* or, *"When did you realize the event was over . . . that you survived?"*
- Choice/Control: *What happened next?"* may help the officer realize forthcoming actions and decisions where control was exercised. Asking, *"Given the circumstances* (or your perception of circumstances at the time), *could anybody have done more?"* can help the officer realize that, *"There is a boundary where being a human stops and God begins."*

Early Mental Health Interventions for the Police Including the Recent Traumatic Events Protocol Script

Frame-by-Frame

Go throuth the incident in detail identifying the perceptions, thoughts, and feelings associated with each "stand-out" moment. This helps identify significant moments that may need to be processed with the Protocol for Recent Traumatic Events.

Phase 1: Client History

Brief overview of recent critical incident: _____

_____

_____

Impact on LEO: _____

_____

_____

Brief history of previous critical incidents: _____

_____

_____

_____

_____

Phase 2: Preparation

Explanation of EMDR   ☐ Completed

Resources Used: _____

_____

Positive Moments of Effective Action, Courage, and/or Ability to React Competently:

_____
_____
_____
_____

Phase 3: Assessment

Past Memories

1. Narrative History Frame-by-Frame

Event Narrative: _____

_____
_____
_____
_____
_____

2. Target Most Disturbing Aspect or Moment of the Memory

Target/Memory/Image: _____
_____

NC: _____
PC: _____
VoC: _____ /7
Emotions: _____
SUD: _____ /10
Sensation: _____

3. Target Remainder of the Narrative in Chronological Order

Target/Memory/Image: _____
_____

NC: _____
PC: _____
VoC: _____ /7
Emotions: _____
SUD: _____ /10
Sensation: _____

4. Visualize Entire Sequence of Event With Eyes Closed With Full Association

If disturbance, reprocess.

Client can view entire event from start to finish, without emotional, cognitive, or somatic distress.   ☐ Completed

5. Visualize Entire Sequence With Eyes Open and Install PC

Visualize sequence of events with eyes open + PC + BLS. Stop signal
when finished.   ☐ Completed

Phase 6: Body Scan

6. Do Body Scan Only at the end of processing all targets and memories of event

Original memory + PC + Scan Body
Unresolved tension/tightness/unusual sensation: _____

_____

Do BLS until subsides.

Phase 7: Closure

Closure: ☐ Completed

Phase 8: Reevaluation

SUDs of Incident:_____/10
New material: _____

_____

Reprocessed necessary targets: ☐ Completed

EMDR helpful in daily life: ☐ Completed

Present Triggers

7. Present Stimuli That Trigger the Disturbing Memory/Reaction

List of Triggering Situations, Events, or Stimuli for LEOs

1. _____
2. _____
3. _____

Target/Memory/Image: _____

NC: _____

PC: _____

VoC: _____ /7

Emotions: _____

SUD: _____ /10

Sensation: _____

Triggers: ☐ Completed

Future Template

8. Create a Future Template

IMAGE AS FUTURE TEMPLATE: IMAGINING POSITIVE OUTCOMES

Incorporate a detailed template for dealing adaptively with an appropriate future
situation (e.g., coping with a similar situation or coping with present triggers/
reminders, see above).

Image of coping effectively with/or in goal in future: _____

_____

PC: _____

New quality/attribute needed: _____

What you see as handling the situation: _____

Thinking, Feeling, and Experiencing in Body: _____

Blocks/Anxieties/Fears in future scene: _____

1. _____

2. _____

3. _____

Do BLS. If they do not resolve, ask for other qualities needed to handle the situation. Other new information, resources, or skills to comfortably visualize coping in the future:

1. _____

2. _____

3. _____

If blocks are not resolved, identify unprocessed material and process with Standard EMDR Protocol:

1. _____

2. _____

3. _____

    Target/Memory/Image: _____

    _____

    NC: _____

    PC: _____

    VoC: _____ /7

    Emotions: _____

    SUD: _____ /10

    Sensation: _____

If there are no blocks, move on.

Future Image + PC + Sensations associated with future scenes + BLS

Do a Body Scan. (Close eyes + Image of Future + PC + Attention to Different Parts of Your Body + Report Tension, Tightness/Unusual Sensation) _____

If there is a sensation, process until the sensation subsides and the VoC = 7/ecological resolution and move on to the movie as a future template.

VoC: _____ /7

Image as Future Template: ☐ Completed

MOVIE AS A FUTURE TEMPLATE OR IMAGINAL REHEARSING

Close eyes and play a movie adaptively coping with a difficult situation with a beginning, middle, and end.

    Coping effectively with problem/in the location: _____

    PC: _____

New Quality/Attribute: _____

Step into the future and imagine coping with ANY challenges. Movie has a beginning middle, and end.

Thinking, feeling, and experiencing in body: _____

Blocks/Anxieties/Fears in Future Scene:

1. _____

2. _____

3. _____

If blocks, use BLS until disturbance dissipates or check for other qualities/resources needed.

Other qualities/Resources needed:

1. _____

2. _____

3. _____

If blocks are not resolved, identify unprocessed material and process with Standard EMDR Protocol:

1. _____

2. _____

3. _____

    Target/Memory/Image: _____

    NC: _____

    PC: _____

    VoC: _____ /7

    Emotions: _____

    SUD: _____ /10

    Sensation: _____

If client can play movie from beginning to end with confidence and satisfaction, play the movie one more time from beginning to end + BLS: ☐ Completed

Movie as Future Template: ☐ Completed

EMDR and Effective Management of Acute Stress Injuries: Early Mental Health Intervention From a Military Perspective

Mark C. Russell, Tammera M. Cooke, and Susan Rogers

> *One of our cultural myths has been that only weaklings break down*
> *psychologically (and that) strong men with the will to do so*
> *can keep going indefinitely.*
>
> —Beebe and Appel (1958, p. 164)

Introduction

January 2012 ushered in a new year, but an old, recurring problem for war veterans. At the mid-month mark alone, media accounts reflected the terrible toll of war on the "enlisted soldier." News headlines and streaming video posted on the Internet inundate the public with stories concerning United States soldiers:

1. *Iraq War Veteran Arrested for the Brutal Murder of Five Homeless Men After His Friend's Death in Afghanistan;*
2. *Video Released Showing U.S. Marines Urinating on Taliban Corpses* (Rudolf, 2012);
3. *19-year-old Army Private Dies From a "self-inflicted gunshot wound" in Afghanistan, After Unrelenting Physical, Racial, and Emotional Torment From His Fellow Soldiers* (Deepti as cited by Russell, 2012);
4. *Iraqi War Veteran Kills a Washington State Park Ranger, Then Dies From Exposure* (Baker as cited by Russell, 2012).

Defense Secretary Leon Panetta—during a Pentagon press conference—reported on sexual assaults in the military. He noted there were 3,191 reported sexual assaults in 2011, a slight increase from the 3,158 reported in 2010. He went on to say that the real number is closer to 19,000 assaults, because so few victims reported the crime. He concluded:

> *It is an affront to the basic American values we defend, and it is a stain on the good honor of the great majority of our troops and our families. Our men and women in uniform put their lives on the line every day to try to keep America safe, therefore, we have a moral duty to keep them safe from those who would attack their dignity and their honor.* (Jelanek & Burns, 2012)

These incidents exemplify what the U.S. military calls "misconduct stress behaviors," and "occupational hazards" present during every armed conflict (Russell & Figley, in press). Military personnel are a unique population whose job description includes being on the front lines of battle and in "operational" environments (e.g., combat, training accidents, military sexual trauma, disaster relief, peace keeping, etc.) that place them at risk for acute and chronic stress injuries. In a climate heightened by crises on international, domestic, and economic fronts, the media coverage of our nation's military personnel reminds us that "the fevers of war are once again upon us" at a profound cost to the bodies, minds, and souls of our military (Marin, 1995, p. 85).

This chapter describes the current goals, classification, and guiding principles being used in the management of combat stress reactions; outlines a proposed system of classification of stress reactions; and describes considerations and protocols for the integration of EMDR into frontline intervention.

The Goal of Frontline Psychiatric Interventions

The military's expressed goal and purpose for implementing forward psychiatry in war-zones is singular—*to preserve manpower in frontline (combat) units.* Individuals who break down in combat or military operations are provided brief interventions to return them to their frontline units as soon as possible. Every effort is made to reduce attrition and avoid an *evacuation syndrome* by the military by keeping individuals in the fight as long as they can possibly endure until their condition is so severe they can no longer be returned to duty (Department of the Army [DoA], 2006).

A common misconception—outside and within the military—is that frontline interventions are *treatment* aimed to prevent chronic disability (e.g., PTSD). That has never been the mission of military psychiatry. In fact, Combat Stress Control (COSC) doctrine stringently avoids confusion of COSC procedures and *psychotherapy.* Psychotherapy is not considered appropriate by the military for treatment of ASR/COSR until individuals are evacuated away from the front lines of combat and military operations after being deemed as having acute stress injuries too severe to be returned to their units (DoA, 2006).

Military Definitions of Acute Stress-Related Disorders and Syndromes

The U.S. military classifies acute stress responses as Acute Stress Reaction, Combat Stress Reaction, and Combat and Operational Stress Reaction, and discourages the pathologizing of these universal reactions as "symptoms" in the sense of being indicative of a mental disorder, as doing so may prevent spontaneous recovery (DoA, 2006).

Acute Stress Reaction and Combat Stress Reaction

According to the Department of Veterans Affairs (DVA) and Department of Defense (DoD) *Clinical Practice Guidelines for Traumatic Stress Disorders* (DVA/DoD, 2010), *Acute Stress Reaction (ASR) is defined as a transient condition triggered in response to a traumatic event (e.g., sexual assault, body recovery),* whereas *Combat Stress Reaction (CSR) refers specifically to traumatic war events (e.g., being shot at, witnessing violent death, killing).* Onset of at least some signs and symptoms may be simultaneous with the trauma itself or within minutes of the traumatic event and may follow the trauma after an interval of hours or days. In most cases, symptoms will disappear within days (even hours) (DVA/DoD, 2010).

Combat Operational Stress Reactions

Combat Operational Stress Reactions (COSRs) is the U.S. military's approved term replacing earlier terminology like *battle fatigue* or *combat exhaustion,* incorporating *"normal"* universal ASR and CSR responses of human beings adapting to acute combat or *"operational"* stressors (e.g., family separation, environmental exposure, disaster relief deployments, etc.) lasting between 2 to 5 days (DVA/DoD, 2010). As reflected in Table 1, both ASR and COSR represent a broad constellation of physical, cognitive, social, behavioral, and spiritual responses to stress ranging from adaptive to maladaptive reactions including *"misconduct stress behaviors"* (DoA, 2006). Of significance, differences in severity, type, and length of COSR associated with acute breakdown is highly individualized and determined by a wide range of risk and

Table 1   Common Human Stress Response

Physical	Cognitive/Menta	Emotional	Behavioral
• Chills • Difficulty breathing • Dizziness • Elevated blood pressure • Fainting • Fatigue • Grinding teeth • Headaches • Muscle tremors • Nausea • Pain • Profuse sweating • Rapid heart rate • Twitches • Weakness	• Blaming someone • Change in alertness • Confusion • Hypervigilance • Increased or decreased awareness of surroundings • Intrusive images • Memory problems • Nightmares • Poor abstract thinking • Poor attention • Poor concentration • Poor decision making • Poor problem solving	• Agitation • Anxiety • Apprehension • Denial • Depression • Emotional shock • Fear • Feeling overwhelmed • Grief • Guilt • Inappropriate emotional response • Irritability • Loss of emotional control	• Increased alcohol consumption • Antisocial acts • Change in activity • Change in communication • Change in sexual functioning • Change in speech pattern • Emotional outbursts • Inability to rest • Change in appetite • Pacing • Startle reflex intensified • Suspiciousness • Social withdrawal

Source: *October, 2010 DVA/DoD Clinical Practice Guideline for the Management of Post-Traumatic Stress.* The Department of Veterans Affairs and Department of Defense. Download available at: www.healthquality.va.gov/ptsd/ptsd_full.pdf

protective factors. The most important determinant of when and how COSR occurs is the intensity, severity, and duration of war stress. Individual reactions to warzone stressors are idiosyncratic in that military personnel may report some, all, or none of the symptoms (DoA, 2006). While COSR's may result from exposure to a specific traumatic event, they generally emerge from cumulative exposure to multiple and specific types of stressors. Typically, the military delineates stressors into two broad categories: combat and operational stressors.

Combat stressors include single incidents that have the potential to significantly impact the unit or individual service member experiencing them while performing military missions. These include: killing of combatants; being the target of enemy fire; witnessing the death of someone; death or wounding of another unit member; injury resulting in the loss of limb; friendly fire incident; killing of non-combatants; noise, blasts, and detonations.

Operational stressors may include numerous combat stressors or prolonged exposure due to continued operations in hostile environments. These include: boredom and monotony; prolonged exposure to extreme geographical environments such as desert heat, rain, mud, sand, or arctic cold; prolonged separation from significant support systems such as family; exposure to significant injuries over multiple missions; handling or transporting of human remains; illness or injury from close quarters, such as upper respiratory complications.

ONSET OF COMMON COSR SYMPTOMS

Exposure to combat and operational stressors often results in COSRs and the onset of at least some signs and symptoms may be simultaneous with the acute stressor or trauma itself that may follow the event after an interval of hours or days. A partial list of signs and symptoms following exposure to COSR including potentially traumatic events (DVA/DoD, 2010) is provided in Table 1.

Spiritual or Moral Symptoms

Military personnel may experience any of the following acute spiritual symptoms:

- Feelings of despair
- Questioning of old religious or spiritual beliefs

- Withdrawal from spiritual practice and spiritual community
- Sense of doom about the world and the future (Russell & Figley, 2013, p. 9)

Positive Stress Reactions and Post-Traumatic Growth

Adaptive or *positive* stress reactions refer to positive responses to COSRs that enhance individual and unit performance (DoA, 2006) such as:

- Formation of close, loyal social ties or camaraderie never likely repeated in life (e.g., *"band of brothers"* and *"band of sisters"*)
- Improved appreciation of life
- Deep sense of pride (e.g., taking part in history making]
- Enhanced sense of unit cohesion, morale, and esprit de corps
- Profound satisfaction from personal growth, sacrifice, and mastery after accomplishing one's mission under the most arduous circumstances (Russell & Figley, 2013, p. 10)

Guiding Principles of Frontline Mental Health Intervention

Individuals with acute COSR are typically managed by frontline medical and mental health personnel applying the BICEPS principles:

- Brevity (respite of 1–4 days)
- Immediacy (when COSR appear)
- Contact (maintain identity as soldier vs. patient)
- Expectancy (return to full duty)
- Proximity (near soldier's unit)
- Simplicity (reassure of normality, rest, replenish bodily needs, restore confidence and return to duty)

It should be noted that BICEPS is an elaboration of an older PIE (proximity, immediacy, expectancy) model, referring to the belief that intervention should take place close to the front, that it should be done early, and with the expectation that the service member would be returning to normal duties rather than being evacuated.

And the 6 R's:

- Reassure of normality (normalize the reaction)
- Rest (respite from combat or break from work)
- Replenish bodily needs (such as thermal comfort, water, food, hygiene, and sleep)
- Restore confidence with purposeful activities and talk
- Retain contact with fellow soldiers and unit
- Remind/recognize emotion of reaction (specifically potentially life-threatening thoughts and behaviors) (Russell & Figley, 2013, p. 95)

Reports of 70 to 90% successful treatment or *return-to-duty* (RTD) rates by embedded or frontline mental health providers refer only to combatants returned to their units, regardless of number of relapses, subsequent level of functioning, or development of chronic war stress injuries. Jones and Wessley (2003) conducted an extensive review of the history and effectiveness of frontline psychiatric interventions since WWI, finding wide variability in outcomes reported based on universal absence of systematic scientific research (e.g., random controlled trials) and concluding: *"It remains far from clear how soldiers perform in the short term having been treated using Proximity, Immediacy, Expectancy & Simplicity (PIES) methods as there are few reliable studies of relapse rates. One investigation found that only about a quarter returned to effective duty"* (Ludwig & Ranson, 1947, pp. 51–62). When COSR is related specifically to combat or other trauma-related stressors it may progress to maladaptive ASR/COSR or what we are referring to as *acute stress injury.*

Proposed Classification Model for Acute Stress Injury Spectrum

Below we outline a classification scheme for the continuum of acute stress injury defined as clinically significant, neurophysiologically based alterations in adaptive psychological and physical functioning lasting up to three months after exposure to cumulative severe stress or potentially traumatic events. It is important to note that acute stress injuries represent a spectrum of stress-related conditions that manifest in a broad array of neuropsychiatric and medically unexplained physical symptoms (MUPS) diagnoses along an adaptive-maladaptive continuum of severity.

Mild Acute Stress Injury

In keeping with U.S. Army doctrine, the mere presence of ASR/COSR signs or symptoms (see Table 1) in the wake of exposure to extreme or traumatic stress is a predictable, universal, adaptive response and not suggestive of an acute stress injury. Therefore, on the lowest end of the severity continuum or "mild" acute stress injury, are moderate to severe maladaptive ASR/COSR characterized by the following:

- Intense, debilitating, yet time-limited alterations in adaptive functioning lasting hours to two weeks
- Continue to perform primary duties of obligations; however, either under extreme duress or with limitations
- Psychotic symptoms, if present, are fleeting and remit within days of initial presentation
- Suicidal and/or homicidal ideation may be present, but fleeting and without intent or plan

These transitory *"breakdowns"* do not present as imminent safety risks to self or others, and generally manifest as distressing symptoms of peri-traumatic dissociation, post-traumatic anger, acute depressive reaction, uncomplicated grief, guilt, brief conversion reactions, diffuse MUPS (Medically Unexplained Physical Symptoms) (e.g., persistent tremor, intermittent, severe headache, sleep disturbance, extreme fatigue), and behavioral "acting-out" problems (e.g., American Psychiatric Association, 2000, V-codes).

If applicable, individuals with mild acute stress injury have not responded to initial early interventions. As level of subjective distress and/or signs of impaired functioning increase, individuals may warrant more "mild" or "atypical" forms of neuropsychiatric and/or medical diagnosis such as Depressive Disorder Not Otherwise Specified (NOS), Anxiety Disorder NOS, Somatoform Disorders NOS, Eating Disorder NOS, Dissociative Disorder NOS, Substance Misuse, Acute Pain, Atypical Headaches, Insomnia, Essential Hypertension, Irritable Bowel Syndrome, Chronic Fatigue, Fibromyalgia, and so on.

Moderate Acute Stress Injury

Moderate acute stress injuries are further along the severity continuum in terms of duration, level of impairment, and safety risk posed to self and others. Moderate stress injuries are characterized as either:

- Persistent, marked ASR/COSR lasting between five days to three months and/or
- Intense, moderately debilitating neuropsychiatric and MUPS that interfere with an individual's ability to fully perform primary duties or obligations, and/or
- If present, psychotic symptoms, suicidal/homicidal ideation, panic attacks, traumatic grief/guilt, post-traumatic anger, and MUPS (e.g., sleep disturbance, pain, fatigue), are more persistent (e.g., lasting greater than 5 days), distressing, and intense than "mild," but less debilitating than "severe."

As the intensity, duration, and/or impact of stress injuries increases in terms of nature, duration, and severity, the greater likelihood of manifesting one or more maladaptive and debilitating neuropsychiatric and MUPS diagnosis such as Acute Adjustment Disorder, Acute Stress Disorder, Conversion Disorder, Brief Reactive Psychosis, Substance Abuse, Impulse Control Disorder, Anxiety Disorder, Psychogenic Amnesia, Eating Disorder, and severe MUPS (e.g., pseudo-seizures, sleep disorder, atypical arrhythmia, etc.).

Severe Acute Stress Injury

At the farthest end of the severity continuum, "severe" acute stress injuries are characterized as either:

- Typically persisting longer than one month,
- If less than one month in duration, symptoms are grossly incapacitating, and/or
- Present clear danger to self or others, including attempted suicide or homicide.

Severe acute stress injuries may manifest as severe Acute Traumatic Grief, Somatoform Disorder, Acute Substance Dependence, Mood Disorder with or without psychotic features, Psychotic Disorder NOS, Acute PTSD, Dissociative Disorder, interpersonal violence including commission of atrocity, and debilitating MUPS (e.g., Anorexia, Non-Cardiac Chest Pain, Lupus, pseudo-dementia, etc.), including possibly premature death (e.g., wasting, suicide).

Early Identification of Acute Stress Injury (ASI)

Individuals developing ASI like ASD (ASD is one of the manifestations of ASI) are at greater risk of developing PTSD and should be identified and offered treatment as soon as possible (Bryant, 2007). In the aftermath of a traumatic event, clients may not complain about ASD symptoms, but in its place they will complain of sleeping problems, pain, or other somatic concerns. After addressing immediate needs and providing education and intervention, alleviating these symptoms will make it easier for survivors to cope and recover from their traumatic experience. It is recommended that clients presenting with acute stress injury symptoms and/or functional impairment be screened for the following risk factors:

Pre-Traumatic Factors

- Ongoing life stress
- Lack of social support
- Young age at time of trauma
- Preexisting psychiatric disorders or substance misuse
- History of traumatic events (e.g., MVA)
- History of post-traumatic stress disorder (PTSD)
- Other pre-traumatic factors, including: female gender, low socioeconomic status, lower level of education, lower level of intelligence, race (Hispanic, African American, American Indian, and Pacific Islander), reported abuse in childhood, report of other previous traumatization, report of other adverse childhood factors, family history of psychiatric disorders, and poor training or preparation for the traumatic event

Peri-Traumatic or Trauma-Related Factors

- Severe trauma
- Physical injury to self or others
- Type of trauma (combat, interpersonal traumas such as killing another person, torture, rape, or assault convey high risk of PTSD)
- High perceived threat to life of self or others
- Community (mass) trauma
- Other peri-traumatic factors, including history of peri-traumatic dissociation

Post-Traumatic Factors

- Ongoing life stress
- Lack of positive social support

- Bereavement or traumatic grief
- Major loss of resources
- Negative social support (shaming or blaming environment)
- Poor coping skills
- Other post-traumatic factors, including children at home and a distressed spouse

Source: *October, 2010 DVA/DoD Clinical Practice Guideline for the Management of Post-Traumatic Stress.* The Department of Veterans Affairs and Department of Defense. Download available at www. healthquality.va.gov/ptsd/ptsd_full.pdf

Screening for Acute Stress Injuries

Acute Stress Disorder

ASD refers to clinically significant (causing significant distress or impairment in social, occupational, or other important areas of functioning) symptoms lasting longer than two days but less than one month after exposure to a trauma, as defined above (may progress to PTSD if symptoms last longer than one month). Criteria for diagnosis include:

- Either while experiencing or after experiencing the distressing event, the individual has at least three dissociative symptoms including numbing, reduced awareness of surrounding, derealization, depersonalization, or dissociative amnesia.
- The traumatic event is persistently reexperienced in at least one of the following ways: recurrent images, thoughts, dreams, illusions, flashback episodes, a sense of reliving the experience, or distress on exposure to reminders of the traumatic event.
- Marked avoidance of stimuli that arouse recollections of the trauma (e.g., thoughts, feelings, conversations, activities, places, people, sounds, smells).
- Marked symptoms of anxiety or increased arousal (e.g., difficulty sleeping, irritability, poor concentration, hypervigilance, exaggerated startle response, and motor restlessness).

Acute Post-Traumatic Stress Disorder (PTSD)

Acute Post-Traumatic Stress Disorder (PTSD) is defined as clinically significant symptoms lasting up to three months after exposure to traumatic events that are causing significant distress or impairment in social, occupational, or other important areas of functioning and occur more than one month after exposure to a trauma (adapted from the, *DVA/DoD clinical practice guideline for management of posttraumatic stress, October 2010*). Symptoms may include:

- *Reexperiencing Symptoms:* The traumatic event is persistently reexperienced in one (or more) of the following ways: intrusive recollection of the event, recurring dreams, flashbacks, distress, and/or physiological reactivity on exposure to reminders
- *Avoidance Symptoms:* Persistent avoidance of stimuli associated with the trauma and numbing of general responsiveness (not present before the trauma), as indicated by three or more of the following: avoidance of reminders, psychogenic amnesia for aspects of the event, diminished interest in activities, social detachment, restricted range of affect, sense of foreshortened future
- *Hyperarousal Symptoms:* Persistent symptoms of increased arousal (not present before the trauma), as indicated by at least two of the following: sleep disturbance, irritability, difficulty concentrating, hypervigilance, startle response

Acute Traumatic Grief Reactions

Pivar (2004) makes the distinction between acute and chronic traumatic grief with chronic being complicated bereavement persisting for six months or longer. Below we will summarize some of the symptoms and signs of traumatic grief reactions as well as exacerbating factors. The therapist will want to pay attention to the client's narrative and the presence or absence of the following:

Acute Traumatic Grief Reaction

- Reacting with rage at the enemy
- Risking their lives with little thought, "gone berserk" or "kill crazy"
- Intense agitation
- Experiences of shock, disbelief, and self-blame
- Self-accusations
- High-risk behaviors
- Suicidal ideation or attempt
- Intense outbursts of anger
- Acute psychotic reaction
- Making heroic efforts to save or recover bodies
- Social withdrawal, becoming loners
- Avoiding making any new friends
- Extreme anger at the events or people that brought them to the battle
- Masking their emotions to avoid a sign of vulnerability or "losing" it

Acute Depression and Suicidality

Reasons for military personnel to develop depression include homesickness from prolonged separation, feeling overwhelmed from painful war experiences or losses, feelings of guilt for actions taken (e.g., killing) or not taken, recent Permanent Change of Station (PCS) transfer and separation from combat support, individual mobilization augmentees separating from their combat support group to return to their home duty station, feeling disconnected from others, sleep deprivation, interpersonal troubles at home or work, and so forth. Suicidal behavior is best assessed with the following criteria: presence of active depression or psychosis, presence of substance abuse, past history of suicidal acts, formulation of plan, a stated intent to carry out the plan, feeling that the world would be better off if the patient were dead, availability of means for suicide (e.g., firearms or pills), disruption of an important personal relationship, and failure at an important personal endeavor.

Acute Post-Traumatic Anger, Aggression, and Violence

In the warzone, or other threatening environments, anger and hyperarousal can be an adaptive human stress response or "survival mode." Conversely, when unregulated, anger and aggression can reflect a central core maladaptive reaction to trauma resulting in uncontrolled expressions that can be harmful to the service member and those they confront. Anger can range from mild annoyance to rage associated with domestic violence and abuse, road rage, and workplace violence, even if there is no intent to cause harm to others. It is important to distinguish between anger and aggression. Aggression is behavior that is *intended* to cause harm to another person or damage property. This behavior can include verbal abuse, threats, or violent acts. Anger, on the other hand, is an emotion and does not necessarily lead to aggression. Therefore, a person can become angry without acting aggressively.

Acute Stress Injury in the Medically Wounded

There is a high comorbidity of war stress injury for those wounded in action (WIA). However, it is not unusual for the medical needs of physically wounded clients to be well managed, while mental health aspects go undetected and untreated. Therapists should routinely screen clients who have deployed for WIA status, including being awarded a Purple Heart. For example, Grieger et al. (2006) found that the rates of depression and PTSD among severely wounded American service members increased significantly between the initial 1-month post-injury assessment (where 4.2% had PTSD symptoms and 4.4% had depression) to seven months post-injury (where 12.0% had PTSD and 9.3% met criteria for depression).

In every war a certain number of battle wounds are "self-inflicted," whether to avoid combat, commit suicide, get a medal, or some other reason—it happens. As of September 2010, a total of 260 deployed military personnel died by self-inflicted wounds. Clients whose wounds are self-induced often carry a burdensome secret and fear eventual discovery.

Acute Medically Unexplained Symptoms (MUPS) and Pain

The DoD's Post-Deployment Health Assessment and Re-Assessments (PDHA/RA) surveys can provide a potential baseline measure of physical complaints originating during or after deployment, that may eventually be categorized as "medically unexplained" or symptoms, signs, and ill-defined conditions (SSID-VA system). If the therapist has access to the client's military medical record then a review of the post-deployment health surveys and medical treatment history could provide at least a landscape view of the client's physical health standing and the overall number of physical complaints. Mental health intake question-naires also may (or should) solicit client feedback on a range of medical symptoms and/ or conditions. It is important, however, that the therapist does not assume that a medical diagnosis of a syndrome (e.g., irritable bowel, chronic fatigue, fibromyalgia) or unexplained medical condition (e.g., pseudoseizure, NCCP, etc.) is automatically an indicator of a stress injury.

The clinical intake, record review (if applicable), and clinical interview can help assess the client for changes in overall health status before, during, and after the precipitating event(s) that might indicate a possible temporal relationship. Therapists might consider use of standardized questionnaires such as the Somatoform Dissociation Questionnaire (SDQ-5 and SDQ-20) or other health-related surveys to obtain additional health background. Practi-tioners employed by DoD and DVA hospitals or medical clinics are already familiar with the requirement for screening every client for pain using a numeric analog rating (e.g., 0–10). We describe these screening measures later on.

Screening for Pain

The literature indicates a robust association between pain and war stress injuries like PTSD, regardless of whether the pain is being evaluated from clients diagnosed with PTSD, or PTSD is being assessed in those with chronic pain (e.g., 10–50% PTSD rate [Schwartz et al., 2006 as cited in DVA/DoD, 2010]). The high prevalence of chronic pain (pain longer than three months) places military personnel at high risk for long-term problems associated with impaired functioning, poor mental health, interpersonal conflict, substance abuse, and vocational problems.

Acute Pain and Prevention of PTSD

A recent link has emerged between the experience of acute pain caused by physical injury and the onset of PTSD, and when pain is treated early and aggressively, patients may have the best chance of getting better. For instance, within 24 to 48 hours after serious injury, client self-reported pain levels are significantly related to the development of PTSD (Norman, Stein, Dimsdale, & Hoyt, 2008 as cited in DVA/DoD, 2010). Moreover, in another study, 35% of 696 wounded Operation Iraqi Freedom (OIF) veterans developed PTSD, however, the authors found that those receiving morphine immediately after injury had significantly reduced PTSD rates (Holbrook, Galarneau, Dye, Quinn, & Dougherty, 2010, as cited in DVA/DoD, 2010).

Acute Sleep Disturbance

One of the most critical and often overlooked determinants for physical-mental health is sleep. Sleep disturbances can be both a symptom of an underlying health condition (e.g., apnea, PTSD, depression, compassion fatigue, dementia, etc.) and/or a catalyst for disorder, especially when persistent (e.g., depression, compassion fatigue, interpersonal violence, etc.). Chronic sleep deprivation can have a major downhill impact on health. Therapists should routinely screen military (any) clients for sleep disturbance and not wait too long before a medical referral. Theoretically, the more sleep impairment and trauma-related nightmares an individual continues to experience, the more likely he/she is to continue to experience the symptoms of ASD and/or subsequently develop PTSD (DVA/DoD, 2010). Hyperarousal behaviors, part of ASD/PTSD symptoms for many people, can be stronger at night and contribute to insomnia. Sleep problems in traumatized clients may be initiated or exacerbated by comorbid conditions such as Traumatic Brain Injury (TBI) or other physical wounds, and/or medically unexplained conditions (e.g., fibromyalgia).

Acute Traumatic Brain Injury

According to the VA and DoD's *Clinical Practice Guidelines for the Management of Post-Traumatic Stress* (October, 2010), therapists working with military personnel should have specific awareness of traumatic brain injury, particularly mild concussion/mTBI in the post-deployment population because of the high incidence of concussion/mTBI during deployment (10–20 percent of combat veterans), and high comorbidity of post-concussive symptoms (PCS) with PTSD. Concussion/mTBI is common in sports injuries, motor vehicle accidents, military training (e.g., hand-to-hand combat), and combat. It is associated with a variety of symptoms that will manifest immediately following the event, and may resolve quickly, within minutes to hours after the injury event. In certain individuals the symptoms persist longer leading to a Persistent Post-Concussion Symptoms (PPCS). Common TBI and PPCS symptoms include:

- Feeling dizzy
- Loss of balance
- Poor coordination, clumsy
- Headaches
- Nausea
- Vision problems, blurring, trouble seeing
- Sensitivity to light
- Hearing difficulty
- Sensitivity to noise
- Numbness or tingling on parts of the body
- Change in taste and/or smell
- Loss of appetite or increased appetite
- Poor concentration, can't pay attention, easily distracted
- Forgetfulness, can't remember things
- Difficulty making decisions
- Slowed thinking, difficulty getting organized, can't finish things
- Fatigue, loss of energy, getting tired easily
- Difficulty falling or staying asleep
- Feeling anxious or tense
- Feeling depressed or sad
- Irritability, easily annoyed
- Poor frustration tolerance, feeling easily overwhelmed by things

As evident above, there is significant overlap between TBI and PPCS symptoms and those found in war stress injuries related to PTSD, depression, and medically unexplained conditions. Military clients with cognitive and behavioral symptoms persisting after one month should be referred for a neuropsychological assessment (DVA/DoD, 2009).

Acute Substance Abuse

A concurrent diagnosis of substance abuse raises a number of challenging issues in the treatment of war stress injury like PTSD. At least 40 to 50% of war veterans diagnosed with PTSD have comorbid substance use problems (DVA/DoD, 2010). Divergent views exists among substance abuse counselors and general mental health practitioners as to the timing of treatment for Axis I conditions like PTSD and depression, when co-occurring with a substance use disorder. Trauma-focused treatments can often lead to increased urges to use substances, therefore, some believe trauma-focused work should not proceed until sobriety is well-established (e.g.,

6–12 months). However, substance use can also be a means of coping (e.g., self-medication) with the consequence of unprocessed traumatic events, and may not end until the underlying traumata or adverse experiences are reprocessed. As a matter of routine, therapists should screen for substance use disorder. Brief screens like CAGE and Alcohol Use Disorders Identification Test (AUDIT) can be useful (Lande, Marin, & Ruzek, 2004, pp. 79–82).

Early Treatment of Acute Stress Injuries

In regard to intervening with severe acute stress injury (ASD), the DVA/DoD (2010) *Clinical Practice Guidelines* recommend the following:

- Acutely traumatized people who meet the criteria for diagnosis of ASD and those with significant levels of post-trauma symptoms after at least two weeks post-trauma, as well as those who are incapacitated by acute psychological or physical symptoms, should receive further assessment and early intervention to prevent PTSD.
- Trauma survivors who present with symptoms that do not meet the diagnostic threshold for ASD, or those who have recovered from the trauma and currently show no symptoms, should be monitored and may benefit from follow up and provision of ongoing counseling or symptomatic treatment.
- Service members with COSR who do not respond to initial supportive interventions may warrant referral or evacuation.

Military Treatment Recommendations for Acute Stress Injury

Therapists should be familiar with the current recommendations for treating Acute Stress Disorder in military populations that are provided in the *DVA/DoD Clinical Practice Guideline for the Management of Post-Traumatic Stress* (October 2010), with the awareness of its inherent limitation in accounting for the spectrum of acute stress injury. The following treatment recommendations should apply to all acutely traumatized people who meet the criteria for diagnosis of acute stress injury (e.g., ASD) and for those with significant levels of acute stress symptoms that last for more than two weeks post-trauma, as well as those who are incapacitated by acute psychological or physical symptoms.

1. Continue providing psychoeducation and normalization.
2. Treatment should be initiated after education, normalization, and Psychological First Aid have been provided and after basic needs following the trauma have been made available.
3. Psychotherapy:
   a. Consider early brief intervention (4 to 5 sessions) of cognitive-based therapy (CBT) that includes exposure-based therapy, alone or combined with a component of cognitive restructuring therapy for patients with significant early symptom levels, especially those meeting diagnostic criteria for ASD.
   b. Routine formal psychotherapy intervention for asymptomatic individuals is not beneficial and may be harmful.
   c. Strongly recommend against individual Psychological Debriefing as a viable means of reducing acute stress disorder (ASD) or progression to post-traumatic stress disorder (PTSD).
   d. The evidence does not support a single session group Psychological Debriefing as a viable means of reducing acute stress disorder (ASD) or progression to post-traumatic stress disorder, but there is no evidence of harm (Note: this is not a recommendation pertaining to Operational Debriefing).

Pharmacotherapy

There is no evidence to support a recommendation for use of a pharmacological agent to prevent the development of ASD or PTSD. There is a strong recommendation *against* the use of benzodiazepines to prevent the development of ASD or PTSD.

Additional Considerations for Managing Acute Stress Disorder

These are the additional considerations for managing Acute Stress Disorder:

1. Symptom-specific treatment should be provided after education, normalization, and basic needs are met.
2. Consider a short course of medication (less than 6 days), targeted for specific symptoms in patients post-trauma:
   a. Sleep disturbance/insomnia
   b. Management of pain
   c. Irritation/excessive arousal/anger.
3. Provide nonpharmacological intervention (e.g., relaxation, breathing techniques, avoiding caffeine) to address both general recovery and specific symptoms (sleep disturbance, pain, hyperarousal, or anger).
4. Immediately after trauma exposure, preserve an interpersonal safety zone protecting basic personal space (e.g., privacy, quiet, personal effects).
5. As part of Psychological First Aid, reconnect trauma survivors with previously supportive relationships (e.g., family, friends, command members, etc.) and link with additional sources of interpersonal support.
6. Assess for impact of PTSD on social functioning.
7. Facilitate access to social support and provide assistance in improving social functioning, as indicated.
8. Continue providing psychoeducation and normalization.
9. Per the *2010 DVA/DoD Clinical Practice Guidelines*, Cognitive-Behavioral Techniques are the current early intervention of choice. Although the military's practice guidelines do not single out EMDR as an early intervention per se, EMDR is explicitly listed by the guidelines as a trauma-focused "cognitive-behavioral" treatment that is evidence-based for the treatment of traumatic stress injuries. Therefore EMDR is a viable frontline option.

EMDR and Early Intervention in the Military

Potential Advantages for Early Intervention With EMDR

Although EMDR is not singled out as evidence-based treatment for ASD per se, according to the DVA/DoD (2010), the evidence-based "trauma-focused" therapies "include a variety of techniques most commonly involving exposure and/or cognitive restructuring" (*Prolonged Exposure, Cognitive Processing Therapy and Eye movement Desensitization and Reprocessing*, p. 115 as cited in DVA/DoD, 2010). After four weeks of symptom presentation, the ASD diagnosis automatically converts to PTSD and EMDR is recognized as one of a few "A-level" trauma-focused psychotherapies for PTSD. It is completely arbitrary and empirically unsupported to distinguish a client's response to an evidence-based trauma-focused intervention at three weeks and 6-days (ASD) and four weeks and a day (PTSD). Furthermore, given several peer-reviewed publications of clinical case studies on EMDR treatment for combat-related ASR and ASD in active-duty military (Russell, 2006; Wesson & Gould, 2009), as well as in the civilian sector (Shapiro, 2009), there appears to be more than sufficient empirical justification and clinical rationale for including EMDR as a viable trauma-focused treatment option for acute stress injury. One of the truly unique advantages of EMDR treatment is that it allows the therapist to assist the client in reprocessing multiple components of acute war/ traumatic stress injury simultaneously—as opposed to a piecemeal approach whereby one package of interventions is for addressing guilt, another for grief, depression, PTSD, MUPS, and so forth (Russell, Silver, & Rogers, 2007).

EMDR Research on Treating Acute Stress Injury in Military Settings

Military clinicians have published small and large EMDR case studies with active-duty clientele treated across medical and operational settings (Russell, Lipke, & Figley, 2011). Subsequently, EMDR's effectiveness in military treatment settings has been demonstrated at a field hospital where four Iraqi War battlefield evacuees were treated for acute stress injuries (Russell, 2006). Each client was referred due to a high level of disturbance and medical instability and was to be transported to a stateside treatment facility. All four service members received a single session of modified-EMDR and reported significant post symptom stabilization and primary symptom reduction, corroborated at 1 to 3 day follow up (Russell, 2006).

Wesson and Gould (2009) successfully treated a U.K. soldier, experiencing ASR, at a frontline combat stress control, following a recent landmine incident. After four EMDR sessions, on four consecutive days, the soldier's ASR was resolved and he was returned to full-duty status with sustained improvement at 18 months (Wesson & Gould, 2009). In addition, single-case studies of EMDR treatment in military outpatient clinics involving phantom-limb pain from traumatic amputation (Russell, 2008b) have shown positive results. Studies of combat-related medically unexplained conditions (Russell, 2008c) and outpatient PTSD cases (Silver, Rogers, & Russell, 2008) also reported significant symptom reduction after an average of four EMDR sessions, eight if wounded-in-action (Russell, Silver, Rogers, & Darnell, 2007)—all of which signify EMDR's potential utility as a frontline early intervention. Because there is a very tight window for intervening with EMDR in military settings, and the extent of client history taking and rapport building is extremely compressed, effective treatment planning is a necessity.

Seven Considerations for Treatment Planning and Adaptation of EMDR to Military Settings

In the vast majority of acute cases, standard trauma-focused EMDR that includes comprehensive reprocessing by utilizing the three-pronged protocol is contraindicated (Russell & Figley, 2013). Russell and Figley (2013) introduced a system for treatment planning and adapting EMDR to military settings based on *seven* key considerations:

- *Referral Question*
- *Strength of the Therapeutic Alliance*
- *Client Treatment Goals*
- *Timing and Environmental Constraints*
- *Clinical Judgment Regarding Client Safety*
- *Suitability for Standard Trauma-Focused EMDR Reprocessing Protocol*
- *Utilization of Any Adjunctive Intervention and Referral Need*

Consideration 1: Referral Question

"Probably the most clinically salient and important issues to clarify for treatment planning purposes is the reason for referral, limits of confidentiality, therapist role expectations, and desired outcomes. The reason for referral provides crucial information regarding who is concerned about the client's behavior, ethical implications in regards to confidentiality (e.g., who has a need to know client's mental health status), potential ramifications for the client, and what is the expected treatment outcome or goal. Most importantly, the referral question provides essential information in regard to potential timing issues related to determining the suitability for EMDR treatment in general, or the need to incorporate modifications of the Standard EMDR Protocol in the treatment plan" (Russell & Figley,

2013, p. 56). Approach to treatment planning will be different depending on deployment status. For example, it is important to know if the client is forward deployed and the referral is for primary symptom reduction or stabilization; or if the client is pending deployment or Permanent Change of Station (PCS) transfer in three weeks; or the Judge Advocate General (JAG) officer (military lawyer) informs the therapist that the client is testifying about military sexual trauma. All of these scenarios depict common timing considerations in developing a treatment plan.

Three Types of Referral Questions

Within the military health system the underlying severity of the problem and sense of urgency for requested services is communicated by characterizing three types of referrals:

- *Routine*—the client presents a noncrisis situation without major safety or military fitness for duty implications. The problematic condition is typically in the "mild" to "low moderate" severity range. Start of intervention services should occur within normal 1 to 14 day standard.
- *Emergent*—the client does not present in *immediate* crisis, life threatening, or military fitness for duty issue, however, the underlying condition falls within the "moderate" to "severe" range, and therefore intervention services should occur within 1 to 3 days in order to prevent a potential crisis situation.
- *Urgent*—the client is currently in crisis and/or presents with a "severe" debilitating health and safety condition requiring immediate "same day" intervention.

Appreciating the context or implications of the reason for referral as either routine, emergent, or urgent, as well as practical considerations surrounding the reason for referral itself, is essential for accurate and effective EMDR treatment planning. For instance, the standard trauma-focused EMDR protocol is almost never appropriate for clients presenting with "urgent" reason for referral. Instead, variant EMDR protocols emphasizing client stabilization (e.g., ERP) and/or primary symptom reduction (e.g., EMD) should be considered.

Consideration 2: Enhancing the Therapeutic Relationship

There are frequently times and settings within the military (e.g., forward-deployed, operational environment) when the EMDR intervention may be limited to 1 to 2 sessions. Therefore, a workable alliance needs to be established very quickly. Fortunately, in the military, "Docs" are generally revered. Thus the therapist's credibility is usually a given. Client history taking and target selection will naturally be abbreviated significantly and narrowly focused on the precipitant event, while client preparation also moves extremely quickly depending on the nature of the referral. For therapists to support the quick establishment of a therapeutic alliance with military clientele, the following is suggested:

- Briefly introduce yourself to the client, stating the reason and source of the referral.
- Adopt a stance of caring and concerned involvement that takes what the client says at face value, doesn't judge or label.
- Avoid jargon, lecturing, and withdrawing into an "objective, professional" role.
- Become familiar with the experience of your clients by reading basic material on the experience of combat and watching documentaries of the same.
- Develop an understanding that wartime and military service involves some of the most intense human experiences and that feelings of profound rage, fear, and grief can be an expected part of these experiences.
- Ask questions when not understanding something about the military to which the client refers.
- Being transparent in terms of treatment options and imparting a sense of control or agency in military clientele is critical in establishing trust and rapport (see Russell & Figley, 2013).

The amount of time and extent of rapport building needs to be taken into consideration when thinking about enhancing the therapeutic relationship. More time is needed establishing a therapeutic alliance when the referral question requires client stabilization versus requests for primary symptom reduction, or comprehensive reprocessing respectfully. For example, an "emergent" referral of a verbally responsive military client who experienced a sexual assault 3 days prior to the consultation by a coworker at a stateside military base would afford the therapist much greater time to devote to rapport building, history, and preparation as well as choice in EMDR intervention (e.g., Modified EMDR, Recent Events Protocol), compared to the same "emergent" scenario with a verbally unresponsive client seen in a warzone.

Consideration 3: Client Treatment Goals

Military clients in acute situations may have a variety of possible treatment oriented goals including stabilization of symptoms for transportation purposes; reduction of primary symptoms in order to return to duty, to deploy, or to address a family member or work supervisor concerns; or comprehensive reprocessing of the most recent and past traumatic events. Treatment planning should take into account the client's desired outcome through questions such as:

- "What is your goal in coming here?"
- "How would you like for things to be different?"
- "At a minimum, what would you hope to happen as a result of coming to treatment?"
- "How will you know when that goal has been achieved?"
- "What problems do you anticipate might interfere with your goal?"
- "This will sound crazy, but what do you think would be the negative effects, if you reached your goal?"

Consideration 4: Timing and Environmental Constraints

The military is a highly mobile population. Typically, infantry and other ground force units deploy for 6 to 12 months, return back to their home base, then enter a training cycle to prepare for the next deployment. Currently, the military has been trying to implement forced "dwell time" allowing military personnel and their family members longer periods of time before re-entering the deployment cycle. National Guardsmen and active Reserves are "mobilized" to serve on active-duty for 6 to 12 month periods than return back to their civilian jobs.

Environmental considerations are similarly important matters in devising a treatment plan. For instance, is the EMDR intervention to occur at or near the front line, or at some other point within the warzone echelon of care? Is the treatment setting in a field hospital tent, onboard a naval vessel, an inpatient psychiatric ward at a Military Treatment Facility (MTF), an outpatient mental health clinic, or an off-base, civilian agency? Besides obvious privacy and resource implications, the environmental setting for which the military client will be returning must also be considered.

With serious time and environmental constraints, high operational tempo, and a very mobile military population, there is an intrinsic need in the military to work as safely, rapidly, and efficiently as one can. Long-term, week-to-week therapy in the military does not exist for most. Therefore to maximize time, the therapist needs to establish trust and rapport early and fast, and identify a sufficient number of quality targets for reprocessing. At a minimum, it is important to identify preferably 3 affectively charged targets (earliest, worst, and most recent). In the case of acute stress injuries, most often it will be the most disturbing events associated with the presenting complaint. It is critical for the practitioner to be aware and plan for the following:

- Typical stressors, socio-emotional responses, and coping patterns that service personnel and family members endure in adapting to deployments

- When/if to offer EMDR
- What type of EMDR intervention to offer (e.g., symptom stabilization, symptom reduction, comprehensive reprocessing)

Consideration 5: Clinical Judgment Regarding Client Safety

Early interventions in the wake of acute trauma can often be conceptualized as the mental health equivalent of physical first aid, with the goal being to "stop the psychological bleeding." The first, most important measure should be to eliminate (if possible) the source of the trauma or to remove the victim from the traumatic, stressful environment. Once the patient is stabilized and in a safe situation, the provider should attempt to reassure the patient, encourage a professional healing relationship, encourage a feeling of safety, and identify existing social supports. Establishing safety and assurance may enable people to get back on track, and maintain their pre-trauma stable condition. Some want and feel a need to discuss the event, and some have no such need. Respect individual and cultural preferences in the attempt to meet their needs as much as possible. Allow for normal recovery and monitor. In regard to Phase 1 (Client History) of the EMDR Standard Protocol, therapists must assess for a number of potential client safety issues. Contradictions for any trauma-focused intervention may include immediate medical, health, and/or psychological concerns, such as the following.

Seizure Disorder: Therapists should get medical clearance for recent onset of seizures. EMDR has been safely used without the likelihood of initiating genuine epileptic seizure (Leeds, 2009). Pseudo-seizures from conversion are fairly common in clients with histories of Complex-PTSD or other severe traumatic stress injuries. Several EMDR case studies have been published on treating pseudo-seizures (de Roos & van Rood, 2009).

Traumatic Brain Injury (TBI): EMDR should not be used with personnel presenting with acute TBI, until medically cleared. For military clients who have been medically cleared, and/or present with a history of TBI, EMDR reprocessing should be considered, *not* as a treatment for TBI (which it is not), but it may help address the past contributing traumatic events, current triggers related to the past trauma or recovery, and future-oriented client worry, concerns, or coping resources that are needed.

Acute Psychotic Conditions: Acute psychosis represents a medical emergency. Clients with transient, acute psychotic reaction may be suitable for EMDR after the resolution of psychotic features. Military stress will exacerbate client's conditions and place them at risk (re-check previous diagnosis for accuracy).

Severe Agitation or Hostility: Clients exhibiting extreme agitation, restlessness, or hostility and who are unable to self-regulate or calm even with therapist interventions would not be suitable for trauma-focused therapy, including EMDR reprocessing, until their state stabilizes. Instead, therapists will want to assess and, if possible, address the precipitants for the imbalanced state. Extreme psychomotor agitation such as pacing, hand wringing, muttering, an inability to stay seated for brief periods, and pressured speech should be assessed for dangerousness or incapacitation and treated as a medical emergency.

Imminent Suicidal or Homicidal Ideation/Attempts: Therapists need to assess for safety and dangerousness in all clients with war stress injuries and other traumatic stress injuries, including current risk to self or others, as well as historical patterns of risk. Problems with explosive anger, a past history of violent behavior, and substance use problems are all associated with heightened risk for violence.

Dissociative Disorder: Efforts should be made to assist the client to contact military medical personnel to initiate medical evaluation and possible discharge. Generally speaking, EMDR interventions, if used, should focus primarily on stabilization and/or primary symptom reduction versus comprehensive reprocessing of severe dissociative disorder conditions from complex trauma.

Note: Therapists should get medical clearance for clients with a recent history of or treatment for: stroke, heart attack, malignant hypertension, severe bronchial asthma, brain tumor, medical surgery, detached retina, delirium, or any other acute or serious, unstable medical condition.

Once immediate basic safety needs are met, the therapist and client may elect to move onto other treatment planning considerations such as reprocessing the acute traumatic event. Obviously, immediate safety needs take precedence. However, safety considerations in working with military populations can present an ethical challenge for therapists. For instance, as mentioned earlier, the sole purpose of frontline psychiatry is to preserve the fighting force, not treatment of acute stress injuries. Therapists working with military clients deployed or pending deployment to warzones may struggle with ethical implications of successful EMDR intervention to stabilize and/or reduce primary symptoms that will result in return to duty and possible reexposure and exacerbation of an acute or chronic stress injury. Therefore, discussion of "client safety" for the purposes of EMDR treatment planning must be extended to informed consent of the possible benefits and consequences of successful and unsuccessful intervention.

Additionally, treatment planning for "emergent" or "urgent" referral questions requesting immediate assistance to stabilize a client in or near crisis in the aftermath of acute trauma, especially when time/environment constraints are present, will usually limit treatment goals and type of EMDR intervention to client stabilization (e.g., RDI) or primary symptom reduction (e.g., EMD), versus Recent Events protocol or comprehensive reprocessing.

Consideration 6: Suitability for the EMDR Standard Protocol for Trauma

The aforementioned client safety factors are also utilized in determining client suitability for standard EMDR reprocessing, however, in the case of treatment planning and acute stress injuries, assessing client suitability for the EMDR Standard Protocol needs to account for much more. For example, the therapist must assess client suitability for the EMDR Standard Protocol in light of the reason for referral, time and environmental constraints, client treatment goals, and post-treatment support environment. Even clients not in crisis or deemed to be otherwise "good candidates" for comprehensive reprocessing may not be suitable for Standard EMDR and pose greater client safety risks. It is, therefore, essential to examine the potential indicators and contra-indicators of suitability in light of the EMDR treatment goal (e.g., client stabilization, primary symptom reduction, comprehensive reprocessing) while addressing his/her suitability for using the EMDR Standard Protocol for trauma.

Four Acute Stress Injury Treatment Goals

For treatment planning purposes, assessing military client suitability for EMDR Standard reprocessing of acute stress injuries requires matching one of four treatment goals with the appropriate EMDR early intervention. Russell and Figley (2013) identified four treatment goals for utilizing EMDR as an early intervention for acute stress injuries:

1. Client stabilization
2. Primary symptom reduction
3. Comprehensive reprocessing, and
4. Prevention of compassion-stress injury

Below, we briefly describe each treatment goal and recommended EMDR early intervention.

TREATMENT GOAL 1: CLIENT STABILIZATION

"In the immediate aftermath of a traumatic event, the majority of survivors experience normal ASR/COSR. However, some may require immediate crisis intervention to help manage intense feelings of panic or grief. Signs of panic are trembling, agitation, rambling speech, and erratic behavior. Signs of intense grief may be loud wailing, rage, or catatonia. Clients may also develop severe, debilitating ASR/COSR that render them unstable and/or unresponsive to medical or unit personnel". Such clients would present as being conscious and awake, however, in a state of acute peri-traumatic dissociation or "emotional shock" with limited or no responsiveness to verbal interchange.

In such cases, the therapist should attempt to quickly establish therapeutic rapport, ensure the survivor's safety, acknowledge and validate the survivor's experience, and offer empathy. After all basic safety needs have been taken care of and medical triage has been completed, medical/nursing, unit or command, and/or other emergency personnel may request the therapist to assist with psychological stabilization in order to medically assess and/or transport to the next echelon of care (Russell & Figley, 2013, p.86 and p.169).

Recommended EMDR Stabilization Interventions
The three stabilization procedures are Emergency Response Procedure (ERP), Eye Movement Desensitization (EMD), and Resource Development and Installation (RDI).

TREATMENT GOAL 2: PRIMARY SYMPTOM REDUCTION

"A variety of contexts may arise that may preclude comprehensive reprocessing by adherence to the standard EMDR trauma-focused protocol for otherwise stable and suitable military clientele. Such variables include: *time-sensitive constraints* (e.g., impending client or therapist absence, impending client deployment, etc.), *environmental demands* (e.g., forward-deployed, operational settings), and *client-stated treatment goals* (e.g., expressed desire to not address earlier foundational experiences other than such as pre-military incidents), that may lead to the joint decision to deviate from the standard EMDR protocol after full informed consent if provided. Generally speaking, comprehensive EMDR reprocessing that includes reprocessing of pre-military memories, even on consecutive days, will usually not be appropriate if within *two weeks* the client will be deploying or involved in a PCS transfer (relocation) or extended training exercise, and so on. Clinical judgment and full informed consent are necessary to determine if reprocessing can occur safely with a very short window.

In addition, depending on time and environmental constraints and clinical judgment, primary symptom reduction may or may not include the installation or body scan phases, or reprocessing of current triggers and future template that is the Standard EMDR Protocol. Some clinicians (Russell, 2006) have reported successful symptom reduction in operational environments using a modified EMDR approach that was limited to the circumscribed recent or precipitating event (e.g., a current deployment) or a specific past combat or other traumatic incident, and did not reprocess current or future antecedents because of time limitations. Therapists need to be familiar with the existing literature and provide informed consent to clients regarding potential advantages and limitations from deviation of an evidence-based protocol." (Russell & Figley, 2013, pp. 88–99 and pp.169–172).

Recommended EMDR Primary Symptom Reduction Interventions
The two primary symptom reduction interventions are Eye Movement Desensitization (EMD), and Modified or "Mod-EMDR."

TREATMENT GOAL 3: COMPREHENSIVE REPROCESSING

The essential treatment plan for the evidence-based, eight-phased Standard EMDR Protocol has always consisted of what Shapiro (2001) refers to as the *Three-Pronged Protocol:*

- *Past* traumatic events or other foundational emotionally charged experiential contributors, or *small t*, as Shapiro (2001) puts it, that are etiologic to the presenting complaints or psychopathological condition.
- *Current* internal or external triggers or antecedents that activate the maladaptive neural (memory) network.
- *Future* template, of the client's anticipatory anxiety, worries, or concerns, and/or needed coping skills or mastery achieved through imaginal or behavioral rehearsal, to prevent relapse or reactivation of the maladaptive schema.

In 1995, Francine Shapiro introduced the Protocol for Recent Traumatic Events and it has been a mainstay since then, despite no controlled studies. Shapiro hypothesized that recent memories had insufficient time to consolidate, therefore, the traditional focus on past memories did not generalize to other disturbing memories and created the Recent Traumatic

Events Protocol. In terms of military application, Wesson and Gould's (2009) single-case study revealed successful early intervention using four consecutive days of the Recent Traumatic Events Protocol with a United Kingdom soldier experiencing ASR, within two weeks post-event. The military client was returned-to-duty after the intervention and treatment gains were maintained at 18 months. Elan Shapiro (2009) and Foa and Riggs (1994) also put forth the notion of fragmented early memories that require repeated processing for each fragment. It bears emphasizing that no randomized controlled trials have ever been conducted comparing the evidence-based standard EMDR protocol and the Recent Events Protocol in treating acute stress injuries.

Recommended EMDR Comprehensive Reprocessing
The two comprehensive reprocessing interventions are the Standard EMDR Protocol (EMDR) and the Recent Traumatic Events Protocol.

TREATMENT GOAL 4: PREVENTION OF COMPASSION-STRESS INJURY

After intense reprocessing sessions, it is recommended that therapists implement their self-care plan. Therapists whose workload frequently exposes them to highly charged sessions need to be particularly mindful of the insidious effects of compassion stress, and take proactive measures whenever possible to avoid cumulative wear-and-tear that may lead to compassion-stress injury (i.e., compassion fatigue). "In the event the therapist does develop a compassion-stress injury, treatment would be in the form of either modified-EMDR that restricts self-focus attention to particular client(s) or one's clinical practice, or the Standard EMDR Protocol to potentially address other past contributors that increase occupational risk." (Russell & Figley, p. 92).

Recommended EMDR Compassion-Stress Prevention Intervention
The two compassion-stress prevention interventions are the Clinician Self-Care Script and Standard EMDR Protocol (EMDR).

Descriptions of EMDR Early Intervention Protocol and Scripts:

EMERGENCY RESPONSE PROCEDURE (ERP)SCRIPT (QUINN)

Purpose: Stabilization and triage of client by increasing orientation to present focus. Use in the following situations: routine attempts to engage blankly staring clients are not successful; clients are suffering from acute stress reactions; clients are in "shock" and/or unresponsive to verbal questions or commands (Quinn, 2009).

1. Calmly speak in the client's ear to identify yourself, your role in the hospital/setting, and reassure the client of their safety in the hospital/setting.
2. Inform the client that you are going to tap them gently on the shoulder and remind them where they are, that they had survived the bombing (or any other incident), and they are now at a safe place.
3. After brief periods of the bilateral taps, direct their attention to safety, so that clients can became responsive to outside stimuli, be engaged verbally about their medical status, and so on. The total intervention time would be measured in minutes (Quinn, 2009.)
4. If stabilized, and deemed appropriate and consent is given, consider suitability for higher level of EMDR intervention (symptom reduction, comprehensive reprocessing, or resilience building).

EYE MOVEMENT DESENSITIZATION (EMD) (RUSSELL, 2006)

Purpose: Crisis intervention limited to the reduction of primary symptoms associated with the precipitating event. In the immediate or near-immediate aftermath of exposure to a severe or potentially traumatic event, clients present with severe, debilitating ASR/COSR.

The EMD protocol is essentially a behavioral exposure therapy that adds BLS and does not reinforce free associations outside of either a single-incident target memory (e.g., primary presenting complaint), or a representative "worst" memory from a cluster of memories related to a circumscribed event (e.g., a recent deployment). Free associations reported outside the treatment parameters require the client to be returned to target memory whereby SUDs are re-accessed and BLS initiated. Clients may be returned to the target memory at any time by the therapist where SUDs are obtained to assess progress of desensitization effect. Repeat process until target memory has SUDs of 0 is obtained or 1 if ecologically valid. Installation, body scan, current triggers, and future template are not included in EMD. (Russell & Figley, 2010, p. 89).

Note: The idea behind EMD as a stabilizing/primary symptom reducer in acute stress injuries is its time-limited nature and goal of essentially crisis intervention. As a result, there is no expectation of "resolution" per se, whereby we get to the Installation Phase, and so on, especially when working with a single precipitant memory vs. the entire pathogenic neural network. On a practical side, it seems awkward at best to ask people for a positive cognition (PC) immediately or shortly after a traumatic event. Therefore, the PC and Validity of Cognition scale (VoC) are not included in this version of EMD.

These are the advantages and disadvantages of Russell's EMDR Protocol (Russell & Figley, 2013, p. 89)

Advantages

- *Allows more strictly controlled reprocessing by reducing chance for generalization to other memories, which might speed up symptom relief.*
- *When free associations outside of the target occur, the client is immediately returned to the target memory so that this may prevent client from in-depth exposure to other sources of emotionally intense material.*
- *May provide clients a mastery experience with EMDR that may open the door for comprehensive reprocessing with the Standard EMDR Protocol.*
- *Potentially more rapid relief of the most intense symptoms than either modified or standard EMDR.*
- *Primary symptom reduction may prevent escalation or exacerbation of stress injury and more readily improve client functioning at least in the short-term.*
- *May reassure military clients concerned about culture expectations that emphasize self-control and military readiness in the context of accessing earlier life events.*
- *Provides viable option for military clients who otherwise may refuse therapy.*

Disadvantages

- *Desensitization effects may not sustain due to unprocessed other past, current, and future contributors.*
- *Reduction of primary symptoms may result in client termination without addressing other contributors.*
- *Increased possibility of stress injury may persist as sub-chronic, more prone to kindling and relapse, in response to future acute stress.*
- *Client will probably be exposed, even if fleetingly, to other negative associations in the maladaptive neural network—so needs thorough informed consent.*

EMD SCRIPT (RUSSELL)

Phases 1–2: Client History, Preparation, and Informed Consent

Information about the precipitating event and the client's involvement should be obtained from the referral source (e.g., medical, nursing, or unit personnel). Therapist introduces themselves, their role, and the reason for referral asking:

Say, *"Is it okay if I talk to you?"*

_____

_____

Say, *"My name is_____(state name) and I understand that you were referred here because_____(state reason for referral). Is that correct?"*

_____

_____

Phase 3: Assessment

Selecting Target Memory

Only one past memory is selected.

Say, *"What is the most disturbing part to you about what just happened* (or words to that effect)?"

_____

_____

Image/Sensory Memory

Say, *"Is there one image or picture in particular that represents the worst part of that_____(name the incident) scene?"*

_____

_____

Negative Cognition (NC)

Say, *"What negative words go with that_____(state the target) that expresses your negative belief about yourself now?"*

_____

_____

Emotion

Say, *"When you bring up that____(state target) and those words_____(state the negative cognition), what emotion do you feel now?"*

_____

_____

Subjective Units of Disturbance (SUD)

Say, *"I can see you're in a lot of pain_____(state military rank)."* Say, *"On a scale of 0 to 10, where 0 is no disturbance or neutral and 10 is the highest disturbance you can imagine, how disturbing does it feel now?"*

0   1   2   3   4   5   6   7   8   9   10
(no disturbance)   (highest disturbance)

Location of Body Sensation

Say, *"Where do you feel it in your body?"*

_____

_____

Phase 4: Desensitization/Reprocessing

Say, *"I would like you to bring up that____(state target), those negative words ____(state the negative cognition), and notice where you are feeling it in your body. Go with that."*

Bilateral Stimulation (BLS)/Dual-Focused Attention

Maintain the client's dual-focused attention/bilateral stimulation during the reprocessing by talking to the client:

Say, *"That's it"* . . . *"Good"* . . . *"Just keep tracking"* . . . *"You are safe now"* . . . *"That's it"* . . . *"Just notice it"* . . . *"You are safe now"* . . . *"Good"* . . . *"It's in the past"* . . . etc.

Reprocessing to Completion

If during BLS, the client reports a free association that appears unrelated to the precipitating event:

Say, *"OK, now I would like you to go back to_____(state the event), what do you notice now?"*

_____

_____

Obtain a SUDs rating each time the client returns to the target memory.

Say, *"On a scale of 0 to 10, where 0 is no disturbance or neutral and 10 is the highest disturbance you can imagine, how disturbing does it feel now?"*

0   1   2   3   4   5   6   7   8   9   10
(no disturbance)   (highest disturbance)

After obtaining the SUDs:

Say, *"Just think of that."*

Repeat this sequence each time the client self-reports an association outside of the treatment parameter. Repeat the process until target memory reaches a SUDs of 0 or 1, if ecologically valid.

Note: Phases 5 and 6 (Installation and Body Scan), Current Triggers, and Future Template are not included because the intervention goal is simply to either stabilize the client's mental status or reduce primary symptoms associated with a single, discrete memory versus reprocessing traumatic schemas (Russell, 2006).

Phase 7: Closure

Standard EMDR closure whereby clients are informed they may continue to process information and are advised to monitor and record any new associations, dreams, etc.

Phase 8: Reevaluation

Contact the client, their medical attendant, or command within a day to check on the client's condition. If appropriate, additional reprocessing (e.g., EMD, EMDR) or strengthening resilience (e.g., RDI) may be recommended. If stabilized, and deemed appropriate and you have consent, consider suitability for higher level of EMDR intervention (symptom-focused reduction, comprehensive reprocessing, or resilience building).

MODIFIED-EMDR (MOD-EMDR) SCRIPT (RUSSELL, 2006)

Purpose: Crisis intervention limited to the reduction of primary symptoms associated with the precipitating event. In the immediate or near-immediate aftermath of exposure to a severe or potentially traumatic event, clients present with severe, debilitating ASR /COSR.

Note: See *EMD Script* above with the following modifications:

In Mod-EMDR the client's self-focused attention is limited to either a single-incident target memory (i.e., the precipitating event), or a representative worst memory from a cluster of memories related to a circumscribed event (e.g., specific operational mission, a certain deployment).

> Say, *"What is the target that we will be working on today? It can be either the incident that brought you in, or the worst memory from all of the cluster of memories related to____(state the event)?"*

"Negative free associations reported outside the treatment parameters require the client to be returned to the target memory. Installation, Body Scan, Current Triggers, and Future Template are selected in relation to the target memory and reprocessed accordingly. Adaptive or *positive free* associations may be reinforced outside of target parameters; however, if negative associations arise, client is returned to the target memory. SUDs and VoC are measured in accordance with the Standard EMDR Protocol." (Russell & Figley, 2013, p. 89–90). These are the advantages and disadvantages of Russell's Mod-EMDR (Russell & Figley, p. 90).

MOD-EMDR

Advantages
- *Less controlled processing than EMD, but more than standard EMDR, thus lessening change of generalization to other memories and may speed up symptom reduction*
- *Includes reprocessing of adaptive neural networks (Installation, Future Template)*
- *Provides a mastery experience with EMDR that may lead to comprehensive reprocessing down the road*
- *More rapid relief (probably) from presenting symptoms is achieved than in Standard EMDR*
- *Reduces the possibility of relapse more than EMD by targeting current and future antecedents, as well as strengthening adaptive resources via Installation*
- *May reassure military client concerned about culture expectations that emphasize self-control and military readiness in the context of accessing earlier life events*
- *Provides viable option for military clients who otherwise may refuse EMDR or other mental health treatment*

Disadvantages
- *Longer treatment duration than with EMD due to inclusion of Installation, Body Scan, Current Triggers and Future Template*
- *Desensitization effects may not be sufficient after a single memory or cluster is processed that will allow successful Installation and Body Scan*
- *Greater chance of relapse than with Standard EMDR due to remaining unprocessed past memories*
- *Reduction of primary symptoms may result in client termination without addressing other past contributors*
- *Increased possibility that stree injury may persist as sub-chronic, thereby making the client more prone to kindling and relapse in response to acute stress*

RECENT TRAUMATIC EVENTS PROTOCOL SCRIPT

(Shapiro as cited in Luber, 2009, pp. 143–144) *Purpose:* Comprehensive reprocessing of acute traumatic events.

Past Memories

1. Obtain a *narrative* history of the event, that is, each separate disturbing aspect or moment of the memory. Treat each separate aspect or moment as a separate target with the EMDR Standard Procedure and installation of positive cognition (PC).
2. Target the *most disturbing* aspect or moment of the memory (if necessary) otherwise target events in chronological order.
3. Target the *remainder* of the narrative in chronological order.
4. Have client visualize the *entire sequence* of the event with *eyes closed* and reprocess it as any disturbance arises. The client should have a full association with the material as it is being reprocessed. If there is disturbance, the client should stop and inform the clinician. Then, the EMDR Procedure including the negative cognition (NC) and positive cognition (PC) is implemented. Repeat until the entire event can be visualized from start to finish without emotional, cognitive, or somatic distress.
5. Have client visualize the event from start to finish with eyes open, and install the PC.
6. Conclude with the Body Scan. Only do Body Scan at the end of the processing of *all* of the targets.

Present Triggers

7. Process *present stimuli* that may cause a startle response, nightmares, and other reminders of the event that the client still finds disturbing, if necessary.

Future Template

8. Create a future template.

Note: For clients whose *earlier history* contains unresolved events that are associated with lack of safety and control, a longer treatment may be required.

CLINICIAN SELF-CARE SCRIPT

(Daniels, 2009)

Purpose:
Therapist self-care intervention to prevent cumulative effects of compassion stress that may lead to compassion stress injury such as compassion fatigue or burnout.

1. Ask the client to bring up the image of the patient and do BLS.
2. Notice whatever positive cognitions come to mind.
3. Install the positive cognition with the patient's image and do BLS.
4. Notice what happens.

Once the negative affects have been reduced, realistic formulations about the patient's future therapy are much easier to develop. Residual feelings of anger, frustration, regret, or hopelessness have been replaced by clearer thoughts about what can or cannot be done. Positive, creative mulling can proceed without the background feelings of unease, weariness, and ineffectiveness.

CREATING RESOURCES

Purpose:
If the client is unable to reprocess due to temporary time constraints, emotional or behavioral instability, or poor self-regulation skills, access to adaptive, coping resources is needed. Resource Development and Installation (RDI) (Korn & Leeds, 2002) may be necessary if there is a pre-military history of trauma and other adverse childhood experiences (e.g., severe childhood trauma, self-mutilation, medication overdoses, domestic violence/battering, military sexual trauma, and comorbid substance use disorders that increase the risk of suicide). Basic types of resources described by Korn and Leeds (2002) for are the following:

Mastery: Experience of past coping, self-care or self-soothing stance, or movement that evokes needed state.

Relationship: (a) Positive role models, (b) Memories of supportive others.

Symbolic: (a) Natural objects that represent the needed attribute, (b) Symbols from dreams, daydreams, or guided imagery, (c) Cultural, religious, or spiritual symbols, (d) Metaphors, (e) Music, (f) Image of positive goal state or future self.

There are many other different possible resources that can be installed/utilizeds (see Luber, 2009a, Section III, pp. 67–107).

Consideration 7: Utilization of Adjunctive Interventions and Referral Needs

It cannot be emphasized enough that effectively treating acute stress injuries in military population requires a comprehensive, biopsychosocial (and often spiritual) approach. As effective as EMDR is, there is a limitation to the curative effects within the therapy room. Therapists should anticipate that military clientele and their families will feel overwhelmed from dealing with a host of work, family, social, health, and financial stressors and demands that are inherent in the military itself and transitions. Clients often need help to stay focused on their treatment course. Therapists who are proactive in assisting their clients with anticipating, identifying, and prioritizing action plans to address the myriad of concerns can help prevent problems from escalating that could derail the treatment of their war stress injuries. It is impossible for an individual therapist to be able to meet the diverse needs of this population. Therefore it is imperative that practitioners become very familiar with the various military support services and agencies.

As in Phase 2 (Client Preparation) of the Standard EMDR Protocol, therapists may introduce stress reduction techniques. One particularly effective method designed for military populations is "Tactical or Combat Breathing" (Russell & Figley, 2013). Grossman (2007) discusses how law enforcement and the military regularly include "Combat or Tactical Breathing," a simple but effective controlled breathing technique to rapidly gain control over the body's acute stress response and adrenaline rush (sympathetic nervous system response) even in extreme high stress and hostile environments. Like any stress reduction skill, clients are encouraged to practice as regularly as possible, and to use Combat/Tactical Breathing before, during, and after combat or other operational missions using the following four-count method (Grossman, 2007).

Combat/Tactical Breathing Script

The therapist asks the client to sit in a chair and follow these instructions.

Say, *"Breathe in through your nose with a slow count of four (two, three, four)."*

The therapist can have clients place a hand on their stomach to see if they are properly filling the diaphragm with air, as evident when their stomach and hand rise.

Say, *"Place your hand on your stomach, as you breathe in through your nose to the count of four and notice your stomach and hand rise."*

Say, *"Hold your breath for a slow count of four (Hold, two, three, four)."*

Say, *"Now, exhale through your mouth for a count of four until all the air is out (two, three, four)."*

Client's hand should lower as the stomach lowers.

Say, *"Now, notice how your hand lowers as your stomach lowers."*

Say, *"Hold empty for a count of four (Hold, two, three, four)."*

Then repeat the cycle three times (Russell & Figley, 2013, p. 19).

Case Study: EMDR Treatment of Acute Combat-Related PTSD

The following excerpt is from Russell and Figley (2013, pp. 155–156). The client was a 24-year-old, male, Marine Lance Corporal, whose unit was ambushed in Iraq; the client was wounded in action (WIA), but his combat buddy (John, fictional) was the father of a newborn and tragically killed on impact by a rocket-propelled grenade (RPG). The setting is a 250-bed Navy tent hospital. Diagnosis is combat-PTSD.

Goal: To stabilize acute PTS for aeromedical evacuation to next higher echelon of care.
Target Memory: Image of John's mutilated corpse
NC: "I'm not ever going to see my family again."
PC: None elicited
Emotion: Numb feeling
SUDs: 8/10
Location of Physical Sensations: No physical sensations

Transcript:

Therapist:	"Okay Corporal, bring up the memory of John's death and the words 'I'm never going to see my family again, . . . and follow my hand with your eyes . . . that's it . . . good . . . just notice . . ." etc.
Therapist:	"Alright blank it out and take a breath . . . what do you notice now?"
Client:	"As soon as you started the hand movements . . . everything got a lot more vivid . . . like I can remember everything . . . like when I was there . . ."
Therapist:	[More vivid, more detail connotes change] "Okay . . . just stay with that and track my hand . . . good . . . keep noticing whatever comes up . . . just observe it . . . it's not happening now . . . blank it out, take a breath, what are you aware of now?"
Client:	"Man . . . I see everything . . . not just John but we lost three or four other guys, good guys too . . . and a whole bunch of dead Iraqi combatants."
Therapist:	[More details in the memory connote change] "Stay with it. Add BLS etc. What do you get now?" [About 4 to 5 BLS sets later—repeating the above sequence]
Client:	"There was a lot of messed up people . . . and John, man he just had a kid, he was so jazzed about being a dad, I never saw him happy like that before ." [sobbing—lengthier BLS set].
Therapist:	[Softly] "I know it hurts Corporal, just stay with it" [Add BLS but slower rate, and sweep was about cheek to cheek when crying] "What comes up now?"
Client:	"Man . . . this is weird. I'm at the bridge now, another attack, there's an explosion, it knocked me down, then I noticed a wet feeling in my leg, I looked down and I can see blood everywhere, and I'm just thinking I'm going to die!"

Therapist:	"OK . . . just think of it [Add BLS] and anything else that comes up . . . remember you're safe here; these are things that already happened . . . etc. What do you get now?"
Client:	"I remembered an old, rag-tag Iraqi man with an AK-47 got out of a car . . . and I killed him." [An additional 7 BLS sets were added]
Therapist:	"What do you notice now?"
Client:	"I remember rolling into South Baghdad and there were a lot of Iraqi kids smiling and waving and they all looked like they were starving . . . I gave one of them an MRE (Meal, Ready to Eat) the kid smiled and said America OK"
Therapist:	"Stay with that . . . What are you aware of now?"
Client:	"Wow. I forgot about this . . . but when we got to Baghdad there was a big crowd smiling and cheering for us . . . I felt like a hero."

Concluding Remarks

As we are inundated on a daily basis with pronouncements and news stories "escalating appropriations for arms" (Marin, 1995, p. 85; Russell, 2012), it is clear that the tentacles of America's War on Terror are far reaching and deeply seated in the fabric of our culture and we will continue to grapple with the reality of war and all the dilemmas it poses. We are only beginning to understand and fully comprehend more deeply the moral and physical complexities and nuances with which the "enlisted soldier" contends. At the core, however, and of primary concern, is the responsibility we bear as a society in attending to and addressing the pain of those whom we commission to fight and kill on our behalf, and who place themselves on the front line of disaster on all fronts (Marin, 1995; Russell, 2012). Our hope is that by elucidating the "occupational hazards" unique to military personnel and by examining effective early interventions to treat what troubles these individuals and their families, we will be closer to alleviating this suffering and diminishing the darkness of war and its effect on the human condition.

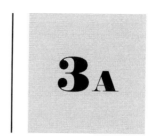

SUMMARY SHEET:
EMDR and Effective Management of Acute Stress Injuries: Early Mental Health Intervention From a Military Perspective

3A

Mark C. Russell, Tammera M. Cooke, and Susan Rogers
SUMMARY SHEET BY MARILYN LUBER

Name: _____ Diagnosis: _____

☑ Check when task is completed, response has changed, or to indicate symptoms or diagnosis.

Note: This material is meant as a checklist for your response. Please keep in mind that it is only a reminder of different tasks that may or may not apply to your incident.

The Goal of Frontline Psychiatric Interventions

The military's expressed goal and purpose for implementing forward psychiatry in warzones is singular—*to preserve manpower in frontline (combat) units. Frontline interventions are not treatment.* Psychotherapy is not considered appropriate by the military for treatment of ASR/COSR until individuals are evacuated away from the front lines of combat and military operations after being deemed as having acute stress injuries too severe to be returned to their units (DoA, 2006).

Military Definitions of Acute Stress-Related Disorders and Syndromes

☐ Acute Stress Reaction (ASR)

A transient condition triggered in response to a traumatic event (e.g., sexual assault, body recovery)

☐ *Combat Stress Reaction (CSR)*

Refers specifically to traumatic war events (e.g., being shot at, witnessing violent death, killing).

☐ COMBAT OPERATIONAL STRESS REACTIONS (COSRS)

Incorporating *normal* universal ASR and CSR responses of human beings adapting to acute combat or *operational* stressors (e.g., family separation, environmental exposure, disaster relief deployments, etc.) lasting between two to five days (DVA/DoD, 2010).

☐ STRESSORS IN THE MILITARY

    ☐ Combat Stressors = single incidents that can impact the unit/individual while performing a military mission

    ☐ Operational Stressors = combat stressors/prolonged exposure to continued operations in hostile environments.

ONSET OF COMMON COSR SYMPTOMS

Table 1   Common Human Stress Response

Physical	Cognitive/Mental	Emotional	Behavioral
☐ Chills	☐ Blaming someone	☐ Agitation	☐ Increased alcohol consumption
☐ Difficulty breathing	☐ Change in alertness	☐ Anxiety	☐ Antisocial acts
☐ Dizziness	☐ Confusion	☐ Apprehension	☐ Change in activity
☐ Elevated bloodpressure	☐ Hypervigilance	☐ Denial	☐ Change in communication
☐ Fainting	☐ Increased or decreased awareness of surroundings	☐ Depression	☐ Change in sexual functioning
☐ Fatigue	☐ Intrusive images	☐ Emotional shock	
☐ Grinding teeth	☐ Memory problems	☐ Fear	☐ Change in speech pattern
☐ Headaches	☐ Nightmares	☐ Feeling overwhelmed	☐ Emotional outbursts
☐ Muscle tremors	☐ Poor abstract thinking	☐ Grief	☐ Inability to rest
☐ Nausea	☐ Poor attention	☐ Guilt	☐ Change in appetite
☐ Pain	☐ Poor concentration	☐ Inappropriate emotional response	☐ Pacing
☐ Profuse sweating	☐ Poor decision making	☐ Irritability	☐ Startle reflex intensified
☐ Rapid heart rate	☐ Poor problem solving	☐ Loss of emotional control	☐ Suspiciousness
☐ Twitches			☐ Social withdrawal
☐ Weakness			

Spiritual or Moral Symptoms

☐ Feelings of despair
☐ Questioning of old religious or spiritual beliefs
☐ Withdrawal from spiritual practice and spiritual community
☐ Sense of the doom about the world and the future (Russell & Figley, 2013)

Positive Stress Reactions and Post-Traumatic Growth

☐ Formation of close, loyal social ties or camaraderie never likely repeated in life (e.g., *"band of brothers" and "band of sisters"*)
☐ Improved appreciation of life
☐ Deep sense of pride (e.g., taking part in history making)
☐ Enhanced sense of unit cohesion, morale, and esprit de corps
☐ Profound satisfaction from personal growth, sacrifice, and mastery after accomplishing one's mission under the most arduous circumstances.

Guiding Principles of Frontline Mental Health Intervention

BICEPS principles:

☐ Brevity (respite of 1–4 days)
☐ Immediacy (when COSR appear)
☐ Contact (maintain identity as soldier vs. patient)
☐ Expectancy (return to full duty)
☐ Proximity (near soldier's unit)
☐ Simplicity (reassure of normality, rest, replenish bodily needs, restore confidence, and return to duty)

It should be noted that BICEPS is an elaboration of an older PIE (proximity, immediacy, expectancy) model, referring to the belief that intervention should take place close to the front, that it should be done early, and with the expectation that the service member would be returning to normal duties rather than being evacuated.

And the 6 Rs:

☐ Reassure of normality (normalize the reaction)
☐ Rest (respite from combat or break from work)
☐ Replenish bodily needs (such as thermal comfort, water, food, hygiene, and sleep);
☐ Restore confidence with purposeful activities and talk
☐ Retain contact with fellow soldiers and unit
☐ Remind/Recognize emotion of reaction (specifically potentially life-threatening thoughts and behaviors)

Proposed Classification Model for Acute Stress Injury Spectrum

Acute Stress Injury Spectrum = clinically significant, neurophysiologically based alterations in adaptive psychological and physical functioning lasting up to three months after exposure to cumulative severe stress or potentially traumatic events. Continuum along an adaptive-maladaptive continuum.

Mild Acute Stress Injury

☐ Brief in duration
☐ Can perform duties under extreme duress/with limitations
☐ Psychotic symptoms, if present, fleeting and remit within days
☐ Suicidal and/or homicidal ideation may be present but fleeting, without intent or plan
☐ No imminent safety risk to self or others
☐ Peri-traumatic dissociation
☐ Post-traumatic anger
☐ Acute depressive reaction
☐ Uncomplicated grief
☐ Guilt
☐ Brief conversion reactions
☐ Diffuse Medically Unexplained Physical Symptoms (MUPS)
☐ Behavioral "acting out" problems
☐ R/O Depressive Disorder Not Otherwise Specified (NOS), Anxiety Disorder NOS, Somatoform Disorders NOS, Eating Disorder NOS, Dissociative Disorder NOS, Substance Misuse, Acute Pain, Atypical Headaches, Insomnia, Essential Hypertension, Irritable Bowel Syndrome, Chronic Fatigue, Fibromyalgia, etc.

Moderate Acute Stress Injury

☐ Persistent, marked ASR/COSR lasting 5 days to 3 months and/or
☐ Intense, moderately debilitating neuropsychiatric and MUPS interfere with ability to fully perform primary duties or obligations, and/or
☐ If present, psychotic symptoms, suicidal/homicidal ideation, panic attacks, traumatic grief/guilt, post-traumatic anger, and MUPS (e.g., sleep disturbance, pain, fatigue) are more persistent (e.g., lasting longer than 5 days), distressing, and intense than "mild," but less debilitating than "severe."
☐ R/O Acute Adjustment Disorder, Acute Stress Disorder, Conversion Disorder, Brief Reactive Psychosis, Substance Abuse, Impulse Control Disorder, Anxiety Disorder, Psychogenic Amnesia, Eating Disorder, and severe MUPS (e.g., pseudo-seizures, sleep disorder, atypical arrhythmia, etc.).

Severe Acute Stress Injury

☐ Longer than one month
☐ If less than one month, symptoms grossly incapacitating, and/or present clear danger to self or others, including attempted suicide or homicide

☐ R/0 Severe Acute Traumatic Grief, Somatoform Disorder, Acute Substance Dependence, Mood Disorder with or without psychotic features, Psychotic Disorder NOS, Acute PTSD, Dissociative Disorder, interpersonal violence including commission of atrocity, and debilitating MUPS (e.g., Anorexia, Non-Cardiac Chest Pain, Lupus, pseudo-dementia, etc.), including possibly premature death (e.g., wasting, suicide)

Early Identification of Acute Stress Injury

Pre-Traumatic Factors

☐ Ongoing life stress
☐ Lack of social support
☐ Young age at time of trauma
☐ Preexisting psychiatric disorders or substance misuse
☐ History of traumatic events (e.g., MVA)
☐ History of post-traumatic stress disorder (PTSD)
☐ Other: female gender, low socioeconomic status, lower level of education, lower level of intelligence, race (Hispanic, African American, American Indian, and Pacific Islander), reported abuse in childhood, report of other previous traumatization, report of other adverse childhood factors, family history of psychiatric disorders, and poor training or preparation for the traumatic event

Peri-Traumatic or Trauma Related Factors

☐ Severe trauma
☐ Physical injury to self or others
☐ Type of trauma (combat, interpersonal traumas such as killing another person, torture, rape, or assault convey high risk of PTSD)
☐ High perceived threat to life of self or others
☐ Community (mass) trauma
☐ Other, including history of peri-traumatic dissociation

Post-Traumatic Factors

☐ Ongoing life stress
☐ Lack of positive social support
☐ Bereavement or traumatic grief
☐ Major loss of resources
☐ Negative social support (shaming or blaming environment)
☐ Poor coping skills
☐ Other post-traumatic factors, including children at home and a distressed spouse.

Screening for Acute Stress Injuries

☐ Acute Stress Disorder

Clinically significant (causing significant distress or impairment in social, occupational, or other important areas of functioning) symptoms more than two days but less than one month after exposure to a trauma, as defined above (may progress to PTSD if symptoms last longer than one month). Symptoms include three dissociative symptoms; reexperiencing of the event; avoidance of stimuli related to trauma; marked symptoms of anxiety or increased arousal

☐ Either while experiencing or after experiencing the distressing event, the individual has at least three dissociative symptoms including numbing, reduced awareness of surrounding, derealization, depersonalization, dissociative amnesia.
☐ The traumatic event is persistently re-experienced in at least one of the following ways: recurrent images, thoughts, dreams, illusions, flashback episodes, or a sense of reliving the experience or distress on exposure to reminders of the traumatic event.

☐ Marked avoidance of stimuli that arouse recollections of the trauma (e.g., thoughts, feelings, conversations, activities, places, people, sounds, smells, or others).

☐ Marked symptoms of anxiety or increased arousal (e.g., difficulty sleeping, irritability, poor concentration, hypervigilance, exaggerated startle response, and motor restlessness).

☐ Acute Post-Traumatic Stress Disorder (PTSD)

Clinically significant symptoms lasting up to three months after exposure to traumatic events that are causing significant distress or impairment in social, occupational, or other important areas of functioning and occur more than one month after exposure to a trauma. Symptoms may include reexperiencing symptoms; avoidance symptoms; hyper-arousal symptoms

☐ *Re-experiencing symptoms:* The traumatic event is persistently re-experienced in one (or more) of the following ways: intrusive recollection of the event, recurring dreams, flashbacks, distress and/or physiological reactivity on exposure to reminders.

☐ *Avoidance symptoms:* Persistent avoidance of stimuli associated with the trauma and numbing of general responsiveness (not present before the trauma), as indicated by three or more of the following: avoidance of reminders, psychogenic amnesia for aspects of the event, diminished interest in activities, social detachment, restricted range of affect, sense of foreshortened future.

☐ *Hyper-arousal symptoms:* Persistent symptoms of increased arousal (not present before the trauma), as indicated by at least two of the following: sleep disturbance, irritability, difficulty concentrating, hyper-vigilance, startle response.

☐ Acute Traumatic Grief Reactions

☐ Reacting with rage at the enemy

☐ Risking their lives with little thought, "gone berserk" or "kill crazy"

☐ Intense agitation

☐ Experiences of shock, disbelief, and self-blame

☐ Self-accusations

☐ High-risk behaviors

☐ Suicidal ideation or attempt

☐ Intense outbursts of anger

☐ Acute psychotic reaction

☐ Making heroic efforts to save or recover bodies

☐ Social withdrawal, becoming loners

☐ Avoiding making any new friends

☐ Extreme anger at the events or people that brought them to the battle

☐ Masking their emotions to avoid a sign of vulnerability or "losing" it

☐ Acute Depression (Risk Factors)

☐ Homesickness from prolonged separation

☐ Feeling overwhelmed from painful war experiences or losses

☐ Feelings of guilt for actions taken (e.g., killing) or not taken

☐ Recent PCS transfer and separation from combat support

☐ Individual mobilization *augmentees* separating from their combat support group to return to their home duty station

☐ Feeling disconnected from others

☐ Sleep deprivation

☐ Interpersonal troubles at home or work

☐ Suicidality

☐ Presence of active depression or psychosis

☐ Presence of substance abuse

☐ Past history of suicidal acts

☐ Formulation of plan
☐ A stated intent to carry out the plan
☐ Feeling that the world would be better off if the patient were dead
☐ Availability of means for suicide (e.g., firearms or pills)
☐ Disruption of an important personal relationship
☐ Failure at an important personal endeavor

☐ Acute Post-Traumatic Anger, Aggression, and Violence

☐ Can be adaptive in warzone
☐ Unregulated can be core maladaptive reaction to trauma and result in uncontrolled behaviors

☐ Acute Stress Injury in the Medically Wounded

Screen when wounded in action (WIA)   ☐ Completed

☐ *Acute Medically Unexplained Symptoms and Pain*

Review medical record, post-deployment health surveys, and medical
treatment history for understanding of client's medical complaints   ☐ Completed

Assess for changes in overall health status before, during, and after
precipitating event   ☐ Completed

☐ *Screening for Pain*

Often association between pain and war stress injuries

☐ *Acute Pain and Prevention of PTSD*

Link between acute pain from physical injury and onset of PTSD (receiving early
treatment makes a difference)

☐ *Acute Sleep Disturbance*

Sleep disturbances can be both a symptom of an underlying health condition (e.g., apnea,
PTSD, depression, compassion fatigue, dementia, etc.) and/or a catalyst for disorder,
especially when persistent (e.g., depression, compassion fatigue, interpersonal violence,
etc.). Chronic sleep deprivation can have a major downhill impact on health.
    Screen for sleep disturbance   ☐ Completed

☐ *Acute Traumatic Brain Injury*

☐ Feeling dizzy
☐ Loss of balance
☐ Poor coordination, clumsy
☐ Headaches
☐ Nausea
☐ Vision problems, blurring, trouble seeing
☐ Sensitivity to light
☐ Hearing difficulty
☐ Sensitivity to noise
☐ Numbness or tingling on parts of my body
☐ Change in taste and/or smell
☐ Loss of appetite or increased appetite
☐ Poor concentration, can't pay attention, easily distracted
☐ Forgetfulness, can't remember things
☐ Difficulty making decisions
☐ Slowed thinking, difficulty getting organized, can't finish things
☐ Fatigue, loss of energy, getting tired easily

☐ Completed
☐ Completed
☐ Difficulty falling or staying asleep
☐ Feeling anxious or tense
☐ Feeling depressed or sad
☐ Irritability, easily annoyed
☐ Poor frustration tolerance, feeling easily overwhelmed by things

☐ Acute Substance Abuse

☐ Screen for Substance Use Disorders "CAGE"   ☐ Completed
☐ Alcohol Use Disorders Identification Test (AUDIT) ☐ Completed

Early Treatment of Acute Stress Injuries Guidelines

☐ Acutely traumatized people, meet the criteria for ASD, significant levels of post-trauma symptoms after at least two weeks post-trauma, and those incapacitated by acute psychological or physical symptoms, should receive further assessment and early intervention to prevent PTSD.

☐ Trauma survivors, symptoms do not meet the diagnostic threshold for ASD, or those recovered from the trauma and currently show no symptoms, should be monitored and may benefit from follow up and provision of ongoing counseling or symptomatic treatment.

☐ Service members with COSR who do not respond to initial supportive interventions may warrant referral or evacuation

Military Treatment Recommendations for Acute Stress Injury

☐ Continue providing psychoeducation and normalization

☐ Treatment should be initiated after education, normalization, and Psychological First Aid have been provided and after basic needs following the trauma have been made available.

Psychotherapy:

- Consider early brief intervention (4 to 5 sessions) of cognitive-based therapy (CBT) that includes exposure-based therapy, alone or combined with a component of cognitive restructuring therapy for patients with significant early symptom levels, especially those meeting diagnostic criteria for ASD.
- Routine formal psychotherapy intervention for asymptomatic individuals is not beneficial and may be harmful.
- Strongly recommend against individual Psychological Debriefing as a viable means of reducing acute stress disorder (ASD) or progression to post-traumatic stress disorder (PTSD).
- The evidence does not support a single session group Psychological Debriefing as a viable means of reducing acute stress disorder (ASD) or progression to posttraumatic stress disorder, but there is no evidence of harm (Note: this is not a recommendation pertaining to Operational Debriefing).

Pharmacotherapy

There is no evidence to support a recommendation for use of a pharmacological agent to prevent the development of ASD or PTSD. There *is* a strong recommendation against the use of benzodiazepines to prevent the development of ASD or PTSD.

Additional Considerations for Managing Acute Stress Disorder

☐ 1. Symptom-specific treatment should be provided after education, normalization, and basic needs are met.

☐ 2. Consider a short course of medication (less than 6 days), targeted for specific symptoms in patients post-trauma:

☐ Sleep disturbance/insomnia
☐ Management of pain
☐ Irritation/excessive arousal/anger.

☐ 3. Provide nonpharmacological intervention to address specific symptoms (e.g., relaxation, breathing techniques, avoiding caffeine) to address both general recovery and specific symptoms (sleep disturbance, pain, hyperarousal, or anger).

☐ 4. Immediately after trauma exposure, preserve an interpersonal safety zone protecting basic personal space (e.g., privacy, quiet, personal effects).

☐ 5. As part of Psychological First Aid, reconnect trauma survivors with previously supportive relationships (e.g., family, friends, command members, etc.) and link with additional sources of interpersonal support.

☐ 6. Assess for impact of PTSD on social functioning.

☐ 7. Facilitate access to social support and provide assistance in improving social functioning, as indicated.

☐ 8. Continue providing psychoeducation and normalization.

☐ 9. EMDR: Per the *2010 VA/DoD Clinical Practice Guidelines*, Cognitive-Behavioral Techniques are the current early intervention of choice. Although the military's practice guidelines do not single out EMDR as an early intervention per se, EMDR is explicitly listed by the guidelines as a trauma-focused "cognitive-behavioral" treatment that is evidence-based for the treatment of traumatic stress injuries. Therefore EMDR is a viable frontline option.

EMDR and Early Intervention in the Military

Seven Considerations for Treatment Planning and Adaptation of EMDR to Military Settings

Consideration 1: Referral Question   ☐ Completed

Reason for referral: _____

_____

_____

Who is concerned about the client's behavior:

_____

Who needs to know client's mental health status (confidentiality): _____

_____

Ramifications for the client: _____

_____

Expected treatment outcome/goal: _____

_____

What type of referral?
☐ *Routine*—non-crisis; no major safety/military fitness for duty implications; intervention within 1 to 14 day standard.
☐ *Emergent*—not presenting in immediate crisis, life threatening, or military fitness for duty issue; moderate to severe range so intervention within 1 to 3 days to prevent potential crisis
☐ *Urgent*—in crisis and/or presents with severe debilitating health and safety condition; *same day* intervention

Consideration 2: Enhancing the Therapeutic Relationship   ☐ Completed

☐ Briefly introduce yourself to the client, stating the reason and source of the referral
☐ Adopt caring stance
☐ Avoid "objective, professional" role
☐ Familiarize yourself with experience of clients
☐ Understand intensity of wartime and military
☐ Ask questions when you don't understand
☐ Be transparent in terms of treatment options
☐ Impart a sense of control/agency critical to establishing trust and rapport

(See Russell & Figley, 2013.)

Consideration 3: Client Treatment Goals—find out client's desired outcome   ☐ Completed

Goal for coming: _____

How would you like things to be different: _____

Outcome of coming for treatment: _____

How will you know when goal achieved: _____

What problems might interfere with goal: _____

What might be negative effects of reaching goal: _____

Consideration 4: Timing and Environmental Constraints   ☐ Completed

☐ Timing: Note the "dwell time" _____

☐ Environmental Constraints: Where is the treatment to occur: _____

☐ Identify 3 affectively charged targets (earliest, worst, most recent) _____

1. Earliest _____

2. Worst _____

3. Most recent _____

☐ Plan for the following:

1. Typical stressors, socio-emotional responses, and coping patterns of personnel and family adapting to _____

2. Offer EMDR?   ☐ Yes ☐ No

3. Type of EMDR Intervention: _____

Consideration 5: Clinical Judgment Regarding Client Safety

After "stopping the psychological bleeding." Get medical clearance and/or issue resolves before working with EMDR with the following: ☐ Completed

☐ *Seizure Disorder*—medical clearance indicated
☐ *Traumatic Brain Injury (TBI)*—EMDR not for acute TBI, for psychologically related issues
☐ *Acute Psychotic Conditions*—only after resolution of psychotic features
☐ *Severe Agitation or Hostility*—would have to stabilize; assess as medical emergency
☐ *Imminent Suicidal or Homicidal Ideation/Attempts*—must assess for current risk to self/others
☐ *Dissociative Disorder*—contact military medical personnel for med evaluation and possible discharge. EMDR only for stabilization/primary symptom reduction
☐ *Medical Issues*—get medical clearance if recent history
☐ *Ethical Issues*—treatment result into return to duty and further exposure

Consideration 6: Suitability for Standard Trauma-Focused EMDR Reprocessing Protocol   ☐ Completed

Four Acute Stress Injury Treatment Goals (Check Appropriate Goal)

TREATMENT GOAL 1: CLIENT STABILIZATION

When intense feelings of panic or grief or severe, debilitating ASR/COSRs and are unstable and/or unresponsive to medical personnel

- ☐ Establish rapport quickly
- ☐ Ensure survivor's safety
- ☐ Acknowledge/validate survivor's experience
- ☐ Offer empathy

Recommended EMDR Stabilization Interventions

- ☐ Emergency Response Procedure (ERP)
- ☐ Eye Movement Desensitization (EMD)
- ☐ Resource Development and Installation (RDI)

TREATMENT GOAL 2: PRIMARY SYMPTOM REDUCTION

Circumstances where comprehensive treatment is precluded:

- ☐ Time-sensitive constraints—impending departure
- ☐ Environmental demands—setting is inappropriate
- ☐ Client-stated treatment goals—patient does not want

Recommended EMDR Stabilization Interventions

- ☐ EMD
- ☐ Modified-EMDR (Mod-EMDR)

TREATMENT GOAL 3: COMPREHENSIVE REPROCESSING—3-PRONGED EMDR PROTOCOL

- ☐ Past Traumatic Events
- ☐ Current Internal or External Triggers/Antecedents
- ☐ Future Template

Recommended EMDR Stabilization Interventions

- ☐ Standard EMDR Protocol (EMDR)
- ☐ Recent Traumatic Events Protocol

TREATMENT GOAL 4: PREVENTION OF COMPASSION STRESS INJURY

Recommended EMDR Stabilization Interventions

- ☐ Standard EMDR Protocol (EMDR)
- ☐ Clinician Self-Care Script

Consideration 7: Utilization of Adjunctive Interventions and Referrel Needs

- ☐ Requires a comprehensive, biopsychosocial (and often spiritual) approach
- ☐ Tactical or Combat Breathing

Descriptions of EMDR Early Intervention Protocol and Scripts (Check Intervention Used)

EMERGENCY RESPONSE PROCEDURE (ERP) SCRIPT—QUINN

Purpose: Stabilization—increase orientation to present focus   ☐ Completed

EYE MOVEMENT DESENSITIZATION (EMD)—RUSSELL

Purpose: Reduction of primary symptoms associated with
precipitating event   ☐ Completed

☐ *Time-frame:* Immediate/near-immediate aftermath of exposure to severe/potentially
   traumatic event
☐ *Client presentation:* Severe, debilitating ASR/COSR

EMD SCRIPT

Phases 1–2: Introduction and Referral
Phase 3: Assessment

   Target/Memory/Image: _____

   NC: _____

   Emotions: _____

   SUD: _____ /10

   Sensation: _____

Phase 4: Desensitization/Reprocessing
Target + NC + Feelings + Location + BLS _____

_____

If a free association unrelated to the precipitating event: Go back to target + What do you
notice?

_____

   SUDs: _____/10 (After each return to target)

   Repeat until SUDs = 0/10 or 1 if ecologically valid

Note: Phases 5–6, Current Triggers and Future Template not included

Phase 7: Closure
Phase 8: Reevaluation
Contact client
   ☐ Additional processing needed/strengthening resilience
   ☐ With consent and stabilization higher level of EMDR intervention

MODIFIED-EMDR (MOD-EMDR)—RUSSELL

Purpose: Reduction of primary symptoms associated with
precipitating event   ☐ Completed

☐ *Time-frame:* Immediate/near-immediate aftermath of exposure to severe/potentially
   traumatic event
☐ *Client presentation:* Severe, debilitating ASR/COSR

Modification of EMDR: Limited to either single-incident target memory/representative
worst memory of event

MODIFIED-EMDR (MOD-EMDR) SCRIPT

Phases 1–2: Introduction and Referral
Phase 3: Assessment
Incident You Brought in or Worst Memory or Cluster of Memories Related to an Event

   Target/Memory/Image: _____

   PC: _____

VoC:_____/7

NC: _____

Emotions: _____

SUD:_____/10

Sensation: _____

Phase 4: Desensitization/Reprocessing
Target + NC + Feelings + Location + BLS _____

_____

If a free association unrelated to the precipitating event: Go back to target + What do you notice? _____

_____

SUDs: _____/10 (After each return to target)

Repeat until SUDs = 0/10 or 1 if ecologically valid

Note: Phases 5–6, Installation, Body Scan, Current Triggers, and Future Template are selected in relation to the target memory and reprocessed accordingly. Adaptive or position free associations may be reinforced outside of target parameters; however, if negative associations arise, client is returned to the target memory. SUDs and VoC are measured in accordance with the Standard EMDR Protocol.

Phase 7: Closure
Phase 8: Reevaluation
Contact client
  ☐ Additional processing needed/strengthening resilience
  ☐ With consent and stabilization higher level of EMDR intervention

PROTOCOL FOR RECENT TRAUMATIC EVENTS SCRIPT (SHAPIRO)

Purpose: Comprehensive reprocessing of acute traumatic events.

Past Memories   ☐ Completed

  ☐ 1. Obtain a *narrative* history of the event, that is, each separate disturbing aspect or moment of the memory. Treat each separate aspect or moment as a separate target with the EMDR Standard Procedure and installation of positive cognition (PC).
  ☐ 2. Target the *most disturbing* aspect or moment of the memory (if necessary) otherwise target events in chronological order.
  ☐ 3. Target the *remainder* of the narrative in chronological order.
  ☐ 4. Have client visualize the *entire sequence* of the event with *eyes closed* and reprocess it as any disturbance arises. The client should have a full association with the material as it is being reprocessed. If there is disturbance, the client should stop and inform the clinician. Then, the EMDR Procedure including the negative cognition (NC) and positive cognition (PC) is implemented. Repeat until the entire event can be visualized from start to finish without emotional, cognitive, or somatic distress.
  ☐ 5. Have client visualize the event from start to finish with eyes open, and install the PC.
  ☐ 6. Conclude with the Body Scan. Only do Body Scan at the end of the processing of *all* of the targets.

Present Triggers   ☐ Completed

☐ 7. Process *present stimuli* that may cause a startle response, nightmares, and other reminders of the event that the client still finds disturbing, if necessary.

Future Template   ☐ Completed

☐ 8. Create a future template.

Note: For clients whose *earlier history* contains unresolved events that are associated with lack of safety and control, a longer treatment may be required.

CLINICIAN SELF-CARE SCRIPT—DANIELS

Purpose: Therapist self-care intervention to prevent cumulative effects of compassion stress that may lead to compassion stress injury such as compassion fatigue or burnout.

☐ Ask the client to bring up the image of the patient and do BLS.
☐ Notice whatever positive cognitions come to mind.
☐ Install the positive cognition with the patient's image and do BLS.
☐ Notice what happens.

CREATING RESOURCES

Purpose: If the client is unable to reprocess due to temporary time constraints, emotional or behavioral instability, or poor self-regulation skills, an access to adaptive, coping resources is needed.

RDI   ☐ Completed
Other Resources: _____

Consideration 7: Utilization of Any Adjunctive Intervention and Referral Need

Be familiar with military support services and agencies   ☐ Completed

COMBAT/TACTICAL BREATHING SCRIPT

Purpose: To rapidly gain control over body's acute stress response and adrenaline rush even in high stress and hostile environments

Say, *"Breathe in through your nose with a slow count of four (two, three, four)."*

The therapist can have clients place a hand on their stomach to see if they are properly filling the diaphragm with air, as evident when their stomach and hand rise.

Say, *"Place your hand on your stomach, as you breathe in through your nose to the count of four and notice your stomach and hand rise."*

Say, *"Hold your breath for a slow count of four (Hold, two, three, four)."*

Say, *"Now, exhale through your mouth for a count of four until all the air is out (two, three, four)."*

Client's hand should lower as the stomach lowers.

Say, *"Now, notice how your hand lowers as your stomach lowers."*

Say, *"Hold empty for a count of four (Hold, two, three, four)."*

Then repeat the cycle three times.

EMDR Early Intervention for Special Situations

EMDR can be helpful in many types of special situations. In this section of the book, we focus on underground traumas for mining and related trauma and how to work with people who would prefer not to divulge information about the nature of their particular trauma.

When the term "mine disaster" is used, it means that the mining accident resulted in the deaths of five or more lives. Although there have been decades of research, technology, and preventive programs, and although mine disasters have declined over the years, they still occur. In 2010, we remember the 33 Chilean miners who were trapped underground for 4 months before they were rescued, or the 2002 Quecreek, Pennsylvania, disaster where nine miners were trapped underground and subsequently saved after 78 hours. There are many other mining disasters where there were no survivors at all, leaving families, friends, and fellow miners grief stricken and mourning.

David Blore introduces us to this facet of the earth that exists underground. These types of situations demand a different vocabulary and way of viewing the world. He takes us below the surface of the earth into the depths of mines, tunnels, caves, and other underground areas. David has provided EMDR to miners from the early 1990s and has put together a modified EMDR protocol that he calls "The Underground Trauma Protocol (UTP)." In fact, David himself has mining experience. He made his first trip down a 700-meter shaft with a miner who had a fear of heights. The colliery manager in charge was so impressed by his effort to return this miner to work that he inscribed a pewter tankard for him (Luber, Match, 1998)!

As in any area where there are specific circumstances, it is the practitioner's job to understand the nature of the environment in which clients find themselves when experiencing the trauma. People who work underground have a different experience of trauma than those who are above ground. To understand our clients who work underground, we need to appreciate this world and the types of experiences our clients have, before we can have a meaningful interchange with them. In these situations, traumatized individuals speak about heat, darkness, and disorientation and they are concerned about the "integrity" of the underground environment. Their concerns are different and in his chapter, "EMDR for Mining and Related Trauma: The Underground Trauma Protocol," David sensitizes us to the kinds of language and situations that are meaningful when talking to clients with underground trauma occurrences.

Out of experiences working with miners and related trauma, David often found that his clients were uncomfortable talking about their memories when they came into direct conflict with the type of person they expected themselves to be. By initially asking them to talk about memories as A, B, C, and so on, he went on to create the "Blind to Therapist Protocol."

Summary sheets accompany each of these chapters, to remind us of the salient points in the chapter and to provide a place to enter our data.

Knowing the language to assist in treating underground traumas will be useful to those therapists with clients in these situations. This is important when working with any new group of people who have their own community. Whether they base it on religious beliefs, cultural values, and/or professional culture, we always need to make sure that we understand what our clients are saying to us. At other times, however, it is helpful to know that, if a client is reticent or fearful of divulging information to us for any reason, the EMDR "Blind to Therapist Protocol" is available for our use.

EMDR for Mining and Related Trauma: The Underground Trauma Protocol

David Blore

Introduction

David Blore has now been providing EMDR to traumatized miners since 1993. As with other specialized client groups, the Single Trauma Protocol (STP) and Recent Trauma Protocol (RTP) have required modifications. The author has collated the modifications made, and presented them here as the Underground Trauma Protocol (UTP). The UTP is intended to provide a rapid and effective method of conducting EMDR with traumatized miners and other similar, very specific, client groups.

The Underground Trauma Protocol Script Notes

The principal use of the UTP is for traumatized miners of coal, gold, nickel, gems, and so forth. It has also been used with the following populations: traumatized tunnelers (e.g., excavators of tunnels in both war and peace); those traumatized in rail accidents in tunnels (e.g., fire in Channel Tunnel, Kings Cross tube fire); those traumatized in underground leisure pursuits (e.g., exploration of caves, pot holing); those traumatized by being trapped (e.g., in collapsed buildings as in Turkish earthquakes); and those traumatized during 9/11 in New York and the 7/7 bombings in London.

There are three golden rules to follow when working with traumatized miners.

1. If possible, visit a coal mine and check out the underground environment for yourself—there's nothing better for getting an idea of working conditions and increasing your standing among the miners themselves, as well as picking up some of the jargon.
2. *Always* remember that the underground environment is *totally different* from a trauma on the surface. The environment can be *so* different it is difficult to believe you are on planet Earth!
3. *Never* underestimate the significance of *heat* in relation to traumatic memories of the underground environment.

The author recommends that the treatment of this client group only be undertaken by fully trained EMDR clinicians who have experience with modifying protocols and clinical experience using cognitive interweave. In addition to Shapiro's instructions (Shapiro, 2001), it is important to cover the following points for miners.

Important information to ask for during history taking is clarification of how much of the underground environment was involved in the incident. *Integrity* of the underground environment refers to the whole underground environment, not just the immediate site of the incident in question. It is important to remember that the underground environment is not like the surface; it is a world in miniature. If the integrity of the underground environment is affected, in essence the whole underground world is affected.

Checking whether safety procedures were followed is important. In the United Kingdom, this information can be gleaned after investigations via Her Majesty's Mines Inspectorate. Her Majesty's Mines Inspectorate comes under Health and Safety Executive (HSE) www .hse.gov.uk; when on the website, do a search for Her Majesty's Mines Inspectorate. Other countries have equivalent systems. Another good place to look in the U.S. Department of Labor Web site: www.msha.gov, as it covers mining safety organizations in 17 countries.

During the Assessment Phase, use the Standard Trauma Protocol (STP) for all memories, *except for those below ground*. As a result of the author's experience, an efficient order of tackling targets is the following: heat, darkness, and then disorientation. This probably because they are related to fear (thus negative affect), which in turn relates to survival.

For underground memories, target the "hottest" or most affect-laden first or use the Recent Trauma Protocol, starting with the memories below ground. For underground memories, target the memories of the actual event in the following order: associated heat, associated darkness, and associated disorientation.

Note: For the miner, "hottest" means the most affect-laden and "cool" is the equivalent of relaxed or chilled out. In fact, SUDs can become SUTs (Subjective Units of Temperature Scale), if necessary.

> Say, *"On a scale of 0 to 10 where 0 is cool or cold and 10 is the hottest you can imagine. . . ."*

Some useful process material can be gleaned from Blore (1997). Bear in mind that images specifically relating to damage to the integrity of the underground environment are frequently associated with a tactile sense of heat. These memories can be very intense and distressing to recall and can challenge the strongest machismo. Emotions are a foreign commodity to most miners and these memories feature in virtually all underground memory abreactions. All *other* abreactions generally relate to subsequent above ground events such as attending colleagues' funerals, for example, of which there can be many.

Since miners are medically checked regularly, they are not going to be physically weak, but their pretrauma beliefs are likely to be inaccurate. It is very common for miners to have given no thought whatsoever—prior to an accident—to the potential for disaster (e.g., when there is a mile of rock above you). On the other hand, most miners can expect injuries at some time in their working life, but generally not to the extent that they will realize their invulnerability belief exists or needs to be challenged. Miners are known for having no cognitions; so it does help to be mindful of these points when it comes to treating them.

Related to the previous comments is the issue of the client identifying memories that clash with perceived machismo. One way around this is to initially label memories A, B, C, and so on. Although this may smack of covert avoidance to the cognitive-behavioral among us, EMDR is the only psychotherapy that the author knows of that can be conducted blind to even the therapist. The author considers that it is a means to an end. If images can be readily and rapidly treated this way, there is no reason why later on some judicious cognitive therapy cannot be added to the EMDR to challenge belief structures. Shapiro frequently tells us that EMDR is not a stand-alone treatment and that it should be part of an overall therapeutic program.

The Underground Trauma Protocol Script

Phase 1: Client History

When working with clients presenting with underground trauma, there are important types of information that are crucial to creating effective case conceptualization and treatment.

> Say, *"During the traumatic event was there damage to the integrity of the underground environment? For instance, did the traumatic event damage a*

significant part of the underground environment such as a roof collapse or affect a component of the working environment that could affect the entire environment as in damage to ventilation or airflow?"

_____

_____

_____

If the answer is yes, the following are the types of events to look for:

1. Roof collapse or cave-in
2. Gas blowout (fractured pocket of gas under high compression)
3. Oil inrush (fractured pocket of oil under high compression)
4. Explosion, fire, or major disruption to airflow
5. Major equipment failures
6. Some "tripping-out" incidents (e.g., failure in situ of winding gear)

If one of the above occurred, proceed to Question 3.

In complex traumas—at a colliery—it is helpful to obtain a sketch of the underground layout and identify the direction of airflow prior to the traumatic event. Then, estimate how long the client had been underground and, if possible, how much fluid the client consumed during the time underground.

If the answer is no, it is likely that the trauma involved a very local incident, possibly even a single coal miner in a specific situation, then ask the following:

Say, *"During the traumatic event if there was no damage to the integrity of the underground environment, what happened?"*

_____

_____

_____

_____

These are the types of events that can occur:

1. Fatal accident (client in immediate proximity of fatal event)
2. Serious injury to colleague
3. First aid responsibilities to colleague (successful or otherwise)
4. Serious injury to self
5. Dehydration is another factor unique to the underground environment. The possibility of dehydration is ever-present because of geothermal issues, the use of underground equipment, the depth of mining level and/or inadequate fluid intake during heavy manual work. Dehydration can alter memory quality and become a small trauma on its own. Also dehydration relates to heat and heat (see later) communicates trauma around the underground environment.
6. Witness to extreme anxiety in another miner (including panic attacks underground)
7. Other personal incidents (unless widespread such as in "tripping-out")

Now ask the following questions, tailored to the specific event just identified:

Say, *"How, specifically, did you become aware of the traumatic event?"*

_____

_____

Note: Heat, or sudden rise in environmental temperature underground, is thus a "language of trauma" and a potential treatment target in itself. Clinical experience seems to suggest that the heat sensation relates to increasing ambient temperature brought about by disruption to underground airflow management. This means that a major accident can, and is, communicated around the underground environment by means of methods other than direct verbal communication. In addition, increase in heat can increase the risk of dehydration, which can also bring about distortions to memories. Consequently miners who were underground at the time of the accident, yet who were neither in the direct vicinity of the accident nor involved in the rescue, can easily have traumatic memories characterized by a sensation of heat. It is possible to assess to what extent this was a problem at the time by reviewing underground site plans that usually contain information about airflow.

Say, *"Was there an increase in environmental temperature?"*

_____

_____

Say, *"What were the reactions of your colleagues?"*

_____

_____

Note: Memories of smells can be particularly resistant memories and seem to play a large part in reactivating traumatic memories at a later date. Large quantities of disinfectant can be used (even pumped through airflow systems) to mask smells of decomposition—rescue working conditions are already hampered by rapid decomposition because of increased temperatures and humidity. Unfortunately, what helps to facilitate rescue working conditions at the time ends up being part of the traumatic memory repertoire that requires treatment. More problematic still are the actual images themselves that can easily seem to produce evidence that the client didn't cope.

Say, *"Were there any changes in smells?"*

_____

_____

Note: Disruption to airflow throughout the underground tunnels during a major traumatic event very quickly communicates the trauma around the underground tunnels, in some instances several miles underground.

Say, *"Were there any changes in airflow?"*

_____

_____

Say, *"Were there any other changes that you noticed?"*

_____

_____

Say, *"What other things did you notice that were not from what others told you?"*

_____

_____

Note: Communications themselves are traumatic and damage to the underground environment may mean that low-tech methods of communication (word of mouth) predominate until communication can be restored. In the meanwhile, something similar to the games "Chinese whispers" or "telephone" can result in unintentional secondary traumas.

Say, *"Were there things that people told you that bothered you and that you cannot get out of your mind?"*

_____

_____

Say, *"At the time, what was your perception of what happened?"*

_____

_____

Note: A perennial problem underground is dust. Coal dust mixed with air is a highly explosive cocktail. The problem is kept under control in coal mines by mixing the coal dust and air with stone dust. However, this can't be controlled during a major incident such as a roof collapse. The amount of dust is vast and tends to obscure vision in the disaster site. The degree of lack of visibility thus indicates proximity to the primary site of the disaster.

Say, *"Was it that you did not see what happened through a loss of visibility or are you unable to recall what happened?"*

_____

_____

Say, *"What were you doing at the time?"*

_____

_____

Say, *"What had been your work instructions?"*

_____

_____

Say, *"Who gave you those instructions?"*

_____

_____

Note: Perhaps "location" should be "distance from the shaft" as the farther from the shaft, the longer underground the traumatized miner is likely to be. Remaining effectively trapped underground—even if not physically injured—can greatly intensify the trauma. It therefore follows that the farther from the shaft a traumatized miner is, the more dehydrated he is likely to be. Clearly the question on losing track of time and disorientation will assist the history taking.

Say, *"Where were you underground?"*

_____

_____

Note: United Kingdom rules on the wearing of equipment including watches and carrying cigarette lighters (obviously) underground are very strictly enforced—loss of time is easy with no access to daylight and is even worse during emotionally charged situations such as mines rescue work.

Say, *"At any point, did you lose track of time or were you disoriented?"*

_____

_____

Say, *"Do you have any images associated with 'heat'?"*

See earlier explanation about the important role of heat in mining disaster memories.

_____

_____

Note: Coal miners are an extremely close-knit community, much more so than virtually all other occupational groups with the possible exception of the armed forces. Often dads and sons may work together—thus emotional ties form a critical mass to the trauma itself.

Say, *"Did you know the individual(s) involved personally?"*

_____

_____

Note: Under normal circumstances, underground miners often work in small teams. They rely upon each other, but small incidents may cause serious injuries to others. If memories are associated with guilt, it may well be because the individual miner feels personally responsible for his colleagues' injuries. During mine rescue work where time is of the essence, corners can be cut in practice for the sake of the rescue. In either case, Her Majesty's Mines Inspectorate will hold an inquiry and interview each person involved—this can also be a traumatic experience. Knowing whether relevant procedures were or were not followed will help identify all manner of secondary and subsequent issues, even secondary gain.

Say, *"Were there specific safety procedures being followed?"*

_____

_____

Say, *"How long were you underground?"*

_____

_____

Say, *"Approximately how much fluid did you consume during the time underground?"*

_____

_____

Note: Miners worldwide have a reputation for alcohol consumption. The author has encountered miners who consume well over 200 + units (a unit is defined as 10 milliliters/ 8 grams of ethanol) per week. They have built an enormous tolerance to alcohol. It is unrealistic in many cases to ask them to cut down on alcohol consumption prior to EMDR. However, this subject should be addressed as alcohol comes as a very natural method of blotting out traumatic memories.

Say, *"What is the approximate minimum number of drinks you consume in an average working week?"*

_____

_____

Say, *"What is the approximate maximum number of drinks you consume in an average working week?"*

_____

_____

Say, *"How frequently do you drink the maximum?"*

_____

_____

Note: Also, miners may hugely underestimate other coping strategies such as smoking. They can't smoke underground so asking how much is smoked will not help. Ask if they chew tobacco or take snuff or both while working. This may be important, as there is anec-dotal evidence that snuff can also mask smells.

Say, *"Do you chew tobacco while working? If so, in what quantity?"*

_____

_____

Say, *"Do you take snuff while working? If so, in what quantity?"*

_____

_____

Ask any other questions deemed appropriate here that are important for the therapist's history taking.

Phase 2: Preparation

Forming a Bond With the Client

If at all possible, familiarize yourself with the basics of mining jargon. Just as languages vary worldwide, so does jargon. If you don't understand a term, ask. This is important to your clients' faith in your ability to understand who they are and what they have been through.

Alcohol should not be consumed on the day of the EMDR session—this author once had a miner who had convinced me he had not drunk any alcohol that day and who sub-sequently lost his balance while tracking eye movements and fell off the seat (fortunately without injury)!

The Safe Place for Miners Script

Safe places involving images relating to fishing, the family, open air, sunlight, gardening, and holidays were the most popular among a group of 20+ miners treated. One miner picked being a mile underground at a colliery with a better safety record as his safe place image, but this had to be replaced!

IMAGE

Say, *"I'd like you to think about some place you have been or imagine being that feels very safe or calm. Perhaps being on holiday somewhere or doing something relaxing such as gardening or fishing."* (Pause) *"What might you be doing?"*

_____

_____

EMOTIONS AND SENSATIONS

Say, *"As you think of that safe* (or calm) *place or activity, notice what you see, hear, and feel right now."* (Pause) *"What do you notice?"*

_____

_____

ENHANCEMENT

Say, *"Focus on your safe* (or calm) *place or activity, its sights, sounds, smells, and body sensations. Tell me more about what you are noticing."*

_____

_____

BILATERAL STIMULATION (BLS)

Say, *"Bring up the image of that place or activity. Concentrate on where you feel the pleasant sensations in your body and allow yourself to enjoy them. Now concentrate on those sensations and follow my fingers* (or whatever BLS you use)."

_____

_____

Use four to six sets.

Say, *"How do you feel now?"*

_____

_____

Repeat several times if the process has enhanced the client's positive feelings and sensations.

If positive, say the following:

Say, *"Focus on that."*

Repeat BLS.

Say, *"What do you notice now?"*

_____

_____

CUE WORD

Note: An interesting choice of cue word that cropped up from time to time was "cool" or even "cold"—especially given the importance of "heat" in the traumatic memories described earlier.

Say, *"Is there a word or phrase that represents your safe* (or calm) *place or activity?"*

_____

_____

Then say, *"Think of_____*(cue word) *and notice the positive feelings you have when you think of that word. Now concentrate on those sensations and the cue word and follow_____*(state BLS using)."

Use short sets (four to six) of BLS with any positive responses.

Say, *"How do you feel now?"*

_____

_____

Repeat several times. Enhance positive feelings with BLS several times.

SELF-CUING

Say, *"Now I'd like you to say that word _____* (cue word) *and notice how you feel."*

_____

_____

CUING WITH DISTURBANCE

Say, *"Now imagine a minor annoyance and how it feels."* (Pause)

_____

_____

Say, *"Now bring up your safe* (or calm) *place or activity _____ and notice any shifts in your body."*

_____

_____

Do BLS.

Guide the client through the process until he is able to experience the positive emotions and sensations. Repeat as often as necessary.

SELF-CUING WITH DISTURBANCE

Say, *"Now I'd like you to think of another mildly annoying incident and bring up your safe* (or calm) *place or activity by yourself, again, especially noticing any changes in your body when you have gone to your safe* (or calm) *place."*

PRACTICE

Say, *"I'd like you to practice using your safe place or activity, between now and our next session, any time you feel a little annoyed. Keep track of how things go and we'll talk about it next time we meet."*

Past Memories

Phase 3: Assessment

Above Ground Trauma Targets

Use the Standard Trauma Protocol (STP) for all memories, *except for those below ground* (see below). For above ground trauma related to underground events, tackle targets according to the following order: heat, darkness, and then disorientation.

Say, *"Let's list the issues we are going to tackle according to how hot they are, for instance on a scale from 0 to 10 where 0 = Cold memories or no sense of heat; 10 = Hottest memories of all."*

0   1   2   3   4   5   6   7   8   9   10
(cold memories or no sense of heat)   (highest disturbance)

"Let's start with the hottest problem and then all those that follow."

_____

_____

_____

_____

_____

_____

Incident

When a picture is unavailable, Shapiro advises the clinician to have the client "think of the incident." An alternative, and one that in the past this author has used instead of locating any picture, is the following:

Say, *"Think of anything you remember about the accident that is hot* (failing this, substitute hot with dark or disorientated)*."*

_____

_____

Note: See Phase 1 above, relating to memories associated with heat.

Picture

Say, *"What image represents the worst part of the memory or incident?"*

_____

_____

Negative Cognition (NC)

Mining still has a huge machismo problem and it can hamper rapid treatment if the client feels he must identify perceived failings such as admission of certain negative cognitions. The following have been the negative cognitions most encountered clinically:

"I am useless."
"I am worthless."
"I am weak."
"I'm a waste of space."
"I can't cope."
"I let my colleagues down."

Say, *"What words go best with the picture that express your negative belief about yourself now?"*

_____

_____

Positive Cognition (PC)

Say, *"When you bring up that picture or incident, what would you like to believe about yourself now?"*

_____

_____

Validity of Cognition (VoC)

Say, *"When you think of the incident* (or picture), *how true do those words*
_____(clinician repeats the positive cognition) *feel to you now on a scale of*
1 to 7, where 1 feels completely false and 7 feels completely true?"

1   2   3   4   5   6   7
(completely false)   (completely true)

Emotions

Say, *"When you bring up the picture* (or incident) *and those words*_____
(clinician states the negative cognition), *what emotion do you feel now?"*

_____

_____

Subjective Units of Disturbance (SUD)

ADAPTING THE SUD SCALE TO THE MINER POPULATION

There is no reason to stick with "distress" as the criterion for your SUD scales. Others may
be more appropriate; try any of these suggestions:

0 = Cold memories or no sense of heat;   10 = Hottest memories of all
0 = Light memories (e.g., daylight);   10 = Very dark memories (i.e., zero visibility)
0 = Normal size or oriented content;   10 = Very large or completely disorientated
                                              content

Say, *"On a scale of 0 to 10, where 0 is*_____(state scale using: no disturbance,
cold memories, no sense of heat, light memories as in daylight, normal
size, or oriented content) *or neutral and 10 is the*_____ (state scale using: highest disturbance, hottest memory of all, very dark memories with
zero visibility, very large, or completely disorientated content) *that you can
imagine. How*_____(disturbing, hot, dark, large, or disorientated) *does it
feel to you* now?"

0   1   2   3   4   5   6   7   8   9   10
(no disturbance)   (highest disturbance)

Location of Body Sensation

Say, *"Where do you feel it* (the disturbance) *in your body?"*

_____

_____

After this list is processed, using Phases 4 to 7, go on to the next list if it is necessary.

Say, *"Let's list the issues we are going to tackle according to how dark they are,
for instance, on a scale from 0 to 10 (0 = Light memories [e.g., daylight];
10 = Very dark memories [i.e., zero visibility])."*

0   1   2   3   4   5   6   7   8   9   10
(light memories)   (very dark memories)

"Let's start with the darkest problem and then all those that follow."

_____

_____

_____

_____

_____

After this list is processed, using Phases 4 to 7, go on to the next list if it is necessary.

Say, *"Let's list the issues we are going to tackle according to how disorientated they feel, for instance, on a scale from 0 to 10 where 0 = Normal size or oriented content* (10 = Very large or completely disorientated content)."

0	1	2	3	4	5	6	7	8	9	10

(normal size or oriented)   (very large or completely disorientated content)

"Let's start with the most disorientated problem and then all those that follow."

Use Phases 4 to 7 of the Standard EMDR Protocol to process this list completely.

_____

_____

_____

_____

_____

_____

Underground Trauma Memory Targets. For underground memories, target the "hottest" or most affect-laden first or use the Recent Trauma Protocol, starting with the memories below ground. When targeting the actual event, use the following order: associated heat, associated darkness, and associated disorientation. See above for scripts.

Phase 4: Desensitization

Present Triggers

Use the Standard EMDR Protocol format for the past memories and any present triggers. The latter can include many current problems including news broadcasts, changes in circumstances relating to any injury, changes in income, loss of contact with colleagues, issues relating to being trapped, the post-incident inquiry, or merely uncertainty about the future and so on.

Future Template

Regarding the future template, it is useful to know the miner's intentions. Is he returning to work underground, working as redeployed to surface work, or leaving mining altogether? It is likely that a single image will be insufficient if the miner is returning to work underground because the process of returning is complicated so installing the future template as multiple images in the form of a video can be useful.

If the miner is returning to surface working or leaving mining altogether, use the standard future template with a single image of coping or readjusting.

If the miner is returning to underground work in the mine, do the following:

Say, *"Which of the following elements of your return to work underground create anxiety when you think of them now?"*

- Sight of the headstocks to the colliery (the headstock is the visible—sometimes from several miles—metal structure usually with a single, large cable winding-wheel showing at the top)
- Clothing and equipment
- Top of shaft (sometimes called the tally room)
- Descending or ascending in the cage (also called the chair—the term for the lift in the shaft)
- The shaft bottom
- Underground transport (underground trains are sometimes referred to as Paddys)
- Coal face itself or other working location
- Other aspects of working underground, particularly any awareness of increases in temperature

Image as a Future Template

Identify each component and desensitize as per normal as follows:

Say, *"I would like you to imagine yourself coping effectively with_____(insert item from list above) in the future. With the positive belief_____and your new sense of_____(i.e., strength, clarity, confidence, calm), imagine stepping into this scene.*
Notice what you see and how you are handling the situation.
Notice what you are thinking, feeling, and experiencing in your body.
Are there any blocks, anxieties, or fears that arise as you think about this future scene?"

_____

_____

_____

_____

If yes, say the following:

Say, *"Then focus on these blocks and follow my fingers* (or any other BLS)."

If the blocks do not resolve quickly, evaluate if the client needs any new information, resources, or skills to be able to comfortably visualize the future coping scene. Introduce needed information or skills.

Say, *"What would you need to feel confident in handling the situation?"*
Or say, *"What is missing from your handling of this situation?"*

_____

_____

If the block still does not resolve and the client is unable to visualize the future scene with confidence and clarity, use direct questions, the Affect Scan, or the Float-Back Technique to identify old targets related to blocks, anxieties, or fears. Use the EMDR Standard Protocol to address these targets before proceeding with the template. (See Worksheets in the Appendix.)

When there are no apparent blocks and the client is able to visualize the future scene with confidence and clarity, say the following:

Say, *"Please focus on the image, the positive belief, and the sensations associated with this future scene and follow my fingers* (or any other BLS)."

Do several sets until the future template is sufficiently strengthened.

Then say, *"Close your eyes and keep in mind the experience that you will have in the future. Then bring your attention to the different parts of your body, starting with your head and working downward. Any place you find any tension, tightness, or unusual sensation, tell me."*

_____

_____

If any sensation is reported, do BLS.

If it is a positive or comfortable sensation, do BLS to strengthen the positive feelings.

If a sensation of discomfort is reported, reprocess until the discomfort subsides. Check the VoC.

Say, *"When you think of the incident* (or picture) *how true do those words _____(clinician repeats the positive cognition) feel to you now on a scale of 1 to 7, where 1 feels completely false and 7 feels completely true?"*

1   2   3   4   5   6   7
(completely false)   (completely true)

Movie as a Future Template

Next, ask the client to move from imagining one scene or snapshot to imagining a movie about coping in the future, with a beginning, middle, and end. Encourage him to imagine coping effectively in the face of specific challenges or triggers. Make some suggestions to help inoculate him for future problems.

Say, *"This time, I'd like you to close your eyes and play a movie, imagining yourself coping effectively with_____(state where client will be) in the future. With the new positive belief_____(state positive belief) and your new sense of_____(strength, clarity, confidence, calm), imagine stepping into the future. Imagine yourself coping with ANY challenges that come your way. Make sure that this movie has a beginning, a middle, and an end. Notice what you are seeing, thinking, feeling, and experiencing in your body. Let me know if you hit any blocks. If you do, just open your eyes and let me know. If you don't hit any blocks, let me know when you have viewed the whole movie."*

_____

_____

If the client hits blocks, address as above with BLS, interweaves, new skills, information, resources, direct questions, Affect Scan, Float-Back, and so forth.

If the client is able to play the movie from start to finish with a sense of confidence and satisfaction, ask the client to play the movie one more time from beginning to end and introduce BLS. In a sense, you are installing this movie as a future template.

Say, *"Okay, play the movie one more time from beginning to end. Go with that."*

Phase 5: Installation

Say, *"How does_____(repeat the PC) sound?"*

_____

_____

Say, "Do the words_____(repeat the PC) *still fit, or is there another positive statement that feels better?"*

_____

_____

If the client accepts the original positive cognition, the clinician should ask for a VoC rating to see if it has improved.

Say, "As you think of the incident, how do the words feel, from 1 (completely false) to 7 (completely true)?"

1   2   3   4   5   6   7
(completely false)   (completely true)

Say, "Think of the event, and hold it together with the words_____ (repeat the PC)."

Do a long set of BLS to see if there is more processing to be done.

Phase 6: Body Scan

Say, *"Close your eyes and keep in mind the original memory and the positive cognition. Then bring your attention to the different parts of your body, starting with your head and working downward. Any place you find any tension, tightness, or unusual sensation, tell me."*

_____

_____

Phase 7: Closure

Say, *"Things may come up or they may not. If they do, great. Write it down, and it can be a target for next time. If you get any new memories, dreams, or situations that disturb you, just take a good snapshot. It isn't necessary to give a lot of detail. Just put down enough to remind you so we can target it next time. The same thing goes for any positive dreams or situations. If negative feelings do come up, try not to make them significant. Remember, it's still just the old stuff. Just write it down for next time. Then use the tape or the Safe Place exercise to let as much of the disturbance go as possible. Even if nothing comes up, make sure to use the tape every day and give me a call if you need to."*

Phase 8: Reevaluation

It is important to pay attention to the following questions when the client returns after doing EMDR work.

Say, *"When you think of whatever is left of the problem that we worked on last time, how disturbing is it now on a scale of 0 to 10, where 0 is no disturbance or neutral and 10 is the highest disturbance you can imagine, how disturbing does it feel now?"*

0   1   2   3   4   5   6   7   8   9   10
(no disturbance)   (highest disturbance)

Say, *"Have you noticed any other material associated with the original memory since the last session?"*

_____

_____

_____

Say, *"Have all the necessary targets been reprocessed so that you can feel at peace with the past, empowered in the present, and able to make choices for the future?"*

_____

_____

_____

Say, *"Has the work that we have done with EMDR helped you be more adaptive in your day-to-day life?"*

_____

_____

_____

The author welcomes feedback on use of the Underground Trauma Protocol. If using this protocol, free help is available via e-mail: help@davidblore.co.uk

SUMMARY SHEET:
EMDR for Mining and Related Trauma:
The Underground Trauma Protocol

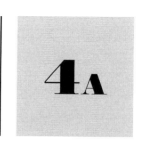

David Blore
SUMMARY SHEET BY MARILYN LUBER

Name: _____ Diagnosis: _____

Medications: _____

Test Results: _____

☑ Check when task is completed, response has changed, or to indicate symptoms.

Note: This material is meant as a checklist for your response. Please keep in mind that it is only a reminder of different tasks that may or may not apply to your incident.

Phase 1: Client History Taking

Important Information Crucial for Case Conceptualization and Treatment

1. Damage to integrity of underground environment

   - Roof collapse or cave in ☐ Yes ☐ No _____ Time

   - Gas blowout ☐ Yes ☐ No _____ Time

   - Oil inrush ☐ Yes ☐ No _____ Time

   - Explosion, fire/disruption to airflow ☐ Yes ☐ No _____ Time

   - Major equipment failures ☐ Yes ☐ No _____ Time

   - "Tripping-out" incidents ☐ Yes ☐ No _____ Time

   If yes, go to #3.

   Obtain sketch or underground layout, identify airflow prior to event ☐ Completed

   Client underground: ☐ Hours ☐ Days ☐ Weeks ☐ Months

   Fluid consumed: _____ ozs/mL/ ☐ Other

2. If no damage to integrity of underground environment, what happened?

   - Fatal accident ☐ Yes ☐ No _____ Time

   - Serious injury to colleague ☐ Yes ☐ No _____ Time

   - First aid responsibilities to colleague ☐ Yes ☐ No _____ Time

   - Serious injury to self ☐ Yes ☐ No _____ Time

   - Dehydration ☐ Yes ☐ No _____ Time

- Witness to extreme anxiety in another miner   ☐ Yes ☐ No _____ Time
- Other personal incidents   ☐ Yes ☐ No _____ Time

3. How specifically became aware of traumatic event: _____

_____

4. Increase in environmental temperature: ☐ Yes ☐ No _____ Time
5. Colleague reactions: _____

_____

6. Changes in smells: ☐ Yes ☐ No _____ Time
7. Changes in airflow: ☐ Yes ☐ No _____ Time
8. Other changes noticed: _____

_____

9. Other things noticed that were not from what others told you: _____

_____

10. Bothersome words or words sticking in mind: ☐ Yes ☐ No _____ Time

_____

11. Your perception of what happened: _____

_____

12. Recall: Did not see (lack of visibility)   ☐ Yes ☐ No

    No recall   ☐ Yes ☐ No

13. Doing at time of incident: _____

_____

14. Work instructions: _____

_____

15. Person who gave instructions _____
16. Location underground (distance from shaft): _____
17. Lost track of time/disoriented: ☐ Yes ☐ No _____ Time
18. Images associated with heat: _____

_____

19. Know individuals personally: ☐ Yes ☐ No
20. Specific safety procedures followed: ☐ Yes ☐ No
21. Underground: _____Hours _____Days _____Weeks _____Months
22. Fluid consumed: _____ozs/mL/ccm/_____ Other
23. Minimum number of alcoholic drinks consumed in average working week: _____minimum drinks consumed
24. Maximum number of alcoholic drinks consumed in average working week: _____maximum drinks consumed
25. Frequency of maximum alcoholic drinks consumed: _____
26. Chew tobacco while working: ☐ Yes ☐ No   Amount: _____
27. Snuff while working: ☐ Yes ☐ No   Amount: _____

Phase 2: Preparation

☐ Therapist understands basic mining jargon
☐ No alcohol on day of EMDR

The Safe Place for Miners Script

Safe Place Installed: □ Completed

SAFE PLACE: _____

      Image: _____

EMOTIONS AND SENSATIONS: _____

      See: _____

      Hear: _____

      Feel/Body Sensations: _____

      Smells: _____

ENHANCEMENT (Safe Place + Sights + Sounds + Smells + Body Sensations + Notice)

      Notice: _____

    Image + Location of Pleasant Sensations + Enjoy + BLS (repeat several times):

    _____

    _____

CUE WORD FOR SAFE/CALM PLACE: _____

      Cue Word + Positive Feelings + BLS (repeat several times):

      Notice: _____

SELF CUE + FEELINGS (NOTICE): _____

MINOR ANNOYANCE: _____

      Feelings: _____

    Minor Annoyance + Feelings + Safe/Calm Place + Notice Shift in Body + BLS
(repeat as needed):

    _____

ANOTHER MINOR ANNOYANCE (2): _____

    2nd Minor Annoyance + Safe/Calm Place + Notice Changes in Body:

    _____

    _____

PRACTICE THE SAFE/CALM PLACE WHEN ANNOYED AND KEEP TRACK BETWEEN SESSIONS.

Phase 3: Assessment

Past Memories

□ Completed

Above Ground Trauma Targets Related to Underground Events List:
(Adapting the SUD Scale to the Miner Population)

  0 = cold memories   10 = hottest memories/heat
  0 = daylight memories   10 = very dark memories or visibility memories
  0 = Normal size/oriented content 10 = very large/disoriented memories

Heat

1. _____ SUDs: _____ /10

2. _____ SUDs: _____ /10

Darkness

3. _____ SUDs: _____ /10

4. _____ SUDs: _____ /10

Disorientation

5. _____ SUDs: _____ /10

6. _____ SUDs: _____ /10

Heat Memories

Hottest Target/Memory/Image: _____

_____

NC: _____

PC: _____

VoC: ____ /7

Emotions: _____

SUD: ____ /10

Sensation: _____

Dark Memories

Darkest Target/Memory/Image: _____

_____

NC: _____

PC: _____

VoC: ____ /7

Emotions: _____

SUD: ____ /10

Sensation: _____

Memories of Disorientation

Darkest Target/Memory/Image: _____

NC: _____

PC: _____

VoC: ____ /7

Emotions: _____

SUD: ____ /10

Sensation: _____

Underground Trauma Targets List

0= cold memories   10= hottest memories/heat
0= daylight memories   10= very dark memories or visibility memories
0= normal size/oriented content   10= very large/disoriented memories

Associated Heat

    1. _____ SUDs: _____/10

    2. _____ SUDs: _____/10

Associated Darkness

    3. _____ SUDs: _____/10

    4. _____ SUDs: _____/10

Associated Disorientation

    5. _____ SUDs: _____/10

    6. _____ SUDs: _____/10

Associated Heat Memories

Hottest Target/Memory/Image: _____

_____

NC: _____

PC: _____

VoC:____/7

Emotions: _____

SUD:_____/10

Sensation: _____

Associated Dark Memories

Darkest Target/Memory/Image: _____

_____

NC: _____

PC: _____

VoC:____/7

Emotions: _____

SUD:_____/10

Sensation: _____

Associated Memories of Disorientation

Most Disoriented Target/Memory/Image: _____

_____

NC: _____

PC: _____

VoC:____/7

Emotions: _____

SUD:_____/10

Sensation: _____

Phase 4: Desensitization

Present Triggers   ☐ completed

☐ News broadcasts
☐ Changes in circumstances related to injury
☐ Changes in income
☐ Loss of contact with colleagues
☐ Issues related to being trapped
☐ Post-incident inquiry
☐ Uncertainty about the future

List of Present Triggers

1. _____
2. _____
3. _____
4. _____
5. _____
6. _____
7. _____
8. _____
9. _____
10. _____

Memory/Image: _____

_____

NC: _____

PC: _____

VoC:____/7

Emotions: _____

SUD:____/10

Sensation: _____

Future Template

Miner returning to work   ☐ Yes   ☐ No _____ Time

If NOT returning, use the standard future template with a single image of coping or readjusting (see Image as Future Template below):
If RETURNING to work, check elements concerning return creating anxiety:

☐ Sight of headstocks to colliery:
☐ Clothing and equipment:
☐ Top of shaft/tally room:
☐ Descending/ascending in the cage:
☐ The shaft bottom:
☐ Underground transport:
☐ Coal face itself /other working location:
☐ Other, especially awareness of temperature increase:

Image as Future Template

Image of Coping Effectively: _____

PC: _____

New Quality/Attribute Needed: _____

Seeing Self Handling the Situation: _____

Thinking, Feeling, and Experiencing in Body: _____

Blocks/Anxieties/Fears in Future Scene: _____

1. _____

2. _____

3. _____

Other Qualities Needed:

1. _____

2. _____

3. _____

Image + PC + Sensations = BLS

If resolved, move on.

Body Scan, if sensation, do BLS until subsides (Close eyes + Image of Future + PC + Attention to Different Parts of Your Body + Report Tension, Tightness, Unusual Sensation).

VoC:_____/7

If Yes, identify unprocessed material and process with Standard Protocol:

1. _____

2. _____

3. _____

Target/Memory/Image: _____

_____

NC: _____

PC: _____

VoC:_____/7

Emotions: _____

SUD:_____/10

Sensation: _____

Completed Image as Future Template: ☐ Completed

Movie as Future Template/Imaginal Rehearsing—Returning to Work

Problem Element/Location: _____

PC: _____

New Quality/Attribute: _____

Seeing Self Handling the Situation: _____

Thinking, Feeling, and Experiencing in Body: _____

Blocks/Anxieties/Fears in Future Scene: _____

1. _____

2. _____

3. _____

Other Qualities Needed:

1. _____

2. _____

3. _____

If resolved, move on.

Play movie one more time from beginning to end + BLS:

If Yes, identify any unprocessed material:

1. _____

2. _____

3. _____

Completed Movie as Future Template: ☐ Completed

Phase 5: Installation

PC: ☐ Completed

New PC (if new one is better): _____

VoC: _____/7

Incident + PC + BLS

Phase 6: Body Scan

Unresolved tension/tightness/unusual sensation: _____

_____

Unresolved tension/tightness/unusual sensation + BLS

Phase 7: Closure

Closure: ☐ Completed

Phase 8: Reevaluation

SUDs of Incident:_____/10

New material: _____

_____

Reprocessed necessary targets: ☐ Completed

EMDR helpful in daily life: ☐ Yes ☐ No

EMDR "Blind to Therapist Protocol"

David Blore and Manda Holmshaw

EMDR "Blind to Therapist Protocol" Script Notes

The "Blind to Therapist Protocol" (B2T) is, essentially, that. It allows a client to go through the Standard EMDR Protocol without revealing the content of the problem. This protocol is often used in conjunction with any client group in which divulging information might be uncomfortable to the individual prior to the use of EMDR. In 1993, the protocol was developed after encountering problems with a client's ability to disclose imagery content. The protocol took well over 10 years to perfect and was first published in 2009. It has been used to treat a wide variety of clients in many types of situations. The workers—including train engineers, airplane pilots, ship captains, police officers, prison guards, doctors, nurses, paramedics, and firemen—are characterized by the need to make life-and-death decisions in a variety of situations for which they are personally responsible. In other words, those who have memories associated with not being in control at precisely the time when they are responsible for being in control.

The most frequent use of the B2T Protocol is among clients who have difficulties with divulging information concerning their own child abuse in which they fear overwhelming or disgusting the therapist with the nature of the material to be treated. In such instances, the protocol is very successful and can be a useful addition to the therapist's repertoire. It helps build the therapeutic relationship by demonstrating to clients that the therapist has trust in them. Once the client has seen how the therapist copes with material being raised, the Standard EMDR Protocol is used.

The B2T Protocol has been successfully used also in the following situations:

- Management of the potential vicarious traumatization of the therapist in which the therapist has been through a similarly traumatic experience to the client's
- Culturally-related and translator-facilitated EMDR situations where expressing strong emotions in front of fellow countrymen and women may be inappropriate
- Culturally-related and translator-facilitated EMDR situations where there are fears that divulging detailed information may result in information being 'leaked' by the translator and potentially put the client's family at risk back in their home country
- Clients with aphasia; the B2T Protocol has been successfully used to treat clients ranging from those with a significant stammer to clients with pronounced aphaisa and limited ability to express themselves.

Note: As yet, we have not used EMDR with clients with "Locked In Syndrome" (a condition in which a patient is aware and awake but cannot move or communicate verbally due to complete paralysis of nearly all voluntary muscles in the body except for the eyes); this is a client group that has previously not had access to any form of psychological 'talking' therapy let alone EMDR but based on our success with other similar populations, the B2T protocol could be helpful (Blore et al., 2013).

EMDR "Blind to Therapist Protocol" Script

Phase 1: Client History

This phase is unchanged. It is likely at this stage that the therapist will become aware of the client's reticence at describing detail relating to the problem.

Phase 2: Preparation

This phase is unchanged, except for when the client does not want to reveal the content of the problem in detail. Suggested text to include:

> Say, *"Typical treatment requires the client to describe, in detail, images and memories that are upsetting. However, it is possible to conduct EMDR without describing the image or memory content.*
>
> *Although you are not describing the image or memory content, treatment will not suffer as a result and you will still be in control throughout treatment. There is no need to tell me about the content of your images, memories, any changes that occur, your evaluation of your memories, or your evaluation of your actions. Remember, treatment will not suffer as a result. Anything you do tell me is entirely confidential anyway and will not be fed back to the company or organization* (or state whomever the client might be concerned about knowing their problem)."

Provide coaching on what change may consist of.

> Say, *"What I mean by change is that after each BLS set, changes may occur in the image, your thoughts, emotions, or feelings in your body. They can be very obvious changes such as the image changing or an emotion changing completely or body sensation moving or disappearing, but they can also be very subtle such as an image fading or going out of focus or a subtle change in emotional intensity. The reason that change is so important is that it indicates that the material is processing to an adaptive resolution for you."*

A metaphor may be useful to explain subtle change.

> Say *"You have probably played the magazine competition where there are two pictures, ostensibly the same. The caption is 'Spot 10 differences.' This illustrates just how subtle change might be. The importance of change of any type and magnitude indicates that information is being processed."*

Past Memories

Phase 3: Assessment

Notice the change in the beginning part of the Assessment to accommodate the client's need to NOT disclose the content of the problem.

Say, *"Please focus on the image or memory you do NOT wish to describe. Do you have it?"*

_____

_____

Say, *"Now, if you would, choose a cue word that* reminds *you of that image or memory without using a word that might give an easy clue about the image content, such as 'failure,' 'out of control,' and so forth.*

Neutral elements of the image work best such as '27,' 'lamp post,' 'nearby,' or words that represent the present, qualitative *nature of that image or memory such as 'It's in my face,' 'Only yesterday,' 'Huge' all work well. What cue word works for you?"*

Cue word: _____

Note: Make no attempt to identify either a negative or a positive cognition as this could give away the content of the image and because it will immediately tap into the negative cognition that the client may find too uncomfortable to acknowledge at this stage. Because there is no attempt to develop a positive cognition at this stage, there can be no rating of the validity of the positive cognition. However, experience shows that some clients while not wishing to discuss a negative cognition *may* nevertheless have sufficient confidence to identify a positive cognition spontaneously. If this happens, it is likely to be along the lines of the client saying: "I would prefer to think I was in control."

PC:_____

If this spontaneous PC occurs don't try developing it, for instance, by getting the wording exactly correct, because the client may feel more vulnerable at a crucial point in which she had felt *just* sufficient confidence. Instead, acknowledge the PC and rate the VoC.

Say, *"When you think of the image you have identified by the cue word _____(state the cue word), how true do your words* (the PC) *feel to you now?"*

If there is no spontaneous PC, do not try to identify one. Only rate the PC if it emerges in Phase 3. If it emerges later, for example in Phase 4, it may well be misleading to rate the PC part way through the processing.

Now proceed as follows:

Say, *"Now, focus on the image you have identified by the cue word_____(state the cue word)."*

Emotions

Say, *"When you bring up the_____(state cue word), what emotion do you feel now?"*

Subjective Units of Disturbance (SUD)

Say, *"On a scale of 0 to 10, where 0 is no disturbance or neutral and 10 is the highest disturbance you can imagine, how disturbing does it feel now?"*

0   1   2   3   4   5   6   7   8   9   10
(no disturbance)   (highest disturbance)

Location of Body Sensation

Say, *"Where do you feel it* (the disturbance) *in your body?"*

_____

_____

Provide coaching about what constitutes processing. Give examples because just saying processing equals change is not sufficient.

Say, *"I cannot assess the amount of processing (or change) that is happening so I need you to understand what processing (or change) means, so you can assess what is happening."*

Keep the coaching simple.

Say, *"During processing, images can change in many different ways. They can move away or seem to get smaller. The images can go out of focus like viewing the image behind frosted glass or there may be more or less detail. You might see totally new images or different images may come to mind; for example, it could be like the magazine competition we talked about earlier where there are two pictures that are ostensibly the same and the caption is 'Spot 10 differences.' Again, this illustrates just how subtle change might be. All of these changes are important to note."*

Phase 4: Desensitization

Commence desensitization with the undisclosed target plus associated emotion plus emotion's bodily location. Here again, ignore cognitions.

Say, *"I would like you to bring up_____(cue word), and notice your emotions and where you feel it or them in your body_____(state BLS you are using)."*

If a PC is revealed in Phase 4, encourage the client to verbalize it *at that point* and explain that this will be returned to in the next phase. Install the PC in Phase 5 as normal.

If a PC is revealed, it is important not to make any attempt to identify the negative equivalent. (Be wary of your own nonverbal body language at this point!) Use the VoC only when, and if, the PC is revealed.

Say, *"Notice those positive words_____(state the PC). We will use them a little later in the processing."*

Validity of Cognition (VoC)

Say, *"When you think of the incident* (or picture), *how true do those words ____(clinician repeats the positive cognition) feel to you now on a scale of 1 to 7, where 1 feels completely false and 7 feels completely true?"*

1   2   3   4   5   6   7
(completely false)   (completely true)

Returning to target: Bring the client back to the undisclosed image or memory (by using the cue word) plus emotion and take SUDs as normal.

Say, *"Please return to whatever is left of_____(state cue word) and on a scale of 0 to 10, where 0 is no disturbance or neutral and 10 is the highest disturbance that you can imagine, how disturbing does it feel to you now?"*

0   1   2   3   4   5   6   7   8   9   10
(no disturbance)   (highest disturbance)

Other Past Events

Make use of the Float-Back Technique to identify any other targets (such as training, instruction, education, apprenticeship) associated with the same emotion or bodily sensation.

Say, *"Are there earlier times in your life when you have had these same emotions or bodily sensations?"*

_____

_____

If so, use the same template as above for each target.

Say, *"Please focus on the image or memory you do NOT wish to describe. Do you have it?"*

_____

_____

Say, *"Now, if you would, choose a cue word that reminds you of that image or memory without using a word that might give an easy clue about the image content, such as 'failure' or 'control,' for example. Neutral elements of the image work best such as '27,' 'lamp post,' 'nearby,' or words that represent the present, qualitative nature of that image or memory such as 'It's in my face,' 'Only yesterday,' 'Huge' all work well."*

Cue word: _____

Make *no attempt* to identify either a negative or a positive cognition as this could give away the content of the image and because it will immediately tap into the negative cognition that the client may find too uncomfortable to acknowledge at this stage.
Now proceed as follows:

Say, *"Now, focus on the image you have identified by the cue word_____* (state the cue word).*"*

Emotions

Say, *"When you bring up the_____*(state cue word), *what emotion do you feel now?"*

_____

_____

Subjective Units of Disturbance (SUD)

Say, *"On a scale of 0 to 10, where 0 is no disturbance or neutral and 10 is the highest disturbance you can imagine, how disturbing does it feel now?"*

0	1	2	3	4	5	6	7	8	9	10
(no disturbance)								(highest disturbance)		

Location of Body Sensation

Say, *"Where do you feel it* (the disturbance) *in your body?"*

_____

_____

Looping

Since you cannot use the cognitive interweave, if basic strategies do not overcome loop-ing, use visual interweaves. The Two-Image Strategy works very well. Morphing is another strategy.

THE TWO-IMAGE STRATEGY

Say, *"Place the 'stuck' image at arm's length on the left. Then, select a 'coping' version of the same image at arm's length on the right."*

Use BLS.

_____

_____

Say, *"Now, go with that."*

Say, *"Did you notice a change?"* or *"What do you get now?"*

MORPHING

Say, *"Stretch the image from the stuck one to an image that looks funny, or one that can easily 'be controlled.'"*

Use BLS.

Say, *"Now, go with that."*

Say, *"Did you notice a change?"* or *"What do you get now?"*

_____

_____

Current Triggers

Experience suggests that current triggers are not a problem with the occupational groups mentioned earlier, but might be with sexual abuse victims. Occasionally, current triggers may need to be handled carefully, especially if they involve a strong sense of smell. Use the Standard EMDR Protocol if memories have been disclosed. If the client still does not wish to disclose an image of a current trigger, merely substitute the opening statement.

Say, *"I would like you to bring up_____ (cue word), and notice your emo-tions and where you feel it or them in your body_____(state BLS you are using)."*

Then continue as per Phase 4 from above.

Future Template

Experience suggests there are not likely to be problems with identifying and disclosing tar-gets relating to a future template even when talking about the worst-case scenario. Since the adaptive information processing (AIP) model predicts that information flows toward an adaptive conclusion, it is possible that by the time the client is focusing on the future tem-plate, there is far less chance of blocks to disclosing material.

Phase 5: Installation

Install any revealed PCs.

> Say, *"Think about whatever is left of the original incident* (or say cue word) *and any positive words that you came up with*_____(state PC).
> *"On a scale of 1 to 7, where 1 feels completely false and 7 feels completely true, how true do they feel* now?"

> 1 2 3 4 5 6 7
> (completely false) (completely true)

> Say, *"Think of*____(state cue word or image if it has now been revealed) *and hold it together with the words*____(repeat the PC)."

Do sets of BLS to fully install the PC (VoC = 7).

Alternatively, merely do usual bilateral stimulation with just the undisclosed target.

> Say, *"Think of*_____(state cue word) *and any positive words that now come to mind that seem linked to it."*

Phase 6: Body Scan

> Say, *"Close your eyes and keep in mind the original memory and* (if appropriate) *the positive cognition. Then bring your attention to the different parts of your body, starting with your head and working downward. Any place you find any tension, tightness, or unusual sensation, tell me."*

_____

_____

Phase 7: Closure

> Say, *"Things may come up or they may not. If they do, great. Write it down, and it can be a target for next time. If you get any new memories, dreams, or situations that disturb you, just take a good snapshot. It isn't necessary to give a lot of detail. Just put down enough to remind you so we can target it next time. The same thing goes for any positive dreams or situations. If negative feelings do come up, try not to make them significant. Remember, it's still just the old stuff. Just write it down for next time. Use the Safe Place exercise to let as much of the disturbance go as possible. Give me a call if you need to."*

Phase 8: Reevaluation

Review the previous session using cue words, unless the client has disclosed the image or memory content already. Be aware that sometimes clients will end one session still having not disclosed the image or memory content, but will disclose the content during Phase 8. If material is disclosed, be prepared to extend the time allocated to Phase 8 to accommodate any explanations the client feels they must make. Alter the wording below according to whether the image or memory content has been disclosed.

> Say, *"When you think of whatever is left of*_____(cue word or disclosed target image) *that we worked on last time, how disturbing is it now on a scale of*

0 to 10, where 0 is no disturbance or neutral and 10 is the highest disturbance you can imagine, how disturbing does it feel now?"

0	1	2	3	4	5	6	7	8	9	10

(no disturbance)   (highest disturbance)

Say, *"Have you noticed any other material associated with_____ (cue word or disclosed target image) in the original memory since the last session?"*

_____

_____

Say, *"Have all the necessary targets been reprocessed so that you can feel at peace with the past, empowered in the present, and able to make choices for the future?"*

_____

_____

Say, *"Has the work that we have done with EMDR helped you be more adaptive in your day-to-day life?"*

_____

_____

Use the answers to these questions to determine what steps to take next. If using this protocol, free help is available via e-mail: help@davidblore.co.uk

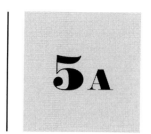

SUMMARY SHEET:
EMDR "Blind to Therapist Protocol"

David Blore and Manda Holmshaw
SUMMARY SHEET BY MARILYN LUBER

Name: _____ Diagnosis: _____

Medications: _____

Test Results: _____

☑ Check when task is completed, response has changed, or to indicate symptoms.

Phase 1: History Taking (As Usual)

Phase 2: Preparation

Say, *"Typical treatment requires the client to describe, in detail, images and memories that are upsetting. However, it is possible to conduct EMDR without describing the image or memory content. Although you are not describing the image or memory content, treatment will not suffer as a result and you will still be in control throughout treatment. There is no need to tell me about the content of your images, memories, any changes that occur, your evaluation of your memories, or your evaluation of your actions. Remember, treatment will not suffer as a result. I merely need to know whether or not change is happening after each bilateral stimulation (BLS) set."*

Provide coaching on what change may consist of.

Say, *"What I mean by change is that after each BLS set, changes may occur in the image, your thoughts, emotions, or feelings in your body. They can be very obvious changes such as the image changing or an emotion changing completely or body sensation moving or disappearing, but they can also be very subtle such as an image fading or going out of focus or a subtle change in emotional intensity. The reason that change is so important is that it indicates that the material is processing to an adaptive resolution for you."*

A metaphor may be useful to explain subtle change.

Say *"You have probably played the magazine competition where there are two pictures, ostensibly the same. The caption is 'Spot 10 differences.' This illustrates just how subtle change might be. The importance of change of any type and magnitude indicates information is being processed."*

Phases 3 and 4: Assessment

Past Memory

PAST

Target/Memory/Image: _____

_____

_____

CUE WORD for Memory: _____

PC (only if volunteered): _____ VoC (optional):_____/7

Emotions: _____

SUD: ___ /10

Sensation: _____

Provide coaching about processing.

Say, *"I cannot assess the amount of processing (or change) that is happening so I need you to understand what processing (or change) means, so you can assess what is happening."*

Keep the coaching simple.

Say, *"During processing, images can change in many different ways. They can move away or seem to get smaller. The images can go out of focus like viewing the image behind frosted glass or there may be more or less detail. You might see totally new images or different images may come to mind; for example, it could be like the magazine competition we talked about earlier where there are two pictures that are ostensibly the same and the caption is 'Spot 10 differences.' Again, this illustrates just how subtle change might be. All of these changes are important to note."*

Phase 4: Desensitization

CUE WORD + Emotions + Sensations + BLS. Indicate "change" or "no change." Other Past Events List Associated with Same Emotion/Bodily Sensation

1. _____ Cue Word: _____

2. _____ Cue Word: _____

3. _____ Cue Word: _____

4. _____ Cue Word: _____

5. _____ Cue Word: _____

CUE WORD for Memory: _____

PC (optional): _____ VoC (optional):_____/7

Emotions: _____

SUD: _____ /10

Sensation: _____

Looping

If looping occurs, use the following:

TWO IMAGE STRATEGY: ☐ Yes   ☐ No

Stuck image arm's length on Left. Coping version of same image on right. BLS

MORPHING: ☐ Yes   ☐ No

Stretch image from the stuck one to image that looks funny/not controllable + BLS

Current Triggers

List of Present Triggers:
1. _____ Cue Word: _____
2. _____ Cue Word: _____
3. _____ Cue Word: _____

CUE WORD for Memory: _____

PC (optional): _____ VoC (optional):_____/7

Emotions: _____

SUD: _____ /10

Sensation: _____

CUE WORD + Emotions + Location = BLS

Future Template

By this point, usually future template can be identified or disclosed

Phase 5: Installation (If PC Revealed)

PC: _____

VoC: ____ /7

CUE WORD/Incident + PC + BLS

Phase 6: Body Scan

Unresolved tension/tightness/unusual sensation: _____

_____

Unresolved tension/tightness/unusual sensation + BLS

Phase 7: Closure (As Usual)   ☐ Completed

Consider need for further resources

Phase 8: Reevaluation

SUDs of incident:_____/10

New material:_____

Reprocessed necessary targets: ☐ Completed

EMDR helpful in daily life: ☐   Yes   ☐   No

Past Memory Worksheet Script (Shapiro, 2001, 2006)

Phase 3: Assessment

Incident

Say, *"The memory that we will start with today is* _____ (select the next incident to be targeted).*"*

_____

_____

_____

Say, *"What happens when you think of the* _____ (state the issue)*?"*

_____

_____

_____

Or say, *"When you think of* _____ (state the issue), *what do you get?"*

_____

_____

Picture

Say, *"What picture represents the entire* _____ (state the issue)*?"*

_____

_____

_____

If there are many choices or if the client becomes confused, the clinician assists by asking the following:

Say, *"What picture represents the most traumatic part of* _____ (state the issue)*?"*

_____

_____

_____

Negative Cognition (NC)

Say, *"What words best go with the picture that express your negative belief about yourself now?"*

_____

_____

Positive Cognition (PC)

Say, *"When you bring up that picture or _____ (state the issue), what would you like to believe about yourself now?"*

_____

_____

Validity of Cognition (VoC)

Say, *"When you think of the incident* (or picture) *how true do those words ____ (clinician repeats the positive cognition) feel to you now on a scale of 1 to 7, where 1 feels completely false and 7 feels completely true?"*

1   2   3   4   5   6   7
(completely false)   (completely true)

Emotions

Say, *"When you bring up the picture or _____ (state the issue) and those words ____ (clinician states the negative cognition), what emotion do you feel now?"*

_____

Subjective Units of Disturbance (SUD)

Say, *"On a scale of 0 to 10, where 0 is no disturbance or neutral and 10 is the highest disturbance you can imagine, how disturbing does it feel now?"*

0   1   2   3   4   5   6   7   8   9   10
(no disturbance)   (highest disturbance)

Location of Body Sensation

Say, *"Where do you feel it* (the disturbance) *in your body?"*

_____

Phase 4: Desensitization

To begin, say the following:

Say, *"Now, remember, it is your own brain that is doing the healing and you are the one in control. I will ask you to mentally focus on the target and to follow my fingers* (or any other BLS you are using). *Just let whatever happens, happen, and we will talk at the end of the set. Just tell me what comes up, and don't discard anything as unimportant. Any new information that comes to mind is connected in some way. If you want to stop, just raise your hand."*

Then say, *"Bring up the picture and the words _____ (clinician repeats the NC) and notice where you feel it in your body. Now follow my fingers with your eyes* (or other BLS)."*

Phase 5: Installation

Say, *"How does _____ (repeat the PC) sound?"*

_____

_____

_____

Say, *"Do the words _____ (repeat the PC) still fit, or is there another positive statement that feels better?"*

_____

_____

_____

If the client accepts the original positive cognition, the clinician should ask for a VoC rating to see if it has improved:

Say, *"As you think of the incident, how do the words feel, from 1 (completely false) to 7 (completely true)?"*

1   2   3   4   5   6   7
(completely false)   (completely true)

Say, *"Think of the event and hold it together with the words _____ (repeat the PC)."*

Do a long set of bilateral stimulation (BLS) to see if there is more processing to be done.

Phase 6: Body Scan

Say, *"Close your eyes and keep in mind the original memory and the positive cognition. Then bring your attention to the different parts of your body, starting with your head and working downward. Any place you find any tension, tightness, or unusual sensation, tell me."*

_____

_____

Phase 7: Closure

Say, *"Things may come up or they may not. If they do, great. Write it down and it can be a target for next time. You can use a log to write down what triggers images, thoughts or cognitions, emotions, and sensations; you can rate them on our 0 to 10 scale where 0 is no disturbance or neutral and 10 is the worst disturbance. Please write down the positive experiences, too."*
"If you get any new memories, dreams, or situations that disturb you, just take a good snapshot. It isn't necessary to give a lot of detail. Just put down enough to remind you so we can target it next time. The same thing goes for any positive dreams or situations. If negative feelings do come up, try not to make them significant. Remember, it's still just the old stuff. Just write it down for next time. Then use the tape or the Safe Place exercise to let as much of the disturbance go as possible. Even if nothing comes up, make sure to use the tape every day and give me a call if you need to."

Phase 8: Reevaluation

There are four ways to reevaluate our work with clients.

1. Reevaluate Since the Last Session

Reevaluate what has come up in the client's life since the last session.

Say, *"Okay. Let's look at your log. I am interested in what has happened since the last session. What have you noticed since our last session?"*

_____

_____

_____

Say, *"What has changed?"*

_____

_____

_____

If the client has nothing to say or does not say much, say the following:

Say, *"Have you had any dreams or nightmares?"*

_____

_____

_____

Say, *"What about _____ (state symptoms you and client have been working on) we have been working on, have you noticed any changes in them? Have they increased or decreased?"*

_____

_____

_____

Say, *"Have you noticed any other changes, new responses, or insights in your images, thoughts, emotions, sensations, and behaviors?"*

_____

_____

_____

Say, *"Have you found new resources?"*

_____

_____

_____

Say, *"Have any situations, events, or other stimuli triggered you?"*

_____

_____

_____

Use the material from your reevaluation to feed back into your case conceptualization and help decide what to do next concerning the larger treatment plan.

2. Reevaluate The Previous Target

Reevaluate the target worked on in the previous session. Has the individual target been resolved? Whether the previous processing session was complete or incomplete, use the following instructions to access the memory and determine the need for further processing.

Say, *"Bring up the memory or trigger of _____* (state the memory or trigger) *that we worked on last session. What image comes up?"*

_____

_____

_____

Say, *"What thoughts about it come up?"*

_____

_____

Say, *"What thoughts about yourself?"*

_____

_____

Say, *"What emotions do you notice?"*

_____

_____

Say, *"What sensations do you notice?"*

_____

_____

Say, *"On a scale of 0 to 10, where 0 is no disturbance or neutral and 10 is the highest disturbance you can imagine, how disturbing does it feel now?"*

0   1   2   3   4   5   6   7   8   9   10
(no disturbance)   (highest disturbance)

Evaluate the material to see if there are any indications of dysfunction. Has the primary issue been resolved? Is there ecological validity to the client's resolution of the issue? Is there associated material that has been activated that must be addressed?

If you are observing any resistance to resolving the issue, say the following:

Say, *"What would happen if you are successful?"*

_____

_____

If there are no indications of dysfunction, and SUD is 0, do a set of BLS to be sure that the processing is complete.

Say, *"Go with that."*

Say, *"What do you get now?"*

_____

_____

Check the positive cognition.

Say, "*When you think of the incident* (or picture) *how true do those words* _____ (clinician repeats the positive cognition) *feel to you now on a scale of 1 to 7, where 1 feels completely false and 7 feels completely true?*"

1   2   3   4   5   6   7
(completely false)   (completely true)

If the VoC is 7, do a set of BLS to be sure that the processing is complete.

Say, "*Go with that.*"

Say, "*What do you get now?*"

_____

_____

If there are any signs of dysfunction such as a new negative perspective(s) or new facets of the event or the SUD is higher than 0, say the following:

Say, "*Okay, now please pay attention to the image, thoughts, and sensations associated with* _____ (state the memory or trigger) *and just go with that.*"

_____

_____

Continue with the Standard EMDR Protocol until processing is complete.

If the VoC is less than 7, say the following:

Say, "*What is keeping it from being a 7?*"

_____

_____

Note the associated feelings and sensations, and resume processing.

Say, "*Go with that.*"

Continue with the Standard EMDR Protocol through the Body Scan until processing is complete.

If a completely new incident or target emerges, say the following:

Say, "*Are there any feeder memories contributing to this problem?*"

_____

_____

Do the Assessment Phase on the appropriate target and fully process it. It is not unusual for another aspect of the memory to emerge that needs to be processed.

If the client claims that nothing or no disturbance is coming up (or he can't remember what was worked on in the previous session), and the therapist thinks that the work is probably still incomplete and that the client is simply not able to access the memory, say the following:

Say, "*When you think of* _____ (state the incident that was worked on) and the image _____ (state the image) *and* _____ (state the NC), *what body sensations do you feel now?*"

_____

_____

Say, "*Go with that*".

_____

_____

Continue processing with the Standard EMDR Protocol.

If the client wants to work on a *charged* trigger that came up since the last session instead of the target from the previous session, say the following:

Say, *"Yes, this IS important information. Tell me about what came up for you."*

_____

_____

Then assess the magnitude of the trigger. If it is indeed a severe critical incident, then proceed accordingly, using the Assessment Phase to target the new material and return to the original target when possible.

If it is not, then say the following:

Say, *"Yes this is important, however, it is important that we finish our work on _____ (state what you are working on) before moving to another target. It is like what happens when you have too many files open on your computer and it slows down, or finishing the course of antibiotics even if you feel okay (or any other appropriate metaphor for your client)."*

Fully reprocess each target through the Body Scan and Reevaluation before moving on to the next in order to ensure optimal results.

3. Reevaluate at Critical Points

At various critical points in treatment (before moving on to the next symptom, theme, goal, etc.), reevaluate what has been effectively targeted and resolved and what still needs to be addressed.

Say, *"Now that we have finished this work, let's reevaluate our work so far. Remember _____ (state the work you have done). On a scale of 0 to 10, where 0 is no disturbance or neutral and 10 is the highest disturbance you can imagine, how disturbing does it feel now?"*

0	1	2	3	4	5	6	7	8	9	10
(no disturbance)								(highest disturbance)		

If the SUD is higher than 0, evaluate what else needs to be done by continuing to work with the disturbance in the framework of the Standard EMDR Protocol.

Also evaluate whether the client has been able to achieve cognitive, behavioral, and emotional goals in his life.

Say, *"Have you accomplished all of the goals that we had contracted to work on such as _____ (read the list of agreed upon goals)?"*

_____

_____

_____

If not, evaluate what still needs to be targeted such as feeder memories.

Say, *"Please scan for an earlier memory that incorporates _____ (state the negative cognition). What do you get?"*

_____

_____

Use the Standard EMDR Protocol to process any feeder memories.

Check if previously identified clusters of memories remain charged.

Say, *"Are there any memories left concerning* _____ (state the cluster of memories previously worked on)*?"*

_____

_____

_____

If so, work on the memory(ies), using the Standard EMDR Protocol. Make sure to incorporate the positive templates for all previously disturbing situations and projected future goals. See the Future Template Worksheet Script.

4. Reevaluate Before Termination

Before termination, reevaluate targets worked on over the course of therapy and goals addressed during treatment.

Say, *"Before we end our treatment, let's reevaluate our work to make sure that all of the targets are resolved and goals are addressed. Are there any PAST targets that remain unresolved for you?"*

_____

_____

Or say, *"These are the past targets with which we worked; do any of them remain unresolved? What about the memories that we listed during our history taking and over the course of treatment?"*

_____

_____

Check with the SUDs for any disturbance.

Say, *"On a scale of 0 to 10, where 0 is no disturbance or neutral and 10 is the highest disturbance you can imagine, how disturbing does it feel now?"*

0	1	2	3	4	5	6	7	8	9	10
(no disturbance)								(highest disturbance)		

Check the major negative cognitions to see if there are any unresolved memories still active.

Say, *"These are the main negative cognitions with which we worked. Hold* _____ (state one of the cognitions worked with) *and scan for any unresolved memories. Does anything surface for you?"*

_____

_____

If there is more unresolved material, check with BLS to see if the charge decreases. If not, use the Standard EMDR Protocol.

Say, *"Now scan chronologically from birth until today to see if there are any other unresolved memories. What do you notice?"*

_____

_____

If there is more unresolved material, check with BLS to see if the charge decreases. If not, use the Standard EMDR Protocol.

Progressions can occur during other events or during the processing of a primary target; use your clinical judgment as to whether it is important to return and reevaluate these memories.

Clusters are related memories that were grouped together during treatment planning and can be scanned to identify any memories that were not involved through generalization of treatment effects.

Say, *"Let's check the* _____ (state the cluster) *we worked on earlier. When you think about it are there any other memories that were not involved that you are aware of now?"*

_____

_____

If there is more unresolved material, check with BLS to see if the charge decreases. If not, use the Standard EMDR Protocol.

Participants are significant individuals in the client's life who should be targeted if memories or issues regarding them remain disturbing.

Say, *"Let's check if there are any remaining concerns or memories concerning* ____ (state whoever the client might be concerned about). *Is there anything that still is bothering you about* _____ (state the person's name)*?"*

_____

_____

If there is more unresolved material, check with BLS to see if the charge decreases. If not, use the Standard EMDR Protocol.

Say, *"Are there any PRESENT or RECENT triggers that remain potent?"*

_____

_____

_____

Say, *"Are there any current conditions, situations, or people that make you want to avoid them, act in ways that are not helpful, or cause you emotional distress?"*

_____

_____

If there is more unresolved material, check with BLS to see if the charge decreases. If not, use the Standard EMDR Protocol.

Say, *"Are there any future goals that have not been addressed and realized?"*

_____

_____

_____

Make sure to use the Future Template for each trigger, new goal(s), new skill(s), issues of memory, or incorporating the client's new sense of himself. See Future Template Worksheet Script in this appendix.

Present Trigger Worksheet Script

Target and reprocess present triggers identified during History Taking, reprocessing, and reevaluation. Steps for working with present triggers are the following.

1. Identify the presenting trigger that is still causing disturbance.
2. Target and activate the presenting trigger using the full Assessment procedures (image, negative cognition, positive cognition, VoC, emotions, SUD, sensations).
3. Follow Phases 3 through 8 with each trigger until it is fully reprocessed (SUD = 0, VoC = 7, clear Body Scan) before moving to the next trigger.

   Note: In some situations a blocking belief may be associated with the present trigger requiring a new Targeting Sequence Plan.

4. Once all present triggers have been reprocessed, proceed to installing Future Templates for each present trigger (e.g., imagining encountering the same situation in the future; see Future Template protocols).

Present Stimuli That Trigger the Disturbing Memory or Reaction

List the situations that elicit the symptom(s). Examples of situations, events, or stimuli that trigger clients could be the following: another trauma, the sound of a car backfiring, or being touched in a certain way.

Say, *"What are the situations, events, or stimuli that trigger your trauma* _____ (state the trauma). *Let's process these situations, events, or stimuli triggers one-by-one."*

Situations, Events, or Stimuli Trigger List

_____

_____

_____

_____

_____

Target or Memory

Say, *"What situation, event, or stimulus that triggers you would you like to use as a target today?"*

_____

_____

Picture

Say, *"What picture represents the* _____ (state the situation, event, or stimulus) *that triggers you?"*

_____

_____

If there are many choices or if the client becomes confused, the clinician assists by asking the following:

Say, *"What picture represents the most traumatic part of the _____ (state the situation, event, or stimulus) that triggers you?"*

_____

_____

When a picture is unavailable, the clinician merely invites the client to do the following:

Say, *"Think of the _____ (state the situation, event, or stimulus) that triggers you."*

_____

_____

Negative Cognition (NC)

Say, *"What words best go with the picture that express your negative belief about yourself now?"*

_____

Positive Cognition (PC)

Say, *"When you bring up that picture or the _____ (state the situation, event, or stimulus) that triggers you, what would you like to believe about yourself now?"*

_____

Validity of Cognition (VoC)

Say, *"When you think of the _____ (state the situation, event, stimulus, or picture that triggers), how true do those words _____ (clinician repeats the positive cognition) feel to you now on a scale of 1 to 7, where 1 feels completely false and 7 feels completely true?"*

1   2   3   4   5   6   7
(completely false)   (completely true)

Sometimes, it is necessary to explain further.

Say, *"Remember, sometimes we know something with our head, but it feels different in our gut. In this case, what is the gut-level feeling of the truth of _____ (clinician state the positive cognition), from 1 (completely false) to 7 (completely true)?"*

1   2   3   4   5   6   7
(completely false)   (completely true)

Emotions

Say, *"When you bring up the picture (or state the situation, event, or stimulus) that triggers you and those words _____ (clinician states the negative cognition), what emotion do you feel now?"*

_____

Subjective Units of Disturbance (SUD)

Say, *"On a scale of 0 to 10, where 0 is no disturbance or neutral and 10 is the highest disturbance you can imagine, how disturbing does it feel now?"*

    0   1   2   3   4   5   6   7   8   9   10
(no disturbance)   (highest disturbance)

Location of Body Sensation

Say, *"Where do you feel it* (the disturbance) *in your body?"*

_____

Continue to process the triggers according the Standard EMDR Protocol.

Future Template Worksheet (Shapiro, 2006)

The future template is the third prong in the Standard EMDR Protocol. Work with the future template occurs after the earlier memories and present triggers are adequately resolved and the client is ready to make new choices in the future concerning their issue(s). The purpose of it is to address any residual avoidance, any need for further issues of adaptation, to help with incorporating any new information, and to allow for the actualization of client goals. It is another place, in this comprehensive protocol, to catch any fears, negative beliefs, inappropriate responses, and so forth, to reprocess them and also to make sure that the new feelings and behavior can generalize into the clients' day-to-day lives.

There are two basic future templates:

1. Anticipatory Anxiety
   Anticipatory anxiety needs to be addressed with a full assessment (Phase 3) of the future situation.
2. Skills Building and Imaginal Rehearsal
   These do not need a full assessment of target and can begin directly with "running a movie."

Future Template Script
(Shapiro, 2001, pp. 210–214, 2006, pp. 51–53)

Check the Significant People and Situations of the Presenting Issues for any Type of Distress

It is helpful to check to see if all the material concerning the issue upon which the client has worked is resolved or if there is more material that has escaped detection so far. The Future Template is another place to find if there is more material that needs reprocessing.

Significant People

When the client's work has focused on a significant person, ask the following:

Say, *"Imagine yourself encountering that person in the future* _____ (suggest a place that the client might see this person). *What do you notice?"*

_____

_____

_____

Watch the client's reaction to see if more work is necessary. If a client describes a negative feeling in connection with this person, check to see if it is reality based.

Say, *"Is* _____ (state the person's name) *likely to act* _____ (state the client's concern)?"

_____

_____

If the negative feeling is not matching the current reality, say the following:

Say, *"What do you think makes you have negative feelings toward* _____ (state the person in question)?"

_____

_____

If the client is unsure, use the Float-Back or Affect Scan to see what other earlier material may still be active.

If the negative feelings are appropriate, it is important to reevaluate the clusters of events concerning this person and access and reprocess any remaining maladaptive memories. (See Past Memory Worksheet.)

Significant Situations

It is important to have the client imagine being in significant situations in the future; this is another way of accessing material that may not have been processed.

> Say, *"Imagine a videotape or film of how* _____ (state current situation client is working on) *and how it would evolve* _____ (state appropriate time frame) *in the future. When you have done that let me know what you have noticed."*

_____

_____

If there is no disturbance, reinforce the positive experience.

Say, *"Go with that."*

Do BLS.

Reinforce the PC with the future situation with BLS as it continues the positive associations. For further work in the future, see below.

If there is a disturbance, assess what the client needs: more education, modeling of appropriate behavior, or more past memories for reprocessing.

> Say, *"On a scale of 0 to 10, where 0 is no disturbance or neutral and 10 is the highest disturbance you can imagine, how disturbing does it feel now?"*

> 0   1   2   3   4   5   6   7   8   9   10
> (no disturbance)   (highest disturbance)

Anticipatory Anxiety

When the SUD is above 4, or when the Desensitization Phase is not brief, the clinician should look for a present trigger and its associated symptom and develop another Targeting Sequence Plan using the Three-Pronged Protocol. (See worksheets on Past Memories and Present Triggers.)

When there is anticipatory anxiety at a SUD level of no more than 3 to 4 maximum, it is possible to proceed with reprocessing using the future template. The desensitization phase should be quite brief.

> Say, *"What happens when you think of* _____ (state the client's anticipatory anxiety or issue)*?"*

_____

_____

_____

> Or say, *"When you think of* _____ (state the client's anticipatory anxiety or issue), *what do you get?"*

_____

_____

_____

Picture

Say, *"What picture represents the entire* _____ (state the client's anticipatory anxiety or issue)?"

_____

_____

_____

If there are many choices or if the client becomes confused, the clinician assists by asking the following:

Say, *"What picture represents the most traumatic part of* _____ (state the client's anticipatory anxiety or issue)?"

_____

_____

_____

Negative Cognition (NC)

Say, *"What words best go with the picture that express your negative belief about yourself now?"*

_____

_____

Positive Cognition (PC)

Say, *"When you bring up that picture or* _____ (state the client's anticipatory anxiety or issue), *what would you like to believe about yourself now?"*

_____

_____

Validity of Cognition (VoC)

Say, *"When you think of* _____ (state the client's anticipatory anxiety or issue) *or picture, how true do those words* ____ (clinician repeats the positive cognition) *feel to you now on a scale of 1 to 7, where 1 feels completely false and 7 feels completely true?"*

1   2   3   4   5   6   7
(completely false)   (completely true)

Emotions

Say, *"When you bring up the picture or* _____ (state the client's anticipatory anxiety or issue) *and those words* ____ (clinician states the negative cognition), *what emotion do you feel now?"*

_____

Subjective Units of Disturbance (SUD)

Say, *"On a scale of 0 to 10, where 0 is no disturbance or neutral and 10 is the highest disturbance you can imagine, how disturbing does it feel now?"*

```
 0    1    2    3    4    5    6    7    8    9    10
(no disturbance)                        (highest disturbance)
```

Location of Body Sensation

Say, *"Where do you feel it* (the disturbance) *in your body?"*

_____

Phase 4: Desensitization

To begin, say the following:

Say, *"Now remember, it is your own brain that is doing the healing and you are the one in control. I will ask you to mentally focus on the target and to follow my fingers* (or any other BLS you are using). *Just let whatever happens, happen, and we will talk at the end of the set. Just tell me what comes up, and don't discard anything as unimportant. Any new information that comes to mind is connected in some way. If you want to stop, just raise your hand."*

Then say, *"Bring up the picture and the words* _____ (clinician repeats the NC) *and notice where you feel it in your body. Now, follow my fingers with your eyes* (or other BLS)."

Continue with the Desensitization Phase until the SUD = 0 and the VoC = 7.

Phase 5: Installation

Say, *"How does* _____ (repeat the PC) *sound?"*

_____

Say, *"Do the words* _____ (repeat the PC) *still fit, or is there another positive statement that feels better?"*

_____

If the client accepts the original positive cognition, the clinician should ask for a VoC rating to see if it has improved.

Say, *"As you think of the incident, how do the words feel, from 1* (completely false) *to 7* (completely true)?"

```
 0    1    2    3    4    5    6    7    8    9    10
(no disturbance)                        (highest disturbance)
```

Say, "Think of the event and hold it together with the words _____ (repeat the PC)."

Do a long set of BLS to see if there is more processing to be done.

Phase 6: Body Scan

Say, *"Close your eyes and keep in mind the original memory and the positive cognition. Then bring your attention to the different parts of your body, starting with your head and working downward. Any place you find any tension, tightness, or unusual sensation, tell me."*

_____

_____

Make sure that this anticipatory anxiety is fully processed before returning to the Future Template.

The Future Template for appropriate future interaction is an expansion of the Installation Phase; instead of linking the positive cognition with the past memory or trigger, the PC is linked to the future issues. Once the client's work has been checked and the other known issues in the past and present have been resolved, each client has the choice to do a more formal future template installation. The first option is to work with the situation or issue as an image.

Image as Future Template: Imagining Positive Outcomes

Imagining positive outcomes seems to assist the learning process. In this way, clients learn to enhance optimal behaviors, to connect them with a positive cognition, and to support generalization. The assimilation of this new behavior and thought is supported by the use of bilateral stimulation (BLS) into a positive way to act in the future.

Say, *"I would like you to imagine yourself coping effectively with or in _____
(state the goal) in the future. With the positive belief _____ (state the
positive belief) and your new sense of _____ (state the quality:
i.e., strength, clarity, confidence, calm), imagine stepping into this scene.
Notice what you see and how you are handling the situation. Notice what you
are thinking, feeling, and experiencing in your body."*

_____

_____

_____

Again, here is the opportunity to catch any disturbance that may have been missed.

Say, *"Are there any blocks, anxieties, or fears that arise as you think about this
future scene?"*

_____

_____

_____

If yes, say the following:

Say, *"Then focus on these blocks and follow my fingers (or any other BLS)."*

Say, *"What do you get now?"*

_____

_____

_____

If the blocks do not resolve quickly, evaluate if the client needs any new information, resources, or skills to be able to comfortably visualize the future coping scene. Introduce needed information or skills.

Say, *"What would you need to feel confident in handling the situation?"*

_____

_____

Or say, *"What is missing from your handling of this situation?"*

_____

_____

If the block still does not resolve and the client is unable to visualize the future scene with confidence and clarity, use direct questions, the Affect Scan, or the Float-Back Technique to identify old targets related to blocks, anxieties, or fears. Remember, the point of the Three-Prong Protocol is not only to reinforce positive feelings and behavior in the future but again to catch any unresolved material that may be getting in the way of an adaptive resolution of the issue(s). Use the Standard EMDR Protocol to address these targets before proceeding with the template (see Worksheets in this appendix).

If there are no apparent blocks and the client is able to visualize the future scene with confidence and clarity, say the following:

Say, *"Please focus on the image, the positive belief, and the sensations associated with this future scene and follow my fingers (or any other BLS)."*

_____

_____

Process and reinforce the positive associations with BLS. Do several sets until the future template is sufficiently strengthened.

Say, *"Go with that."*

_____

Then say, *"Close your eyes and keep in mind the image of the future and the positive cognition. Then bring your attention to the different parts of your body, starting with your head and working downward. Any place you find any tension, tightness, or unusual sensation, tell me."*

_____

If any sensation is reported, do BLS.

Say, *"Go with that."*

If it is a positive or comfortable sensation, do BLS to strengthen the positive feelings.

Say, *"Go with that."*

If a sensation of discomfort is reported, reprocess until the discomfort subsides.

Say, *"Go with that."*

When the discomfort subsides, check the VoC.

Say, *"When you think of the incident* (or picture) *how true do those words _____ (clinician repeats the positive cognition) feel to you now on a scale of 1 to 7, where 1 feels completely false and 7 feels completely true?"*

1   2   3   4   5   6   7
(completely false)   (completely true)

Continue to use BLS until reaching the VoC = 7 or there is an ecological resolution. When the image as future template is clear and the PC true, move on to the movie as future template.

Movie as Future Template or Imaginal Rehearsing

During this next level of future template, clients are asked to move from imagining this one scene or snapshot to imagining a movie about coping in the future, with a beginning, middle, and end. Encourage clients to imagine themselves coping effectively in the face of specific challenges, triggers, or snafus. Therapists can make some suggestions in order to help inoculate clients with future problems. It is helpful to use this type of future template after clients have received needed education concerning social skills and customs, assertiveness, and any other newly learned skills.

Say, *"This time, I'd like you to close your eyes and play a movie, imagining yourself coping effectively with or in _____ (state where client will be) in the future. With the new positive belief ___ (state positive belief) and your new sense of ___ (strength, clarity, confidence, calm), imagine stepping into the future. Imagine yourself coping with ANY challenges that come your way. Make sure that this movie has a beginning, middle, and end. Notice what you are seeing, thinking, feeling, and experiencing in your body. Let me know if you hit any blocks. If you do, just open your eyes and let me know. If you don't hit any blocks, let me know when you have viewed the whole movie."*

If the client hits blocks, address as above with BLS until the disturbance dissipates.

Say, *"Go with that."*

If the material does not shift, use interweaves, new skills, information, resources, direct questions, and any other ways to help clients access information that will allow them to move on. If these options are not successful, usually it means that there is earlier material still unprocessed; the Float-Back and Affect Scan are helpful in these cases to access the material that keeps the client stuck.

If clients are able to play the movie from start to finish with a sense of confidence and satisfaction, ask them to play the movie one more time from beginning to end and introduce BLS.

Say, *"Okay, play the movie one more time from beginning to end. Go with that."*

Use BLS.

In a sense, you are installing this movie as a future template.

After clients have fully processed their issue(s), they might want to work on other positive templates for the future in other areas of their lives using the above future templates.

Appendix B: EMDR Worldwide Associations and Other Resources

In the Beginning

The EMDR Institute

Web site: (http://www.emdr.com/)
Contact Person: Robbie Dunton (rdunton@emdr.com)

EMDR Worldwide Associations Contact Information

Africa

Algeria
Contact Person: Mohamed Chakali (chakmed@yahoo.com)

Cameroon
Contact Person: Michelle Depré (emdrcameroun@gmail.com)

Ethiopia
Contact Person: Hiwot Moges (hiwot.moges@gmail.com)
Dorothy Ashman (dorothy.ashman@gmail.com)

Kenya
Association: EMDR Kenya (http://emdrkenya.org)

South Africa
Association: EMDR South Africa/Africa
Contact Person: Reyhana Seedat (rravat@iafrica.com)

Zambia
Contact Person: Sue Gibbons (suegibbonsnow@yahoo.co.uk)
Jack McCarthy (jackmcc5@aol.com)

Asia

EMDR Asia Association: An association of Asian National EMDR Associations (http://www.emdr-asia.org)

Australia
Association: EMDR Association of Australia (http://emdraa.org)

Bangladesh
Contact Person: Shamim Karim (shamim.karim@gmail.com)

Cambodia
Association: EMDR Cambodia Association (http://emdrcambodia.org/)
Contact Person: Bunna Phoeun (bunnasyeng@gmail.com)

China—Mainland
Association: China EMDR (www.emdr.org.cn)
Contact Persons: Jinsong Zhang (zhangjsk@yahoo.com)
Lu Qui-Yun (lvquiyun@263.net)

Hong Kong
Association: The EMDR Association of Hong Kong (http://hkemdr.org)

India
Association: EMDR India (www.emdrindia.org)

Indonesia
Association: EMDR Indonesia (http://www.emdrindonesia.org)

Japan
Association: Japan EMDR Association (http://www.emdr.jp)

Korea
Association: Korean EMDR Association [KEMDRA] (http://emdrkorea.com/fine/)

New Zealand
Association: EMDR New Zealand Association
Contact Person: Astrid Katzur (Astrid.Katzur@emdrnz.org.nz)

Pakistan
Association: EMDR Pakistan (http://emdrpakistan.wordpress.com)

Philippines
Contact Person: Lourdes Medina (lcm50us@yahoo.com)

Singapore
Association: EMDR Singapore (http://www.emdr.sg)

Sri Lanka
Association: Sri Lanka EMDR Association (SEA)
Contact Person: Sr. Janet Nethisinghe (jnethisinghe@yahoo.ca)

Taiwan
Association: Taiwan EMDR Association [TEMDRA] (http://www.temdra.org.tw)

Thailand
Association: EMDR Thailand (http://www.emdrthailand.com)

Vietnam
Contact Person: Dr. Carl Sternberg (pv.carl@gmail.com) Ho Chi Minh City

Europe

EMDR Europe Association: An association of European National EMDR Associations (www .emdr-europe.org)

Austria
Association: EMDR-Netzwerk Osterreich (http://www.emdr-netzwerk.at/)

Belgium
Association: EMDR-Belgium (http://www.emdr-belgium.be)

Denmark
Association: EMDR Danmark (http://www.emdr.dk/)

Finland
Association: Suomen EMDR-Yhdistys (http://www.emdr.fi)

France
Association: Association EMDR France (http://www.emdr-france.org/)

Germany
EMDRIA Deutschland e.V. (http://www.emdria.de)

Greece
Association: EMDR Greece (http://www.emdr.gr/)

Ireland
Association: EMDR UK & Ireland (http://www.emdrassociation.org.uk)

Israel
Association: EMDR-IS (http://www.emdr.org.il)

Italy
Association: EMDR Italie (http://www.emdritalia.it)

Netherlands
Association: Vereniging EMDR Nederland (http://www.emdr.nl)

Norway
Association: EMDR Norge (http://www.emdrnorge.com/)

Poland
Association: PTT EMDR (http://www.emdr.org.pl)

Portugal
Association: EMDR Portugal (http://www.emdrportugal.com)

Serbia
Association: EMDR Serbia (http://www.emdr-se-europe.org)

Slovakia
Contact: Daniel Ralaus (ralaus@hotmail.com)

Spain
Association: Associatión: EMDR-España (www.emdr-es.org)

Sweden
Association: EMDR Sverige (http://www.emdr.se/)

Switzerland
Association: EMDR Schweiz-Suisse-Svizzera-Switzerland (http://www.emdr-schweiz.ch)

Turkey
Association: EMDR Derneği (http://www.emdr-tr.org)

United Kingdom and Ireland
Association: EMDR UK & Ireland (http://www.emdrassociation.org.uk)

EMDR Iberoamérica

EMDR Iberoamérica: An association of South and Central America National EMDR Associations (www.emdriberoamerica.org)

Argentina
Association: EMDR Iberoamérica Argentina (http://www.emdribargentina.org)

Brazil
Association: EMDR Brasil (http://www.emdr.org.br)

Chile
Association: EMDR Chile (http://www.emdrchile.cl)

Colombia
Association: EMDR-IBA Colombia (http://emdrcolombia.com)

Costa Rica
Association: EMDR Costa Rica (http://emdrcostarica.wordpess.com)

Cuba
Contact: Alexis Lorenzo Ruiz (alexis.lorenzo@psico.uh.cu)

Ecuador
Association: EMDR Iberoamérica Ecuador (http://emdrecuador.org)

Guatemala
Association: EMDR Guatemala (http://emdrguatemala.org)
Contact: Ligia Barascout (ligiabps@yahoo.com)

Haiti
Contact: Myrtho Marra Chilosi (emdrhaiti2011@yahoo.fr)

Mexico
Association: EMDR Mexico (http://www.emdrmexico.org)

Panama
Association: EMDR Panama (http://emdribapanama.org/)

Puerto Rico
Association: EMDR Iberoamérica Puerto Rico (http://www.emdribappuertorico.org/)

Uruguay
Association: EMDR Uruguay (http://emdruru.guay.org.uy)

Venezuela
Contact: Deglya Camero de Salazar (deglyac@gmail.com)

North America

Canada
Association: EMDR Canada (http://www.emdrcanada.org)

United States
Association: EMDR International Association (http://emdria.org)

Members of EMDRIA Outside the United States

Iraq
Contact Person: Mona Zaghrout (monazag12@yahoo.com; mzaghrout@ejymca.org)

Lebanon
Association: EMDR Lebanon Association
Contact Person: Lina Ibrahin (lina_f_ibrahim@hotmail.com)

Palestine
Contact Person: Mona Zaghrout (monazag12@yahoo.com; mzaghrout@ejymca.org)

Related EMDR Humanitarian Associations

Asia

Japan
Association: JEMDRA-HAP (http://hap.emdr.jp/)

Europe

HAP-Europe
Association: HAP-Europe (http://www.emdr-europe.org)

France
Association: HAP-France (http://www. http://hap-france.blogspot.fr)

Germany
Association: Trauma Aid (http://www.trauma-aid.org)

Spain
Association: HAP-España (http://www.emdr-es.org)

Switzerland
Association: HAP-Schweiz-Suisse-Svizzera-Switzerland (http://www.emdrschweiz.ch)

Turkey
Association: EMDR-HAP Turkey (www.emdr-tr.com)
Contact Person: Senel Karaman (senelkaraman@gmail.com)

United Kingdom and Ireland
Association: HAP UK & Ireland (www.hapuk.org)

Ibero-America

Argentina
Association: EMDR-Programa de Programa de Ayuda Humanitaria–Argentina
Email: emdrasistenciahumanitaria@fibertel.com.ar(Web site under construction at same address)

Iberoamerica
EMDR Iberoamerica (http://emdriberoamerica.org/progamaayudahumanitaria.html/)

Mexico
Asociacion Mexicana para Ayuda Mental en Crisis A.C. (http://www.amamecrisis.com.mx)

North America

United States
EMDR Humanitarian Assistance Program [EMDR-HAP] (http://www.emdrhap.org)

The Francine Shapiro Library

Francine Shapiro Library's EMDR Bibliography (http://library.nku.edu/)

EMDR Journals and E-Journals

The Journal of EMDR Practice and Research—The official publication of the EMDR International Association (http://www.springerpub.com/emdr)

EMDR-IS Electronic Journal (http://www.emdr.org.il)

Related EMDR Information

EMDR Network (http://www.emdrnetwork.org)

EMDR Research Foundation (http://www.emdrresearch.org)

Related Traumatology Information

American Red Cross (www.redcross.org)

The Australian Trauma Web (http://welcome.to/ptsd)David Baldwin's Trauma Pages (http://www.trauma-pages.com)

Children and War (http://www.childrenandwar.org)

European Federation of Psychologists Associations Task Force on Disaster Psychology [EFPA] (http://www.disaster.efpa.eu)

European Society for Traumatic Stress Studies (http://www.estss.org)

Give an Hour (www.giveanhour.org/)

International Society for the Study of Trauma and Dissociation (http://www.isst-d.org)

The International Critical Incident Stress Foundation (http://www.icisf.org)

National Center for PTSD (http://www.ptsd.va.gov)

National Institute of Mental Health (http://www.nimh.nih.gov/health/topics/post-tra umatic-stress-disorder-ptsd/index.shtml)

United States National Center for Posttraumatic Stress Disorder (http://www.ncptsd .va.gov/ncmain/index.jsp)

Wounded Warrior Project (www.woundedwarriorproject.org)

Adler-Tapia, A. (2012). *Child psychotherapy: Integrating developmental theory into clinical practice.* New York, NY: Springer Publishing.

Adúriz, M. E., Knopfler, C., & Bluthgen, C. (2009). Helping child flood victims using group EMDR intervention in Argentina: Treatment outcome and gender differences. *International Journal of Stress Management, 16(2)*, 138–153.

Alter-Reid, K., Evans, S., & Schaefer, S. (2010, October). *Therapy for Therapists Project: Impact of intensive EMDR treatment post-Katrina.* Paper presented at the EMDRIA Conference, Minneapolis, MN.

American Psychiatric Association. (2000). *Diagnostic and statistical manual of mental disorders-fourth edition text revision.* Washington, DC: Author.

American Psychiatric Association. (2004a). *Diagnostic and statistical manual for mental disorders. DSM-IV-TR* (4th ed., rev. text). Washington, DC: Author.

American Psychiatric Association. (2004b). *Practice Guideline for the treatment of patients with acute stress disorder and post-traumatic stress disorder.* Arlington, VA: Author.

Anderson, M. B., Brown, D., & Jean, I. (2012). *Time to listen, hearing people on the receiving end of international aid.* Cambridge, MA: CDA Collaborative Learning Projects.

Andrews, B., Brewin, C. R., Philpott, R., & Stewart, L. (2007). Delayed-onset posttraumatic stress disorder: A systematic review of the evidence. *American Journal of Psychiatry, 164(9)*, 1319–1326.

Armstrong, K., O'Callahan, W., Marmar, C. R. (1991). Debriefing Red Cross Disaster Personnel: The multiple stressor debriefing model. *Journal of Traumatic Stress 4*, 581–593.

Artigas, L., & Jarero, I. (2009). The butterfly hug. In M. Luber (Ed.) *Eye movement desensitization and reprocessing (EMDR) scripted protocols: Special populations* (pp. 5–7). New York, NY: Springer.

Artigas, L., Jarero, I., Alcalá, N., & Lopez-Cano, T. (2009). The EMDR integrative group treatment protocol (IGTP). In M. Luber (Ed.) *Eye movement desensitization and reprocessing (EMDR) scripted protocols: Basic and special situations* (pp. 279–288). New York, NY: Springer.

Artigas, L., Jarero, I., Mauer, M., López Cano, T., & Alcalá, N. (2000, September). *EMDR and traumatic stress after natural disasters: Integrative treatment protocol and the butterfly hug.* Poster presented at the EMDRIA Conference, Toronto, ON, Canada.

Artwohl, A. (2002). Perceptual and memory distortions in officer involved shootings. *FBI Law Enforcement Bulletin, 10*, 18–24.

Arvay, M. J., & Uhlemann, M. R. (1996). Counsellor stress in the field of trauma: A preliminary study. *Canadian Journal of Counselling, 30*, 193–121.

Ayalon, O. (1976). *Rescue! An emergency handbook.* Haifa, Israel: University of Haifa Press.

Ayalon, O., Lahad, M., & Cohen, A. (1999). *Community Stress Prevention.* Vol 3, 4 1999. The Community Stress Prevention Center, Jerusalem Ministry of Education, Kiryat Shmona, Israel.

Ayalon, O. (2003). The HANDS project: Helpers assisting natural disaster survivors. *Community Stress Prevention Centre, 5*, 127–135.

Bar-Sade, E. (2003a). *Early trauma: Revisited and revised through EMDR, the narrative story and the implementation of attachment theory.* Paper presented at the EMDR European Annual Conference, Rome.

Bar-Sade, E. (2003b). *EMDR and children.* The International Trauma Conference, Jerusalem.

Bar-Sade, E. (2005a). *"Attachment cues" as resources in affect regulation enhancement in children's EMDR Processing.* EMDR European Conference, Stockholm.

Bar-Sade, E. (2005b). EMDR and the challenge of working with children. *EMDR-Israel E-Journal,* www.emdr.org.il (Hebrew).

Bar-Sade, E. (2005c). EMDR with children. *EMDR-Israel E-Journal,* www.emdr.org.il (Hebrew).

Baruch, Y. (2009, January). *Mental health assistance in national emergencies: Initial phase.* Paper presented at the International Conference on Crisis as an Opportunity: Organizational and Professional Responses to Disaster, Ben-Gurion University of the Negev, Beer-Sheva, Israel.

Baum, N. (2010). Shared traumatic reality in communal disasters: Towards a conceptualization. *Psychotherapy Theory, Research, Practice, Training, 47(2),* 249–259.

Beaton, R. D., & Murphy, S. A. (1995). Working with people in crisis: Research implications. In C. R. Figley (Ed.), *Compassion fatigue: Coping with secondary traumatic stress disorder in those who treat the traumatized* (pp. 51–81). New York, NY: Brunner/Mazel.

Beck, A. T., Ward, C., & Mendelson, M. (1961). Beck Depression Inventory (BDI). *Archives for General Psychiatry,* 4(6), 561–571.

Beebe, G. W., & Appel, J. W. (1958). Variation in psychological tolerance to ground combat in World War II. Washington, DC: National Academy of Sciences.

Birnbaum, A. (2005a, February). *Group EMDR with children and families in South Thailand post-tsunami.* Invited presentation at Bangkok Children's Hospital, Bangkok, Thailand.

Birnbaum, A. (2005b, February). *Group EMDR with children and families following the tsunami in Thailand.* Invited presentation at the EMDR-Israel Humanitarian Assistance Program Conference, Ra'anana, Israel.

Birnbaum, A. (2006, July). *Group EMDR: Theory and practice.* Invited presentation at the EMDR-Israel Humanitarian Assistance Program Conference, Netanya, Israel.

Birnbaum, A. (2007, February). *Group EMDR in critical incident stress debriefing with IDF casualty notification officers: A pilot study.* Invited presentation at the EMDR-Israel Conference on EMDR in the Second Lebanese War, Netanya, Israel.

Bleich, A., Gelkopf, M., & Solomon, Z. (2003). Exposure to terrorism, stress related mental health symptoms, and coping behaviours among a nationally representative sample in Israel. *JAMA,* 290, 612–620.

Blore, D. C. (2009). Blind to therapist protocol. In M. Luber (Ed.), *Eye movement desensitization and reprocessing (EMDR) scripted protocols: Basics and special situations* (chap. 25). New York, NY: Springer.

Blore, D. C. (1997). Reflections on "A day when the whole world seemed to be darkened" changes. *International Journal of Psychology and Psychotherapy, 15(2),* 89–95.

Blore, D., Holmshaw, E. M., Swift, A., Standart, S., & Fish, D. M. (2013). The development and uses of the "Blind to Therapist" EMDR Protocol. *Journal Of EMDR Practice and Research, 7,* 2, pp. 95–105.

Boel, J. (1999). The butterfly hug. *EMDRIA Newsletter,* 4(4), 11–13.

Brewin, C. R., Rose, S., Andrews, B., Green, J., Turner, S., & Foa, E. (2002). Brief screening instrument for post-traumatic stress disorder. *British Journal of Psychiatry, 181,* 158–162.

Briere, J., & Scott, C. (2006). *Principles of trauma therapy: A guide to symptoms, evaluation and treatment.* Thousand Oaks, CA: Sage.

Bryant, R. A. (2007). Early intervention for post-traumatic stress disorder. *Early Intervention in Psychiatry, 1,* 19–26.

Bryant, R. A., & Harvey, A. G. (2000). *Acute stress disorder: A handbook of theory, assessment, and treatment.* Washington, DC: American Psychological Association.

Buchanan, M., Anderson, J., Uhlemann, M., & Horwitz, E. (2006, December). Secondary traumatic stress: An investigation of Canadian mental health workers. *Traumatology, 12*, 272–281.

Carlson, E, B., & Putnam, F. W. (1992). *Manual for the dissociative experiences scale.* Lutherville, MD: Sidran Foundation.

Cemalovic, A. (1997). *A saga of Sarajevo children: Coping with life under siege.* Stockholm, Sweden: KTH Hogskoletryckeriet.

Chemtob, C. M., & Dutch, H. (2006). *Bi-national trauma response: Building psychosocial resiliency in Sri Lanka [Evaluation report].* New York, NY: UJA Fed NY.

Chemtob, C. M., Nakashima, J., & Carlson, J. G. (2002). Brief-treatment for elementary school children with disaster-related posttraumatic stress disorder: A field study. *Journal of Clinical Psychology, 58*, 99–112.

Cocco, N., & Sharpe, L. (1993). An auditory variant of eye movement desensitization in a case of childhood post-traumatic stress disorder. *Journal of Behavior Therapy and Experimental Psychiatry, 24, 373–377.*

Connor, K. M., & Davidson, J. R. T. (2001, September). SPRINT: A brief global assessment of post-traumatic stress disorder. *International Clinical Psychopharmacology, 16(5)*, 279–284.

Crespo, M., & Gomez, M. M. (2011). *EGEP Evaluación Global del Estrés Postraumático.* Madrid, Spain: TEA Ediciones.

Daniels, N. (2009). Self-care for EMDR practitioners. In M. Luber (Ed.). *Eye movement desensitization and reprocessing (EMDR) Scripted Protocols: Basics and special situations* (pp. 399–400). New York, NY: Springer.

de Roos, C., & van Rood, Y. R. (2009). EMDR in the treatment of medically unexplained symptoms: A systematic review. *Journal of EMDR Practice and Research, 3*, 248–263.

Department of the Army. (2006). *Combat and operational stress control: Field manual No. 4–02.51 (FM 8 51).* Washington, DC: Headquarters, Department of the Army.

Department of Veteran's Affairs & Department of Defense. (2009). *VA/DoD evidence based clinical practice guideline for management of concussion/mild traumatic brain injury.* Washington, DC: The Office of Quality and Performance & Quality Management Directorate, United States Army MEDCOM, VA.

Department of Veteran's Affairs & Department of Defense. (2010). *VA/DoD clinical practice guideline for the management of post-traumatic stress* (Office of Quality and Performance Publication 10Q-CPG/PTSD-10). Washington, DC: Veterans Health Administration, Department of Veterans Affairs and Health Affairs, Department of Defense. Retrieved from www.healthquality.va.gov/ptsd/ptsd_full.pdf

Derogatis, L. R. (1983). *SCL-90-R administration, scoring & procedures manual-II* (pp. 14–15). Towson, MD: Clinical Psychometric Research.

Derogatis, L. R. (1993). *Brief Symptom Inventory: Administration, scoring, and procedures manual.* Minneapolis, MN: National Computer Systems.

Dyregov, A. (1989). Caring for helpers in disaster situations: Psychological debriefings. *Disaster Management, 2*, 25–30.

Elliott, D. M., & Briere, J. (1992). Sexual abuse trauma among professional women: Validating the Trauma Symptom Checklist-40 (TSC-40). *Child Abuse & Neglect, 16(3)*, 391–398.

Emanuel, Y. (2006, August). Integrating EMDR and a narrative approach in treatment of complex trauma. *EMDR-Israel E-Journal*, www.emdr.org.il (Hebrew).

Errebo, N., Knipe, J., Forte, K., Karlin, V., & Altayli, B. (2008). EMDR-HAP Training in Sri Lanka following 2004 tsunami. *Journal of EMDR Practice & Research, 2(2)*, 124–139.

Escudero, A. (2003). *Healing by thinking. Noesitherapy (Biological basis)* (4th ed.). Impreso en Signo Grafico: Valencia, Espana (web-site: http://dr.escudero.com/comprar.html.)

Etherington, K. (2009). Supervising helpers who work with the trauma of sexual abuse. *British Journal of Guidance and Counselling, 37(2)*, 179–194.

Everly, G. S., Boyle, S. & Lating. J. (1999). The effectiveness of psychological debriefing in vicarious trauma: A meta-analysis. *Stress Medicine, 15*, 229–233.

Everly, G. S., Jr., & Mitchell, J. T. (2008). *Integrative crisis intervention and disaster mental health.* Ellicott City, MD: Chevron.

Fernandez, I. (2002, Dicembre). I disturbi post-traumatici da stress, fattori di rischio, aspetti diagnostici e trattamento con l'EMDR [The post-traumatic stress disorder factors of risk, diagnostic aspects and treatment with EMDR]. Rivista Scientifica di Psicologia, Sommario 01, 15–24.

Fernandez, I., Gallinari, E., & Lorenzetti, A. (2004). A school-based intervention for children who witnessed the Pirelli building airplane crash in Milan, Italy. *Journal of Brief Therapy, 2,* 129–136.

Figley, C. R. (Ed.). (1995). *Compassion fatigue: Coping with secondary traumatic stress disorder in those who treat the traumatized.* New York, NY: Bruner/Mazel.

Figley, C. R. (2002). *Treating compassion fatigue.* New York, NY: Brunner-Rutledge.

Figley, C. R., & Kleber, R. J. (1995). Beyond the "victim": Secondary traumatic stress. In R. J. Kleber, C.R. Figley, & B. P. R. Gersons (Eds.), *Beyond trauma: Cultural and societal dynamics* (pp. 75–98). New York, NY: Plenum Press.

Foa, E. B., Cashman, L., Jaycox, L., & Perry, K. (1997). The validation of a self-report measure of posttraumatic stress disorder: The Posttraumatic Diagnostic Scale. *Psychological Assessment, 9*(4), 445–451.

Foa, E. B., & Riggs, D. S. (1994). Posttraumatic stress disorder and rape. In R. S. Pynoos (Ed.), *Posttraumatic stress disorder: A clinical review* (pp. 133–163). Baltimore, MD: Sidran Press.

Foa, E. B., Riggs, D. S., Dancu, C. V., & Rothbaum, B. O. (1993). Reliability and validity of a brief instrument for assessing post-traumatic stress disorder. *Journal of Traumatic Stress, 6*(4), 459–473.

French, D. P., & Sutton, S. (2010). Reactivity of measurement in health psychology: How much of a problem is it? What can be done about it? *British Journal of Health Psychology, 15*(Pt. 3), 453–468.

Galliano, S., Cervera, M., & Parada, E. (2004). *El CIPR Procesamiento y Recuperación tras Incidentes Críticos.* Retrieved from http://hdl.handle.net/10401/2975

Galliano, S., & Lahad, M. (2002). Debriefing reconsidered. *Counseling and Psychotherapy Journal, 3*(2), 20–21.

Gawrych, A. L. (2010). *PTSD in firefighters and secondary trauma in their wives.* Hempstead, NY: Hofstra University.

Gelbach, R., & Davis, K. (2007). Disaster response: EMDR and family systems therapy under communitywide stress. In F. Shapiro, F. W. Kaslow, & L. Maxfield (Eds.), *Handbook of EMDR and family therapy processes* (pp. 387–406). Hoboken, NJ: Wiley.

Gelinas, D. J. (2003). Integrating EMDR into phase-oriented treatment for trauma. *Journal of Trauma and Dissociation, 4,* 91–135.

Gilbar, O., Plivazky, N., & Gil, S. (2010). Counterfactual thinking, coping strategies, and coping resources as predictors of PTSD diagnosed in physically injured victims of terror attacks. *Journal of Loss and Trauma, 15,* 304–324.

Grainger, R. D., Levin, C., Allen-Byrd, L., Doctor, R. M., & Lee, H. (1997). An empirical evaluation of eye movement desensitization and reprocessing (EMDR) with survivors of a natural disaster. *Journal of Traumatic Stress, 10,* 665–671.

Greenwald, R. (1994). Applying eye movement desensitization and reprocessing to the treatment of traumatized children: Five case studies. *Anxiety Disorders Practice Journal, 1,* 83–97.

Greenwald, R. (1998). Eye movement desensitization and reprocessing (EMDR): New hope for children suffering from trauma and loss. *Clinical Child Psychology and Psychiatry, 3,* 279–287.

Greenwald, R., & Rubin, A. (1999). Brief assessment of children's post-traumatic symptoms: Development and preliminary validation of parent and child scales. *Research on Social Work Practice, 9,* 61–75.

Greenwald, R. (1999). *Eye movement desensitization and reprocessing (EMDR) in child and adolescent psychotherapy.* Northvale, NJ: Jason Aronson Press.

Greenwald, R. (2000). A trauma-focused individual therapy approach for adolescents with conduct disorder. *International Journal of Offender Therapy and Comparative Criminology, 44,* 146–163.

Grenough, M. (2012). *Oasis in the overwhelm.* New Haven, CT: Beaver Hill Press.

Grieger, T. A., Cozza, S. J., Ursano, R. J., Hoge, C., Martinez, P. E., Engel, C. C., & Wain, H. J. (2006). Posttraumatic stress disorder and depression in battle-injured soldiers. *American Journal of Psychiatry, 163*(10), 1777–1783.

Grossman, D. (2007). *On combat: The psychology and physiology of deadly conflict in war and in peace* (2nd ed.). Millstadt, Illinois: PPCT Research.

Herman, J. L. (1992). *Trauma and recovery.* New York, NY: Basic Books.

Hernandez, D. (2002). DRC: District resource center defined. *Insights.* Retrieved from http://www.openinc.org/newsletters/Insights_2002Fall.pdf

Holbrook, T. L., Galarneau, M. R., Dye, J. L., Quinn, K., & Dougherty, A. L. (2010). Morphine use after combat injury in Iraq and post-traumatic stress disorder. *New England Journal of Medicine, 362*, 110–117.

Holgersen, K. H., Klöckner, C. A., Boe, H. J., Weisaeth, L., & Holen, A. (2011). Disaster survivors in their third decade: Trajectories of initial stress responses and long term course of mental health. *Journal of Traumatic Stress, 24(3)*, 334–341.

Honig, A., & Roland, J. (1998). Shots fired: Officer involved. *The Police Chief, 65*, 16–19.

Horowitz, M. J. (1979). Psychological response to serious life events. In V. Hamilton & D. M. Warburton (Eds.), *Human stress and cognition* (pp. 235–263). Chichester, England: Wiley.

Horowitz, M. J., Wilner, M., & Alverez, W. (1979). Impact of Events Scale: A measure of subjective stress. *Psychosomatic Medicine, 41*(3), 209–218.

Ironson, G. I., Freund, B., Strauss, J. L., & Williams, J. (2002). A comparison of two treatments for traumatic stress: A pilot study of EMDR and prolonged exposure. *Journal of Clinical Psychology, 58*, 113–128.

Ivar, Pivar (2004). Traumatic grief: Symptomatology and treatment in the Iraq War veteran. In The Department of Veterans' Affairs National Center of PTSD, *Iraq War clinician guide* (2nd ed., pp. 75–78). Department of Veteran's Affairs, National Centre for PTSD.

Jarero, I. (2011). *El Desastre Después del Desastre: ¿Ya pasó lo peor? Revista Iberoamericana de Psicotraumatología y Disociación* (Volumen 1, Número 1). Retrieved from http://revibapst.com/DESASTRE-REVIBA.pdf

Jarero, I., & Artigas, L. (2009). EMDR integrative group treatment protocol. *Journal of EMDR Practice and Research, 3*(4), 287–288.

Jarero, I., Artigas, L., & Hartung, J. (2006). EMDR integrative group treatment protocol: A post-disaster trauma intervention for children and adults. *Traumatology, 12*, 121–129.

Jarero, I., & Artigas, L. (2010). The EMDR integrative group treatment protocol: Application with adults during ongoing geopolitical crisis. *Journal of EMDR Practice and Research, 4*(4), 148–155.

Jarero, I., Artigas, L., & Hartung, J. (2006). EMDR integrative group treatment protocol: A post-disaster trauma intervention for children and adults. *Traumatology, 12*, 121–129.

Jarero, I., Artigas, L., & Luber, M. (2011). The EMDR protocol for recent critical incidents: Application in a disaster mental health continuum of care context. *Journal of EMDR Practice and Research, 5*(3), 82–94.

Jarero, I., Artigas, L., Mauer, M., López Cano, T., & Alcalá, N. (1999, November). *Children's post traumatic stress after natural disasters: Integrative treatment protocol.* Poster presented at the annual meeting of the International Society for Traumatic Stress Studies, Miami, FL.

Jarero, I., Artigas, L., Montero, M. (2008). The EMDR integrative group treatment protocol: Application with child victims of mass disaster. *Journal of EMDR Practice & Research, 2*(2), 97–105.

Jarero, I., & Uribe, S. (2011). The EMDR protocol for recent critical incidents: Brief report of an application in a human massacre situation. *Journal of EMDR Practice and Research, 5*(4), 156–165.

Jarero, I., & Uribe, S. (2012). The EMDR protocol for recent critical incidents: Follow-up report of an application in a human massacre situation. *Journal of EMDR Practice and Research, 6*(2), 50–61.

Jelinek, P., & Burns, R. (2012, January). *Pentagon works on new plan to curb sex assaults.* Retrieved from http://www.huffingtonpost.com/2012/01/ll/marines-urinate-corpses-video-afghanistan_n_1200513.html

Jelinek, P. & Burns, R. (2012, January). Panetta assures Afghans of full probe into video. OnlineAthens (Athens Banner-Herald), (http://onlineathens.com/do/not/override/panel/taxonomy/term/43481/2)

Johnson, K. (1998). *Trauma in the lives of children*. Alameda, CA: Hunter House.

Jones, E., & Wessley, S. (2003). Forward psychiatry in the military: Its origins and effectiveness. *Journal of Traumatic Stress, 16(4)*, 411–419.

Jones, E., & Wessely, S. (2005). *Shell shock to PTSD: Military psychiatry from 1900 to the Gulf War*. New York, NY: Psychology Press.

Jones, R. (1997). Child's reaction to traumatic event scale (CRTES). In J. Wilson & T. Keane (Eds.), *Assessing psychological trauma and PTSD* (pp. 291–348). New York, NY: Guilford Press.

Jones, R. T., Fletcher, K., & Ribbe, D. R. (2004). Child's reaction to traumatic event scale-revised (CRTES-R). In J. Wilson & T. Keane (Eds.), *Assessing psychological trauma and PTSD* (2nd ed., p. 523). New York, NY: Guilford Press.

Kabat-Zinn, J. (2012). *Mindfulness for beginners*. CT: Sounds True.

Kaplan G. (1975). *Support Systems in Times of War, The Individual and the Community in Emergencies*. Hebrew University, Jerusalem (Hebrew)

Klingman, A., & Ayalon, O. (1976). Preparing the education system for emergency. *Israeli Journal of Psychology and Counseling in Education (Chavat Da'at), 15*, 135–148. (Hebrew)

Konuk, E. (2009, June). Mental health response and training program for developing countries: The Turkish model. In G. Zaal (Chair), *Diverse*. Symposium conducted at the annual meeting of the EMDR Europe Association, Amsterdam, the Netherlands.

Konuk, E., Knipe, J., Eke, I., Yuksek, H., Yurtsever, A., & Ostep, S. (2006). The effects of eye movement desensitization and reprocessing (EMDR) therapy on post-traumatic stress disorder in survivors of the 1999 Marmara, Turkey, earthquake. *International Journal of Stress Management, 13(3)*, 291–308. doi:10.1037/1072–5245.13.3.291

Korkmazlar-Oral, U., & Pamuk, S. (2002). Group EMDR with child survivors of the earthquake in Turkey. *Journal of the American Academy of Child and Adolescent Psychiatry, 37*, 47–50.

Korn, D., & Leeds, A. M. (2002). Preliminary evidence of efficacy for EMDR resource development and installation in the stabilization phase of treatment of complex posttraumatic stress disorder. *Journal of Clinical Psychology, 58*, 1465–1487.

Kristal-Andersson, B. (2000). *Psychology of the refugee, the immigrant and their children: Development of a conceptual framework and applications to psychotherapeutic and related support work*. Lund, Sweden: University of Lund Press.

Kutz, I., Dekel, R., Schreiber, S., Resnick, V., Dolberg, O. T., Barkai, G., . . . Bloch, M. (2008, November). *The effect of a single session of EMDR on intrusive distress in acute stress syndromes*. Symposium/panel conducted at the 24th annual meeting of the International Society for Traumatic Stress Studies, Chicago, IL.

L'Abate, L. (2004). *A guide to self-help mental health workbooks for clinicians and researchers*. Binghamton, NY: Haworth.

Lahad, M. (2005, October). *1st report to JDC & UJA Fed NY, on the progress of the Tri National project*. Unpublished manuscript, Community Stress Prevention Center, Kiryat Shmona, Israel.

Lahad, M. (2009). *Lessons learnt from the Tri-National project in Sri Lanka following the 2004 tsunami: Focusing on culturally sensitive issues of mental health and psychosocial support and the management of such a project*. Paper presented at the International Conference on Crisis as an Opportunity: Organizational and Professional Responses to Disaster, Ben-Gurion University of the Negev, Beer-Sheva, Israel.

Lahad, M. (2011). *Lessons learned: What was effective post natural disaster training 5 years after the MT training in Sri Lanka was over (2007) field visit and group interview*. A report submitted to UJA Fed. NY and to ITC.

Lahad, M. (2013). BASIC Ph: The story of coping resources. In M. Lahad, M. Shacham, & O. Ayalon (Eds.), *The "BASIC PH" model of coping and resiliency—Theory, research and cross-cultural application*. London, England: Jessica Kingsley.

Lahad, M., Baruch, Y., Shacham, Y., Niv, S., Rogel, R, Nacasch, N., . . . Leykin, D. (2011). Cultural sensitivity in psychosocial interventions following a disaster: A trinational collaboration in Sri Lanka. In R. Kaufman, R. L. Edwards, J. Mirsky, & A. Avgar (Eds.), *Crisis as an opportunity: Organizational and professional responses to disaster* (pp. 129–154). Lanham, MD: University Press of America.

Lahad, M., & Cohen, A. (1997). *Community stress preventions* (Vols. 1, 2). Kiryat Shmona, Israel: The Community Stress Prevention Center, Jerusalem Ministry of Education.

Lamphear, M. (2010). *Effectiveness of the post critical incident seminar in reducing critical incident stress among law enforcement officers.* Doctoral dissertation, Walden University.

Lande, R. G., Marin, B. A., & Ruzek, J. I. (2004). Substance abuse in the deployment environment. In The Department of Veterans Affairs National Center of PTSD (Eds.), *Iraq War clinician guide* (2nd ed., pp. 79–82). Department of Veterans Affairs, National Center of PTSD. Retrieved from: www.ptsd.va.gov

Lansen, J. (1993). Vicarious traumatization in therapists treating victims of torture and persecution. *Torture, 3*(4), 138–140.

Lansen, J., & Haans, T. (2004). Clinical supervision for trauma therapists. In J. P. Wilson & B. Drozdek (Eds.), *Broken spirits: The treatment of traumatized asylum seekers, refugees, war and torture victims* (pp. 317–354). New York, NY: Brunner-Routledge.

Laub, B. (2001). The healing power of resource connection in the EMDR protocol [Special edition]. *EMDRIA Newsletter, 21*–27.

Laub, B. (2009). Resource connection envelope (RCE) in the EMDR Standard Protocol. In Luber, M. (Ed.), *EMDR Scripted Protocols: Basic and Special Situations (pp. 93–99).* New York, NY: Springer.

Laub, B., & Bar-Sade, E. (2009). The Imma EMDR group protocol. In M. Luber (Ed.), *Eye movement desensitization and reprocessing (EMDR) scripted protocols: Basic and special situations* (p. 292). New York, NY: Springer.

Laub, B., & Weiner, N. (2007). The pyramid model—Dialectical polarity in therapy. *Journal of Transpersonal Psychology, 39*(2), 199–221.

Laub, B., & Weiner, N. (2011). A developmental/integrative perspective of the recent traumatic episode protocol (R-TEP). *Journal of EMDR Practice and Research, 5*(2), 57–72.

Lee, C., Gavriel, H., Drummond, P., Richards, J., & Greenwald, R. (2002). Treatment of PTSD: Stress inoculation training with prolonged exposure compared to EMDR. *Journal of Clinical Psychology, 58,* 1071–1089.

Leeds, A. M. (2009). *A guide to the standard EMDR protocols for clinicians, supervisors, and consultants.* New York, NY: Springer.

Levine, P. (1997). *Waking the tiger: Healing trauma.* Berkeley, CA: North Atlantic Book.

Leykin, D. (2012, September). *Crisis management in schools (CIMS) preliminary results from a controlled study* [Research report]. Unpublished manuscript, Community Stress Prevention Center, Kiryat Shmona, Israel.

Litz, B. T. (Ed.). (2004). *Early intervention for trauma and traumatic loss.* New York, NY: Guilford Press.

Lovett, J. (1999). *Small wonders: Healing childhood trauma with EMDR.* New York, NY: Free Press.

Luber, M. (2001, December). In the spotlight. Roger Solomon. EMDRIA Newsletter, 6, 4, 20–21.

Laub, B. (2009). Resource Connection Envelope (RCE) in the EMDR standard protocol. In M. Luber (Ed.), *EMDR scripted protocols: Basic and special situations* (pp. 93–99). New York: Springer

Luber, M. (Ed.) (2009a). *Eye movement desensitization and reprocessing (EMDR) scripted protocols: Basics and special situations.* New York, NY: Springer.

Luber, M. (Ed.). (2009a). *Eye movement desensitization and reprocessing (EMDR): Scripted protocols basics and special situations* (pp. 387–392). New York, NY: Springer.

Luber, M. (Ed.). (2009a). *Eye movement desensitization and reprocessing (EMDR): Scripted protocols basics and special situations* (Section, III, pp. 67–106). New York, NY: Springer.

Luber, M. (Scripted by). (2009a). Recent traumatic events protocol. In M. Luber (Ed.), *Eye movement desensitization and reprocessing (EMDR): Scripted protocols basics and special situations* (pp. 387–392). New York, NY: Springer.

Luber, M., & Shapiro, F. (2009). Interview with Francine Shapiro: Historical overview, present issues, and future directions of EMDR. *Journal of EMDR Practice and Research*, 3(4), 217–231.

Ludwig, A., & Ranson, S. (1947). A statistical follow-up of effectiveness of treatment of combat-induced psychiatric casualties: 1. Returns to full combat duty. *Military Surgeon, 100*, 51–62.

Macy, R., Behart, L., Paulson, R., Delman, J., Schmid, L., & Smith, S. F. (2004). Community-based, acute posttraumatic stress management: A description and evaluation of a psychosocial-intervention continuum. *Harvard Review of Psychiatry, 12*, 217–218.

Maguan, S., Lucenko, B. A., Reger, M. A., Gahm, G. A., Litz, B. T., Seal, K. H., . . . Marmar, C. R. (2010). The impact of reported direct and indirect killing on mental health symptoms in Iraq war veterans. *Journal of Traumatic Stress*, 23(1), 86–90.

Maguen, S., Metzler, T., McCaslin, S., Inslicht, S., Henn-Haase, C., Neylan, T., & Marmar, C. (2009). Routine work environment stress and PTSD symptoms in police officers. *Journal of Nervous & Mental Disease*, 197(10), 754–760.

Manfield, P., & Shapiro, F. (2003). The application of EMDR to the treatment of personality disorders. In J. F. Magnavita (Ed.), *Handbook of personality: Theory and practice*. Hoboken, NJ: Wiley.

Marin, P. (1995). *Freedom & its discontents: Reflection on four decades of American moral experience*. South Royalton, VT: Steerforth Press.

Marmar, C. R., Weiss, D. S., & Metzler, T. J. (1996). The Peritraumatic Dissociative Experiences Questionnaire. In J. P. Wilson & C. R. Marmar (Eds.), *Assessing psychological trauma and posttraumatic stress disorder* (pp. 412–428). New York, NY: Guilford Press.

Maslach, C., Jackson, S. E., & Leiter, M. P. (1996). *Maslach Burnout Inventory manual* (3rd ed.). Palo Alto, CA: Consulting Psychologists Press.

Maxfield, L. (2008). EMDR treatment of recent events and community disasters. *Journal of EMDR Practice & Research*, 2(2), 74–78.

Maxfield, L. (2009). Twenty years of EMDR. *Journal of EMDR Practice and Research*, 3(4), 211–216.

Maxfield, L., Melnyk, W. T., & Hayman, C. A. G. (2008). A working memory explanation for the effects of eye movements in EMDR. *Journal of EMDR Practice and Research*, 2(4), 247–261.

McCann, I. L., & Pearlman, L. A. (1990). Vicarious traumatization: A contextual model for understanding the effects of trauma on helpers. *Journal of Traumatic Stress*, 3(1), 131–149.

McCullough, L. (2002). Exploring change mechanisms in EMDR applied to "small t-trauma" in short term dynamic psychotherapy: Research questions and speculations. *Journal of Clinical Psychology, 58*, 1465–1487.

McFarlane, A. C. (2010). The long-term costs of traumatic stress: Intertwined physical and psychological consequences. *World Psychiatry, 9*, 3–10.

McNally, V. J., & Solomon, R. M. (1999, February). The FBI's critical incident stress management program. *FBI Law Enforcement Bulletin*, pp. 20–26.

Mehrotra, S. (1996). *EMDR an integrated approach to psychotherapy*. Paper presented at the Bombay Psychological Association Annual Conference, Bombay, India.

Mehrotra, S. (2008, June). *EMDR in India*. Keynote and paper presented at the 9th EMDR European Conference, London.

Mehrotra, S., & Geng, W. (2011, February). EMDR in India. *Journal of Xihua University (Philosophy & Social Sciences)*. doi:CNKI:SUN:CDSF.0.2011-02-000

Meichenbaum, D. (1994). *A clinical handbook/practical therapist manual for assessing and treating adults with post-traumatic stress disorder (PTSD)*. Waterloo, Canada: Institute Press.

Melville, A. (2003, April). Psychosocial Interventions: Evaluation of UNICEF supported projects (1999–2001). UNICEF Indonesia.

Mitchell, J. T. (1983). When disaster strikes . . . The critical incident stress debriefing. *Journal of Emergency Medical Service, 13*(11), 49–52.

Mitchell, J. T., & Everly, G. S. (1996). *Critical incident stress debriefing: An operations manual*. Ellicott City, MD: Chevron.

Mitchell, J. T., & Everly, G. S. (2003). *Critical incident stress management: Group crisis intervention* (3rd ed.). Ellicott City, MD: International Critical Incident Stress Foundation.

Modell, A. H. (1976). "The holding environment" and the therapeutic action of psychoanalysis. *Journal of the American Psychoanalytic Association, 24,* 285–307.

Motta, R. W., Hafeez, S., Sciancalepore, R., & Diaz, A. B. (2001). Discriminant validation of the Modified Secondary Trauma Questionnaire. *Journal of Psychotherapy in Independent Practice, 2*(4), 17–25.

Muñoz, M., Vázquez, J. J., Crespo, M., & Pérez-Santos, E. P. (2004). We were all wounded on March 11th in Madrid: Immediate psychological affects and interventions. *European Psychologist, 9*(4), 278–280.

National Institute for Clinical Excellence. (2005). *Post traumatic stress disorder (PTSD): The management of PTSD in adults and children in primary and secondary care.* London, England: NICE Guidelines.

National Institute for Clinical Excellence. (2005a). *PTSD clinical guidelines.* United Kingdom: NHS.

National Institute for Clinical Excellence. (2005b). *Posttraumatic stress disorder (PTSD): The management of adults and children in primary and secondary care.* United Kingdom: NHS.

National Institute for Health and Care Excellence (2005, March). *Post-traumatic stress disorder (PTSD): The management of PTSD in adults and children in primary and secondary care* (NICE Clinical Guideline 26). London, England: National Institute for Clinical Excellence.

National Institute of Mental Health. (2002). Mental Health and Mass Violence: Evidence-Based Early Psychological Intervention for Victims/Survivors of Mass Violence. A Workshop to Reach Consensus on Best Practices. NIH Publication No. 02–5138, Washington, D.C.: U.S. Government Printing Office.

Nikapota, A. (2006). After the tsunami: A story from Sri Lanka. *International Review of Psychiatry, 18,* 275–279.

Norman, S. B., Stein, M. B., Dimsdale, J. E., & Hoyt, D. B. (2008). Pain in the aftermath of trauma is a risk factor for post-traumatic stress disorder. *Psychology Medicine Journal, 38,* 533–542.

Norris, F. H., Galea, S., Friedman, M. J., & Watson, P. J. (2006). *Methods for disaster mental health research.* New York, NY: Guilford Press.

Nouwen, H. (2010, February). *Nouwen & the Ministry of Presence.* Retrieved from http://missionalchurchnetwork.com/nouwen-the-ministry-of-presence/

Ogden, P., & Minton, K. (2000, January). Sensorimotor psychotherapy: One method for processing traumatic memory. *Traumatology, 4*(3), V1(3), 149–173.

Palm, K. M., Polusny, M. A., & Follette, V. M. (2004). Vicarious traumatization: Potential hazards and interventions for disaster and trauma workers. *Prehospital and Disaster Medicine, 19*(1), 73–78.

Parada, E., & Cervera, M. (Unpublished manuscript, 1997). *Psychological first aid response.* Madrid, Spain: ICAS Spain.

Pearlman, L. A. (1995). Self-care for trauma therapists: Ameliorating vicarious traumatization. In B. H. Stamm (Ed.), *Secondary traumatic stress: Self-care issues for clinicians, researchers, and educators* (pp. 51–64). Lutherville, MD: Sidran Press.

Pearlman, L. A. (1996a). Psychometric review of TSI Belief Scale, Revision L. In B. H. Stamm (Ed.), *Measurement of stress, trauma, and adaptation* (pp. 415–417). Lutherville, MD: Sidran Press.

Pearlman, L. A. (1996b). Psychometric review of TSI Life Event Questionnaire (LEQ). In B. H. Stamm (Ed.), *Measurement of stress, trauma, and adaptation* (pp. 419–430). Lutherville, MD: Sidran Press.

Pearlman, L. A., & Maclan, I. (1995). Vicarious traumatization: An empirical study of the effects of trauma work on trauma therapists. *Professional Psychology: Research and Practice, 26*(6), 558–565.

Pearlmann, L. A., & Saakvitne, K. W. (1995). Trauma and the therapist: Countertransference and vicarious traumatization in psychotherapy with incest survivors. New York, NY: W. W. Norton.

Pellicer, X. (1993). Eye movement desensitization treatment of a child's nightmares: A case report. *Journal of Behavior Therapy and Experimental Psychiatry, 24*, 73–75.

Pennebaker, J. W. (1997). Writing about emotional experiences as a therapeutic process. *Psychological Science*, 8(3), 162–168.

Perkins, B., & Rouanzoin, C. (2002). A critical examination of current views regarding eye movement desensitization and reprocessing (EMDR): Clarifying points of confusion. *Journal of Clinical Psychology, 58*, 77–97.

Puffer, M. K., Greenwald, R., & Elrod, D. E. (1998). A single session EMDR study with twenty traumatized children and adolescents. *Traumatology*, 3(2), Article 6.

Purandare, M., Bhagwagar, H., & Tank, P. (2010, July). *EMDR on children affected by the earthquake.* Paper presented at the 1st EMDR Asia Conference, Bali, Indonesia.

Quinn, G. (2009). Emergency response procedure. In M. Luber (Ed.), *Eye movement and desensitization and reprocessing: Scripted protocols basics and special situations.* New York, NY: Springer.

Radloff, L. S., & Locke, Z. (2000). Center for Epidemiologic Studies Depression Scale (CES-D). In *American Psychiatric Association, task force for the handbook of psychiatric measures* (pp. 523–526). Washington, DC: American Psychiatric Association.

Raphael, B. (1977). Preventive intervention with the recently bereaved. *Archives of General Psychiatry, 34*, 1450–1454.

Reddemann, L. (2009). The inner safe place. In Luber, M. (Ed.), *EMDR Scripted Protocols: Basic and Special Situations* (pp. 71–72). New York, NY: Springer.

Roberts, N. P., Kitchiner, N. J., Kenardy, J., & Bisson, J. I. (2009, March). Systematic review and meta-analysis of multiple-session early interventions following traumatic events. *American Journal of Psychiatry, 166(3)*, 293–301. doi: 10.1176/appi.ajp.2008. 08040590

Rudolf, J. (2012, January). *Marines appear to urinate on dead Taliban fighters.* Retrieved from http://www.huffingtonpost.com/2012/01/ll/marines-urinate-corpses-video-afghanistan_n_1200513.html

Russell, A., & O'Connor, M. (2002). Interventions for recovery: The use of EMDR with children in a community-based project. *Association for Child Psychiatry and Psychology, Occasional Paper No. 19*, 43–46.

Russell, M. C. (2006). Treating combat-related stress disorders: Multiple case study utilizing eye movement desensitization and reprocessing (EMDR) with battlefield casualties from the Iraqi war. *Military Psychology, 18*, 1–18.

Russell, M. C. (2008b). Treating traumatic amputation-related phantom limb pain: Case study utilizing eye movement desensitization and reprocessing (EMDR) within the armed services. *Clinical Case Studies, 7*, 136–153.

Russell, M. C. (2008c). War-related medically unexplained symptoms, prevalence and treatment: Utilizing EMDR within the armed services. *Journal of EMDR Practice and Research*, 2(2), 212–225.

Russell, M. C. (2012, January 27). *Preventing military misconduct stress behavior* [Blog]. Retrieved from http://www.huffingtonpost.com/mark-c-russell-phd-abpp/ptsd-veterans_b_l 228546.html

Russell, M. C., & Figley, C. F. (2013). *An EMDR practitioners guide to treating traumatic stress disorders in military personnel.* New York, NY: Routledge.

Russell, M. C., & Figley, C. F. (2013). *Treating traumatic stress disorders in military personnel: An EMDR practitioners' guide.* New York, NY: Routledge.

Russell, M. C., Lipke, H. E., & Figley, C. R. (2011). EMDR therapy. In B. A. Moore & W. A. Penk (Eds.), *Handbook for the treatment of PTSD in military personnel.* New York, NY: Guilford Press.

Russell, M. C., Silver, S. M., & Rogers, S. (2007). Responding to an identified need: A joint DoD-DVA training program in EMDR for clinicians providing trauma services. *International Journal of Stress Management*, 14(1), 61–71.

Russell, M. C., Silver, S. M., Rogers, S., & Darnell, J. N. (2007, February). Responding to an identified need: A joint Department of Defense/Department of Veterans Affairs training program in eye movement desensitization and reprocessing (EMDR) for clinicians providing trauma services. International Journal of Stress Management, 14(1), 61–71. doi: 10.1037/1072–5245.14.1.61.

Samec, J. (2001). The use of EMDR safe place exercise in group therapy with traumatized adolescent refugees [Special edition]. *The EMDRIA Newsletter*. 32–34

Scheck, M. M., Schaeffer, J. A., & Gillette, C. S. (1998). Brief psychological intervention with traumatized young women: The efficacy of eye movement desensitization and reprocessing. *Journal of Traumatic Stress, 11*, 25–44.

Schwartz, A. C., Bradley, R., Penza, K. M., Sexton, M., Jay, D., Haggard, P. J., . . . Ressler, K. J. (2006). Pain medicine use among patients with posttraumatic stress disorder. *Psychosomatics, 47*, 136–142.

Shacham, Y. (2009, January). Challenges in extending help cross culturally [Unpublished PowerPoint slides]. Paper presented at the International Conference on Crisis as an Opportunity: Organizational and Professional Responses to Disaster, Ben-Gurion University of the Negev, Beersheva, Israel.

Shalev, A. Y., Ankri, Y., Israeli-Shalev, Y., Peleg, T., Adessky, R., & Freedman, S. (2012). Prevention of posttraumatic stress disorder by early treatment: Results from the Jerusalem Trauma Outreach and Prevention study. *Archives for General Psychiatry, 69*(2), 166–176.

Shani, Z. (2006, July). *Group EMDR with school children following a traumatic event.* Invited presentation at EMDR-Israel HAP conference, Netanya, Israel.

Shapiro, F. (2006). *EMDR: New notes on adaptive information processing with case formulation principles, forms, scripts and worksheets.* Watsonville, CA: EMDR Institute.

Shapiro, E. (2009). EMDR treatment of recent trauma events. *Journal of EMDR Practice and Research, 3*(3), 141–151.

Shapiro, E., & Laub, B., (2008a). Early EMDR intervention (EEI): Summary, a theoretical model, and the recent traumatic episode protocol (R-TEP). *Journal of EMDR Practice and Research, 2*(2), 79–96.

Shapiro, E., & Laub, B., (2008b, May). *Unfinished-traumatic episode protocol (U-TEP) A new protocol for early EMDR interventions.* Paper presented at the EMDR Europe Annual Conference, London, England.

Shapiro, E., & Laub, B. (2009). The recent traumatic episode protocol (R-TEP): An integrative protocol for early EMDR intervention (EEI). In M. Luber (Ed.), *Eye movement and desensitization and reprocessing: Scripted protocols basics and special situations* (pp. 251–270). New York, NY: Springer.

Shapiro, F. (1989). Efficacy of eye movement desensitization procedure in the treatment of traumatic memory. *Journal of Traumatic Stress, 2*(2), 199–223.

Shapiro, F. (1989). Eye movement desensitization. A new treatment for posttraumatic stress disorder. *Journal of Behavior Therapy and Experimental Psychiatry, 20*, 211–217.

Shapiro, F. (1991). Eye movement desensitization and reprocessing procedure: From EMD to EMDR: A new treatment model for anxiety and related traumata. *Behavior Therapist, 14*, 133–135.

Shapiro, F. (1995). *Eye movement desensitization and reprocessing: Basic principles, protocols, and procedures* (1st ed.). New York, NY: Guilford Press.

Shapiro, F. (2001). *Eye movement desensitization and reprocessing: basic principles, protocols, and procedures* (2nd ed.). New York, NY: Guilford Press.

Shapiro, F. [scripted by M. Luber].(2009). Recent traumatic events protocol. In Luber, M. (Ed.), *EMDR scripted protocols: Basic and special situations* (pp. 143–154). New York, NY: Springer.

Shapiro, F. (2006). *New notes on adaptive information processing with case formulation principles, forms, scripts, and worksheets.* Watsonville, CA: EMDR Institute.

Silver, S. M., Rogers, S., Knipe, J., & Colelli, G. (2005). EMDR therapy following the 9/11 terrorist attacks: A community-based intervention project in New York City. *International Journal of Stress Management, 12*, 29–42.

Silver, S. M., Rogers, S., & Russell, M. (2008). Eye movement desensitization and reprocessing (EMDR) in the treatment of war veterans. *Journal of Clinical Psychology: In session, 64*(8), 947–957.

Skovholt, T. M. (2001). *The resilient practitioner: Burnout prevention and self-care strategies for counsellors, therapists, teachers, and health professionals.* Boston, MA: Allyn & Bacon.

Soberman, G. B., Greenwald, R., & Rule, D. L. (2002). A controlled study of eye movement desensitization and reprocessing (EMDR) for boys with conduct problems. *Journal of Aggression, Maltreatment, and Trauma, 6*, 217–236.

Solomon, R. (2008). Critical incident interventions. *Journal of EMDR Practice and Research, 2*, 160–165.

Solomon, R. M. (1988, October). Post-shooting trauma, *Police Chief*, pp. 40–44.

Solomon, R. M., & Horn, J. M. (1986). Post-shooting traumatic. In J. Reese & H. Goldstein (Eds.), *Law enforcement* (pp. 383–393). Washington, DC: United States Government Printing Office.

Spielberger, C. D., Gorssuch, R. L., Lushene, P. R., Vagg, P. R., & Jacobs, G. A. (1983). *Manual for the State-Trait Anxiety Inventory*. Palo Alto, CA: Consulting Psychologists Press.

Stamm, B. H. (2010). *The Concise ProQOL manual* (2nd ed.). Pocatello, ID: ProQOL.org

Stewart, K., & Bramson, T. (2000). Incorporating EMDR in residential treatment. *Residential Treatment for Children & Youth, 17*, 83–90.

Strupp, H. H., & Binder, J. L. (1984). *Psychotherapy in a new key: A guide to time-limited dynamic psychotherapy*. New York, NY: Basic Books.

Tank, P. (2011). *A presentation on EMDR*. Delhi, India: ANCIPS, EMDR.

Taylor, R. (2002). Family unification with reactive attachment disorder: A brief treatment. *Contemporary Family Therapy: An International Journal, 24*, 475–481.

Tedeschi, R., & Calhoun, L. (1995). *Trauma and transformation: Growing in the aftermath of suffering*. Thousand Oaks, CA: Sage.

Tedeschi, R., & Calhoun, L. (2004). Posttraumatic growth: Conceptual foundations and evidence, *Psychological Inquiry, 15(l)*, 1–18.

Tinker, R. H., & Wilson, S. A. (1999). *Through the eyes of a child: EMDR with children*. New York, NY: W. W. Norton.

Turkish Psychological Association. (1999). *Annual bulletin*. Ankara: Author.

U.S. Department of Veterans Affairs & US Department of Defense. (2004). *VA/DoD clinical practice guideline for the management of post-traumatic stress*. Washington, D.C.

Ullmann, E., & Hilweg, W. (2000). *Infancia y Trauma, separación, abuso y guerra*. Auryn colección. Brand. Madrid. (German Original version, 1997).

Van Peski, C. (2006, January). *CSPC crisis intervention training Colombo, Sri Lanka*. Unpublished manuscript, Community Stress Prevention Center, Kiryat Shmona, Israel.

Van Rooyen, M., & Leaning, J. (2005). After the tsunami: Facing the public health challenges. *New England Journal of Medicine, 352*, 435–438.

Weathers, F., Litz, B., Herman, D., Huska, J., & Keane, T. (1993). *The PTSD Checklist (PCL): Reliability, validity, and diagnostic utility*. Paper presented at the annual meeting of the International Society for Traumatic Stress studies, San Antonio, TX.

Weiss, D. S., & Marmar, C. R. (1996). The Impact of Event Scale—Revised. In J. Wilson & T. M. Keane (Eds.), *Assessing psychological trauma and PTSD* (1st ed., pp. 399–411). New York, NY: Guilford Press.

Wesson, M., & Gould, M. (2009). Intervening early with EMDR on military operations. *Journal of EMDR Practice and Research, 3(2)*, 91–97.

White, M., & Epston, D. (1990). *Narrative means to therapeutic ends*. New York: Norton.

Wilson, S., Tinker, R., Hofmann, A., Becker, L., & Marshall, S. (2000). *A field study of EMDR with Kosovar-Albanian refugee children using a group treatment protocol*. Paper presented at the annual meeting of the International Society for the Study of Traumatic Stress, San Antonio, TX.

World Health Organization Quality of Life. (1995). Position paper from the World Health Organization. *Social Science and Medicine, 41*(10), 1403–1409.

Zaghrout-Hodali, M., Alissa, F., & Dodgson, P. (2008). Building resilience and dismantling fear: EMDR group protocol with children in an area of ongoing trauma. *Journal of EMDR Practice and Research, 2, 106*.

Zeidner, M., & Hadar, D. (2012, July). Psychoactualia, secondary traumatization among trauma therapists [Hebrew]. *Quarterly of the Israeli Psychological Association*, 42–52.

Alayarian, A. (2007). Trauma, resilience and creativity: Examining our therapeutic approach in working with refugees. *European Journal of Psychotherapy, Counselling & Health*, 9(3), 313–324.

Altan Aytun, O., Ozcan, G., Ciftci, A., Konuk, E., Yuksek, H., Karakus, D., . . . Vatan Ozcelik, D. (2010, June). The effects of early EMDR interventions (EMD and R-TEP) on the victims of a terrorist bombing in Istanbul. In *Treatment of children/acute stress*. Symposium conducted at the annual meeting of the EMDR Europe Association, Hamburg, Germany.

American Psychological Association. (2003). The road to resilience. Retrieved from http://www.apa.Org/helpcenter/road-resilience.aspx#

Ayalon, O., Lahad, M., & Cohen, A. (1999). *Community stress prevention* (Vols. 3, 4). Kiryat Shmona, Israel: The Community Stress Prevention Center, Jerusalem Ministry of Education.

Bados, A., Toribio, L., & García-Grau, E. (2008). Traumatic events and tonic immobility. *The Spanish Journal of Psychology, 11(2)*, 516–521.

Blore, D., & Holmshaw, M. (2009). EMDR blind to therapist protocol. In M. Luber (Ed.), *Eye movement desensitization and reprocessing (EMDR) scripted protocols: Basic and special situations* (pp. 233–240). New York, NY: Springer.

Bremner, J. D. (2005). *Does stress damage the brain? Understanding trauma-related disorders from a mind-body perspective.* New York, NY: W. W. Norton.

Breslau, N., Chilcoat, H. D., Kessler, R. C., & Davis, G. C. (1999). Previous exposure to trauma and PTSD effects of subsequent trauma: Results from the Detroit area survey of trauma. *American Journal of Psychiatry, 156(6)*, 902–907.

Brill, N. Q., & Beebe, G. W. (1952). Psychoneurosis: Military application of a follow-up study. *U.S. Armed Forces Medicine Journal, 3*, 15–33.

Brunet, A., Weiss, D. S., Metzler, T. J., Best, S. R., Neylan, T. C., Rogers, C., . . . Marmar, C. R. (2001). The Peritraumatic Distress Inventory: A proposed measure of PTSD criterion A2. *American Journal of Psychiatry, 158*, 1480–1485.

Brymer, J., Layne, P., Ruzek, S., & Vernberg, W. (2006). *Psychological first aid (PFA).* Los Angeles, CA: National Child Traumatic Stress Network and National Center for PTSD.

Bui, E., Brunet, A., Allenou, C., Camassel, C., Raynaud, J. P., Claudet, I., . . . Birmes, P. (2010). Peritraumatic reactions and posttraumatic stress symptoms in school-aged children victims of road traffic accident. *General Hospital Psychiatry, 32*, 330–333.

Carlson, J. G., Chemtob, C. M., Rusnack, K., Hedlund, N. L., & Muraoka, M. Y. (1998). Eye movement desensitization and reprocessing for combat-related posttraumatic stress disorder. *Journal of Traumatic Stress, 11*, 3–24.

Carmelo, V., Gonzalo, H., & Perez-Sales, P. (2008). Chronic thought suppression and posttraumatic symptoms: Data from the Madrid March 11, 2004 terrorist attack. *Journal of Anxiety Disorders, 22*, 1326–1336.

Cervera, M. (2006). La técnica EMDR en la práctica Terapéutica. La empresa privada en la intervención psicológica en desastres: ICAS. In R. Ramos (Ed.), *Psicología Aplicada a Crisis, Desastres y Catástrofes*. Melilla, Spain: UNED Centro Asociado.

Cervera, M. (2012). La intervencion en situatciones de crisis en las empresas y los primeros auxilios psicólogos. In L. N. Martin & A. S. Sordo (Eds.), *Tratando Situaciones de Emergencia* (pp. 195–210). Madrid, Spain: Pirámide.

Chossegros, L., Hours, M., Charnay, P., Bernard, M., Fort, E., Boisson, D., . . . Laumon, B. (2011). Predictive factors of chronic post-traumatic stress disorder 6 months after a road accident. *Accident Analysis and Prevention, 43,* 471–477.

Creamer, M., Bell, R., & Failla, S. (2003). Psychometric properties of the Impact of Event Scale-Revised. *Behaviour Research and Therapy, 41,* 1489–1496.

Department of the Army. (2009). *Combat and operational stress control manual for leaders and soldiers: Field Manual No. 6–22-5.* Washington, DC: Headquarters, Department of the Army.

Department of Veteran's Affairs & Department of Defense. (2004). *VA/DoD clinical practice guideline for the management of post-traumatic stress* (Office of Quality and Performance Publication 10Q-CPG/PTSD-04). Washington, DC: Veterans Health Administration, Department of Veterans Affairs and Health Affairs, Department of Defense.

Dyregov, A., & Mitchell, J. (1992). Work with traumatized children; Psychological effects and working strategies. *Journal of Traumatic Stress, 5*(1), 5–17.

Fernández-Liria, A., & Rodríguez-Vega, B. (2002). *Intervención en crisis.* Madrid, Spain: Síntesis.

Figley, C. R., & Nash, W. P. (2007). *Combat stress injury: Theory, research, and management.* New York, NY: Routledge.

Finely, E. P., Baker, M., Pugh, M. J., & Peterson, A. (2010). Intimate partner violence committed by returning veterans with post-traumatic stress disorder. *Journal of Family Violence, 25, 737–743.*

Foa, E. B., Keane, T. M., & Friedman, M. J. (Eds.). (2000). *Effective treatments for PTSD: Practice guidelines from the International Society for Traumatic Stress Studies.* New York, NY: Guilford Press.

Galliano, S. (2002). Debriefing reconsidered. *Counseling and Psychotherapy Journal, 3*(2), 20–21.

Gendlin, E. (2002). *Focusing, proceso y técnica de enfoque corporal.* Bilbao, Spain: Mensajero.

Gentry, J. (1999). *Compassion satisfaction manual* (p. 25). Toronto, Canada: Psych Ink Resources.

Gibson, L. E. (2004). *Acute stress disorder: A brief description.* A National Center for PTSD Fact Sheet (www.ncptsd.org).

Gilbar, O., Plivazky, N., & Gil, S. (2010). Counterfactual thinking, coping strategies, and coping resources as predictors of PTSD diagnosed in physically injured victims of terror attacks. *Journal of Loss and Trauma, 15,* 304–324.

Gordon, R. (2007). Thirty years of trauma work: Clarifying and broadening the consequences of trauma. *Psychotherapy in Australia, 13*(3), 12–19.

Grossman, D. (1996). *On killing: The psychological cost of learning to kill in war and society.* Toronto, ON: Little, Brown.

Guenthner, D. H. (2012). Emergency and crisis management: Critical incident stress management for first responders and business organizations. *Journal of Business Continuing Emergency Plan, 5*(4), 298–315.

Horowitz, M. J. (1976). *Stress response syndromes.* New York, NY: Jason Aronson.

Horowitz, M. J. (1999). Signs and symptoms of posttraumatic stress disorder. In M. J. Horowitz (Ed.), *Essential papers on posttraumatic stress disorder* (pp. 1–17). New York, NY: New York University Press.

Institute of Medicine. (2008). *Gulf War and health: Volume 6. Physiologic, psychologic and psychosocial effects of deployment-related stress.* Washington, DC: National Academies Press.

International Association of Firefighters. (2001). *Guide to developing fire service labor/ employee assistance & critical incident stress management programs.* Retrieved from http://www.iaff.org/hs/LODD_Manual/Resources/IAFF%20Developing %20Fire%20Service%20Labor-Employee%20Assistance%20and%20CISM %20Programs.pdf

Kimbrel, S., Meyer, K., Knight, Z., & Gulliver. (2011). A revised measure of occupational stress for firefighters: Psychometric properties and relationship to posttraumatic stress disorder, depression, and substance abuse. *Psychological Services*, 8(4), 294–306.

Knipe, J., Hartung, J., Konuk, E., Colelli, G., Keller, M., & Rogers, S. (2003, September). *EMDR Humanitarian Assistance Programs: Outcome research, models of training, and service delivery in New York, Latin America, Turkey and Indonesia*. Symposium conducted at the annual meeting of the EMDR at the annual meeting of the EMDR Europe Association, Istanbul, Turkey.

Konuk, E. (2002). *The August and November 1999 Turkish earthquakes: An EMDR HAP progress report*. The EMDR Practitioner. Retrieved from http://www.emdrpractitioner. net/

Korn, D. L., Weir, J., & Rozelle, D. (2004). *Looking beyond the data: Clinical lessons learned from an EMDR treatment outcome study*. Paper presented at the EMDR International Association Conference, Montreal, Canada.

Kutz, I., Resnik, V., & Dekel, R. (2008). The effect of single-session modified EMDR on acute stress syndromes. *Journal of EMDR Practice and Research*, 2(3), 190–200.

Lazarus, A. (1989). *The practice of multimodal therapy*. New York, NY: McGraw-Hill.

Leach, J. (2004). Why people "freeze" in an emergency. Temporal and cognitive constraint on survival response. *Aviation, Space, and Environmental Medicine, 75*, 539–542.

Levine, P. (2008). *Healing trauma: A pioneering program for restoring the wisdom of your body*. Berkeley, CA: North Atlantic Books.

Shapiro, F. [scripted by M. Luber]. (2009). Recent traumatic events protocol. In Luber, M. (Ed.), *EMDR scripted protocols: Basic and special situations* (pp. 143–154). New York, NY: Springer.

Marks, I. M. (1987). *Fears, phobias and rituals: Panic, anxiety and their disorders*. Oxford, England: Oxford University Press. (Spanish translation: *Miedos, fobias y rituals 1: Los mecanismos de la ansiedad*. Barcelona: Martínez Roca, 1991.)

Marshall, G. N., Davis, L. M., & Sherbourne, C. D. (2000). *A review of the scientific literature as it pertains to Gulf War illnesses: Volume 4 stress*. Prepared for the Office of the Secretary of Defense. National Defense Research Institute, RAND, Santa Monica, CA.

McNally, R. J., Bryant, R. A., & Ehlers, A. (2003). Does early psychological intervention promote recovery from posttraumatic stress? *Psychological Science in the Public Interest*, 4(2), 45–79.

Meyer, E. C., Zimering, R., Daly, E., Knight, J., Kamholz, B. W., & Gulliver, S. (2012). Predictors of posttraumatic stress disorder and other psychological symptoms in trauma-exposed firefighters. *Psychological Services*, 9(1), 1–15.

Mitchell, J. T., & Everly, G. S. (2001). Critical incident stress management and critical incident stress debriefing: Evolution, effects and outcomes. In B. Raphael & J. Wilson (Eds.), *Psychological debriefing: Theory, practice and evidence*. Cambridge, UK: Cambridge University Press.

Murphy, S. A., Bond, G. E., Beaton, R. D., Murphy, J., & Clark, L. C. (2002). Lifestyle practices and occupational stressors as predictors of health outcomes in urban firefighters. *International Journal of Stress Management*, 9(4), 311–327.

Neria, Y., DiGrande, L., & Adams, B. G. (2011). Posttraumatic stress disorder following the September 11, 2001, terrorist attacks: A review of the literature among highly exposed populations. *American Psychologist*, 66(6), 429–446.

Ogden, P., Minton, K., & Pain, C. (2006). *Trauma and the body: A sensorimotor approach to psychotherapy*. New York, NY: W. W. Norton.

Rothschild, B. (2006). *Help for the helper: Self-care strategies for managing burnout and stress*. New York, NY: W. W. Norton.

Russell, M. C. (2008a). Scientific resistance to research, training, and utilization of EMDR therapy in treating post-war disorders. *Social Science and Medicine, 67*(11), 1737–1746.

Russell, M. C., & Friedberg, F. (2009). Training, treatment access and research on trauma intervention in the armed services. *Journal of EMDR Practice and Research, 3*, 24–31.

Seyle, H., & Fortier, C. (1950). Adaptive reaction to stress. *Psychosomatic Medicine 12(3)*, 149–157.

Shapiro, E. (2007). 4 Elements exercise. *Journal of EMDR Practice and Research, 2*, 113–115.

Shapiro, E. (2012). EMDR and early psychological intervention following trauma. *European Journal of Applied Psychology (ERAP)*, V. 62(4), 241–251.

Shapiro, F. (1993). Eye movement desensitization and reprocessing (EMDR). *Journal of Traumatic Stress, 6*, 417–421.

Shapiro, F. (1999). Eye movement desensitization and reprocessing (EMDR) and the anxiety disorders: Clinical and research implications of an integrated psychotherapy treatment. *Journal of Anxiety Disorders, 13*(1–2, Excerpt), 35–67.

Shapiro, F. (2004). *Military and post-disaster field manual.* Hamden, CT: EMDR Humanitarian Assistance Program.

Shapiro, F. (In press). Protocol for recent traumatic events. In M. Luber (Ed.), *Implementing EMDR early mental health interventions for man-made and natural disasters: Models, scripted protocols and summary sheets.* New York, NY: Springer.

Silver, S., & Rogers, S. (2001). *Light in the heart of darkness: EMDR and the treatment of war and terrorism survivors.* New York, NY: W. W. Norton.

Slonim, D. (2010, July). *Post traumatic stress disorder.* Paper presented at the NATO Science for Peace conference, Istanbul, Turkey.

Sosa, C. D., & Capafons, J. (2005). *Estrés Postraumático.* Madrid, Spain: Síntesis.

Stapert, M., & Verliefde, E. (2008). *Focusing with children. The art of communicating with children at school and at home.* United Kingdom: PCCS Books. (Spanish versión 2011.)

Ullmann, E., & Hilweg, W. (2000). *Infancia y Trauma, separación, abuso y guerra.* Auryn colección. Madrid: Brand. (German Original version, 1997.) Wittman, L., Zehnder, D., Schredl, M., Jenni, O. G., & Landolt, M. A. (2010). Posttraumatic nightmares and psychopathology in children after a road traffic accidents. *Journal of Traumatic Stress, 23*(2), 232–239.

Yehuda, R. (1999). *Risk factors for posttraumatic stress disorder.* Washington, DC: American Psychiatric Association. Yehuda, R. (2001). Biology of post traumatic stress disorder. *Psychiatric Clinics of North America, 62*(Suppl. 17), 41–46.

Zayfer, C., & Becker, C. B. (2007). *Cognitive—Behavioral therapy for PTSD.* New York, NY: Guilford Press. (Spanish versión, 2008. México: El Manual Moderno.)

63397797R00124

Made in the USA
Lexington, KY
05 May 2017